SECRET SOLDIER

SECRET SOLDIER

The True Life Story of
Israel's Greatest Commando

BY COL. MOSHE "MUKI" BETSER (RET.)

WITH ROBERT ROSENBERG

THE ATLANTIC MONTHLY PRESS
NEW YORK

First edition

Published simultaneously in Canada
Printed in the United States of America

Library of Congress Cataloging-in-Publication Data

Betser, Moshe.
Secret soldier / Moshe "Muki" Betser with Robert Rosenberg.
p.   cm.
ISBN 0-87113-637-6
1. Betser, Moshe. 2. Soldiers—Israel—Biography. 3. Israel—
Armed Forces—Commando troops. I. Rosenberg, Robert, 1951–
II. Title.
U55.B48B47   1996
356'.167'095694—dc20
[B]   96-4396

Design by Laura Hammond Hough

Atlantic Monthly Press
841 Broadway
New York, NY 10003

10 9 8 7 6 5 4 3 2 1

For all my friends
who fell in the campaigns

and to my loving wife, Nomi

CONTENTS

INTRODUCTION

Muki Betser's life is full of cycles that open and close with historic events in the life of the State of Israel.

Twice he is called to war just when he expects to go home to family and farm. On one occassion he returns in the most glorious fashion from a country in Africa that he loved and from which he was ignominiously evicted. And when he finally leaves the field of battle, it is because he has survived combat long enough to see his own son join the unit that Muki helped turn into the most elite in the IDF. But perhaps no cycle is as profound as the one that this book represents.

We began working on it a few weeks before the historic handshake between Yitzhak Rabin and Yasser Arafat on the White House lawn in September 1993. This introduction was written a few weeks after Rabin was assassinated in November 1995, in the very heart of presumably the safest place in Israel—Tel Aviv.

"My commander, my general" is how Muki referred to Rabin, using the term in the way former chief of staff Rabin himself meant it to be used by soldiers of the Israel Defense Forces: as much teacher as officer, as much parent as leader, as much friend as manager—all roles that Muki himself filled in his years as an IDF commander. Indeed, if not for the assassination, Rabin might have written this introduction, for the old general turned statesman knew Muki well, going all the way back to when, as chief of staff in 1965, he pinned Muki's first officers' bars to the then-young lieutenant's epaulets.

So, "if," as Rabin's successor, Shimon Peres, said at the unveiling of the Rabin tombstone on Mount Herzl in Jerusalem, "almost all of Israel is now part of the Rabin family," then Muki is one of the favorite sons in that family.

A scion of the original pioneering families of the Zionist movement in the early twentieth century, a soldier turned civilian who regards deeds as more important than words, a man who spent nearly twenty-five years fighting terrorism but remained constant in his belief that the only way to peace with the Arabs is by sharing the Land of Israel, Muki Betser is of a generation that grew up believing in what Rabin stood for: a strong defense for the sake of a strong peace.

The first question I ever asked Muki, when we finally met face-to-face, was "For years you've kept silent. Why do you want to tell your story now?" Except for two interviews soon after retiring from the IDF in 1986, he refrained from making media appearances despite hundreds of requests over the years. His decision to work on his autobiography was a surprise—even to himself, I think.

"Peace is coming," he told me that hot afternoon in August 1993, before either of us—or the world—knew that in a few weeks Rabin and Arafat would declare the time for bloodshed was over. Nonetheless, it was clear that the Rabin-Peres government was determined to move the peace process forward.

"It's our only choice—because we're now strong enough to make it happen. Reality changed. The Berlin Wall fell; there was a war in the Gulf. The Arab world has changed. So have we.

"If we did not try to make peace, how could we look in the eyes of the next generation when they ask what they are fighting for. And if the peace process does not work, then at least we can look into our own hearts and know that we tried.

"It's important for the next generation to know that all along we fought for peace. My friends say that I have no choice but to tell my story, so that the next generation knows what I know and what all my comrades in the army knew—that when we fought, we fought for peace."

I once asked Muki to show me the Sayeret Matkal pin he was given when he first joined the Unit. He promised to look for it, but he never did turn it up. Medals never interested him.

But framed and hanging in the living room of his home is the personal invitation he received by messenger from then-Prime Minister Yitzhak Rabin's office to attend the ceremonies in the Arava Desert where Israel and Jordan declared peace between the two countries.

That ceremony was, after all, yet another circle closed in Muki's life—it took place almost a stone's throw away from where, in 1968, Muki went on a reconnaissance mission in preparation for the first full-scale battle against the PLO, in Karameh, the place where he was wounded so badly he thought he was already dead.

This, then, is not only the story of a secret soldier. It is the story of a secret dove, for whom peace, not combat, was the purpose of his military service at what the popular press sometimes call "the tip of the IDF's spear." And as such, I believe it is an inspirational tale of both courage and humanity that reaches far beyond the borders of the Middle East.

Robert Rosenberg
Tel Aviv, November 1995

SECRET SOLDIER

CONQUERING FEAR

One night just before my eighth birthday, my father sent me out after supper to close the irrigation sprinklers watering the fields behind our house. Proud to get the job, which meant hiking to the far end of the field behind our house in the Jezreel Valley, I ran quickly past the familiar shadows of the little cow barn, the corral where we kept our horse, and the chicken coop, up to the edge of the field.

My pioneering grandparents founded this place, the village of Nahalal, the first cooperative farming settlement of modern Israel. My birthplace, my home, and my world, until that moment at the edge of the dark field, the valley had seemed the safest place in the world.

Though proud to know my father believed me both strong enough to turn the big iron wheel and responsible enough to make sure no precious water was wasted during the night, I looked out at the dark night and felt fear for the first time in my life. I remembered the old farmers telling stories about wild jackals prowling the valley at night. Their howling sounded like crying babies, a trick to seduce farmers into the fields at night to search for a lost infant—only to be set upon by the ravenous beasts.

To my eight-year-old ears, those folk tales merged easily with other natural fears in Israel in the early 1950s, right after the founding of the state. In the rhythmic whispering of the sprinklers off in the darkness, I could hear a gang of hidden Arabs plotting to kidnap me. I stood at the edge of the darkness, frozen with fear.

3

But in my family's home in the Jezreel Valley, three values ruled: settling the land, defending the land, and remaining stoic in the face of adversity. I knew I could not turn back without completing the mission.

A jackal's cackle broke through the night. It mocked my fright—and left me no choice. Taking a deep breath, I walked stiffly into the dark, listening to my pounding heart. I knew every rut in the dusty path. But the walk that took minutes in daytime became endless, as every sound suddenly seemed foreign.

The distant jackals, a nearby frog, the rustling of wind in the hay—all the sounds seemed to be conspiring against me. Finally, I reached the iron wheel that controlled the flow of water into the irrigation pipes. Grabbing it with both hands, I turned with all my might. Just as it closed, a nearby jackal's howl burst out of the night. And I ran.

Only when I reached the edge of the pool of light in the backyard did I catch the fright in my breath and stop running, conscious of the need to overcome the panic. Panting, I forced myself to listen to the sounds of the night instead of my heart.

The jackals continued to howl. A frog belched from a damp patch inside the orange grove my father had planted that spring. Gradually, as I realized nothing had happened to me, my heart slowed down. I began to recognize and identify the sounds instead of running from them in fear.

Finally, I stepped into the familiar light, knowing that I must overcome the fear, and how I would do it. The next night, even before my father assigned the task, I volunteered. He smiled slightly at my request, as if he knew why I wanted it, and he nodded his approval.

My second trip began as the first, but when I reached the dark edge I took a breath and walked forward slowly and deliberately, forcing myself to listen and learn from the night sounds instead of imagining what they might be.

Controlling my pace and my thoughts, I marched past the rows of citrus trees and into the field until finally the house lights were as distant as the stars and I was at the end of the field, the iron wheel cold and moist under my hands.

Just as I planned, I turned it slowly until the metal screw of the faucet stopped whining and it would close no further. A jackal yelped in the dark.

I did not run. I listened. The muttering of the sprinklers died away. A soft breeze came down the valley, carrying the sound of a truck's engine. Closer, a jackal barked. I clenched the damp soil between my toes, and listened for more.

Finally, when it seemed that every sound, shadow, and movement in the valley became as much a part of me as my callused hands and feet, I began walking back to the distant lights of Nahalal, knowing that I had learned to conquer my fear.

The lesson has stayed with me my entire life. But in 1968, as a twenty-three-year-old lieutenant in the Israel Defense Forces, deputy commander of the paratroops brigade's elite reconnaissance unit, I would discover that it was a lesson to be learned over and over again.

SMOKE OVER KARAMEH

———

Like a driver getting on a crowded highway, every soldier goes into battle believing that it won't happen to him. Except sometimes it does—especially when the plan goes wrong. In 1968, the plan went wrong. The Israel Defense Forces, which had triumphed less than a year before, failed miserably in a battle that could have changed history. And I learned of my own mortality.

My life seemed perfect in early March 1968. I was married to my childhood sweetheart, father to a newborn son; my unit was the most famous of all the special reconnaissance forces the IDF calls a *sayeret*. The newspapers called us the "the tip of the spear."

The Arab world vowed to throw us into the sea in 1967. They failed. Yasser Arafat's Palestine Liberation Organization picked up where the defeated Arab armies had left off. The PLO tried to frighten our people out of Israel. Car bombs killed shoppers in downtown Jerusalem; land mines along lonely roads in the southern desert of the Negev killed tourists on their way to Eilat. By early 1968, the terror incidents had escalated into nearly daily occurrences.

We could not turn the other cheek. The IDF began pressing the government to authorize an operation to put an end to the terrorism by striking at the PLO's bases in the Jordan Rift Valley, across the Jordan River in the Hashemite kingdom of Jordan.

An arid plain rippled with dry riverbeds called wadis, which carry flash floods in winter when rains fall on the yellow Judean

Mountains to the west and the red Edom Mountains in the east; the Rift is all that remains of the great sea that once covered the Afro-Syrian fault dividing Africa and Asia. In the northern half of the Rift, the Jordan River divides the valley with a narrow stream of water fed from the Sea of Galilee. The river flows between a winding ribbon of green banks through the sun-stroked land until it reaches the Dead Sea, the lowest place on earth. South from there is the Arava's flatland, all the way to the Gulf of Aqaba at the tip of the Negev.

Before the generals offered a plan to the government, the army needed intelligence from the other side of the border. In our capacity as a reconnaissance unit, the job fell to the paratroops *sayeret*. I got the job and was sent to lead an overnight foray into Jordan across the Arava, south of the Dead Sea.

One evening just after dusk in mid-March, an armored corps officer and an officer from the airborne sappers (explosives experts), followed me across the cold, shin-deep waters of Nahal Arava after a winter rain on the eastern plateau above the Rift.

The three of us spent the night scouting around two tiny Jordanian villages, Fifi and Dahal, counting a handful of Jordanian military vehicles parked by two little police stations. Back in Israel by dawn, the armored corps officer reported confidently to headquarters that he foresaw no problems for the heavy equipment to get through the mud we had encountered.

I disagreed. The flash floods of winter sweeping across the flatland left behind a deceptively shallow mud. I reported my views to the intelligence officers who took our reports. But in the senior command's eyes, the armored corps officer was the expert, not me. Now, they wanted a second reconnaissance mission, to a place far more dangerous than tiny Fifi and Dahal—a town called Karameh.

A Jordanian farming village north of the Dead Sea just over the Jordan River from Jericho, Karameh became the PLO's main base in Jordan after the Six-Day War. They turned the sleepy village into the center of international terrorism against Israel and the West. Preaching a rhetorical hodgepodge of pan-Arab liberation, Palestinian self-determination, Marxist revolution, and *jihad*—Islamic holy war against infidels—the armed irregulars in Karameh plotted for airline hijackings, urban bombings, and assassinations, often with Soviet-trained instructors.

In Fifi and Dahal we counted a handful of Jordanian military vehicles and even fewer armed Palestinians. But at Karameh, said intelligence, more than two thousand armed Palestinians, as well as a few dozen Soviet-backed terrorists from Western Europe and Japan, trained for terror missions. Planning a recon for such a target takes time. The PLO didn't give us any. A few days after the Fifi-Dahal mission, a land mine blew up a busload of high school children on a Negev road. Several died and dozens were wounded in the worst incident of its kind since 1967.

One of the advantages in our tiny country is that a soldier is never far from home—or the front. I heard the news of the bombing on the radio during a weekend at home in Nahalal with my wife, Nurit, and our baby son, Shaul. Like me, Nurit was a child of Nahalal, and she was a niece of Moshe Dayan's. We lived in a little three-room house shaded by two tall date palms planted by Dayan's father, who, with my grandparents and five other couples, founded the Jezreel Valley settlement in 1922. When we married in February 1967, she inherited Dayan's childhood home, a few doors down the road from my grandparents' house, where I was born.

Hearing the news about the land mine in the Negev, I did not need a radio report to know the government would want the army to react immediately. Like every soldier on active duty in the IDF, even on leave at home I kept my weapon—an AK-47 Kalashnikov—always within reach. I geared up and headed out the front door to my army-issued car, a frog-eyed Citroën Deux Cheveaux.

Back at Tel Nof headquarters in central Israel, *sayeret* commander Matan Vilnai took me along to the brigade planning session. The Jerusalem-born son of Israel's most famous guide to the Holy Land, Matan went to a military high school, choosing an army career early in his life. (He eventually became deputy chief of staff at the end of 1994.)

As the most junior officer in the session, I kept quiet—but listened and watched carefully—while the colonels and generals plotted the brigade's maneuvers around Karameh. IDF chief of staff Haim Bar-Lev wanted a plan to punish the PLO in time for the next morning's government session. He got it.

It was called Operation Inferno, and for the first time since the Six-Day War, the full strength of the IDF would head east over the Jordan River into the Hashemite kingdom.

The Bible calls those lands Gilead, home to three of the twelve Israelite tribes that originally settled the Land of Israel three thousand years ago. But self-defense, not longing for biblical homelands, sent us east over the Jordan River in Operation Inferno.

A precise schedule involving the air force, artillery, armor, and infantry became the blueprint for action. At five-thirty in the morning on March 21, just as dawn broke over the mountains in the east, air force fighter jets would put on a show over the village, dropping leaflets warning Arafat's followers to surrender or be killed. Very straightforward, the leaflets said simply, "The IDF is coming. You are surrounded. Surrender. Obey the army's instructions. Drop your weapons. If you resist, you will be killed."

Meanwhile, tanks and half-tracks would cross the narrow Jordan River over the Allenby Bridge, while north and south of Karameh, the engineering corps put up temporary bridges for more armor to block the village's flanks. Artillery in the foothills of the Judean Mountains on the west bank of the river backed up the operation.

When the enemy woke to the sonic booms and the news of their imminent capture, their natural reaction would be to flee east. The tip of the IDF spear—the paratroops' *sayeret*—would be waiting, helicoptered to a position east of Karameh to control escape routes into the foothills of the Edom Mountains. If the PLO's fighters tried to flee into Jordan's hinterland, we would be in place to catch them. Indeed, if the plan worked, the entire PLO would be arrested in one fell swoop.

Matan divided the company into two groups, one under his command and one under mine. He took forty fighters, while I took thirty. Just before we began loading the helicopters, Matan took me aside. "Listen, Muki," he said. "We have some tagalongs."

"That's bad news, Matan," I said.

Tagalongs are a phenomenon in the IDF—people show up wanting to get in on the action. Sometimes they are former members of the unit, sometimes from other units. The larger an operation, the more likely that the circle of people aware of the secret preparations will grow. And in tiny Israel, word spreads fast.

More often than not, tagalongs get in the way, especially in a special operations mission, where everything is measured out and planned. Vehicles are loaded so perfectly that every soldier and item has a number, the order in which they go in and out of the transport, or a specific position in a formation, or a task to accomplish. Adding a tagalong means taking someone else out. Matan knew this as well as I did.

"No tagalongs," I said. "Not with me."

"Muki, please . . . " Matan asked.

"No way," I insisted. "And you know better," I added, making no effort to hide a reprimanding tone from my captain (something that can only happen in a special operations unit of the IDF, where a soldier's skills are as important—if not more important—than his rank).

Although Matan did know better, as a career soldier he had his own considerations. But I refused to give in—especially when I recognized one of the two tagalongs coming up the walkway.

Tzimel's appearance confirmed everything I felt about late-minute arrivals from outside the unit. A company commander in the brigade when I first reached the *sayeret*, he made a bad impression on me then. Now, trailed by an air force intelligence lieutenant named Nissim, who claimed to have a background in infantry and wanted to be taken along, Tzimel's appearance in the operation gave me a foreboding feeling.

"No way," I said to Matan, shaking my head, not caring if Tzimel overheard. "No tagalongs. Come on," I insisted. "This operation looks like a lot of fun, but it also could get very complicated. Those people will not be any help. They'll just get in the way. And you know it."

"I'll take one and you'll take one," suggested Matan.

I shook my head. If he wanted to take them on, he could. But I wanted neither of them. "No way," I repeated. "No way I'm going to take off someone who knows the plan to put in someone who doesn't. No way." Like many of my generation from the Jezreel Valley, I am stubborn. Matan finally gave in. I hoped he would send Tzimel and Nissim home. Instead, he added them to his force.

We took off in the dark, in eight helicopters. Half an hour into the ride, the pilots went into a holding pattern because of fog. Five minutes went by, then fifteen, while the pilots did figure eights. There is nothing unusual in an operation's schedule changing in real time—as long as the other forces involved know about the new timetable. When the helicopters resumed their flight path down the Jordan Rift Valley, it never occurred to us on board that central command stuck to the same plan, without taking our delay into account.

I am not saying our job was the most important cog in the operation or that if we had arrived on time, everything would have worked like clockwork. But to prevent the enemy's escape from Karameh, they needed us in the right place at the right time.

Nobody warned us that we lost the element of surprise in the swirl of dust before dawn, our landing camouflaged by the fast-changing light of the desert just as the sun rose over the red mountains of Edom.

My teams scrambled out of the rocking choppers, heading to the formation we had practiced. The choppers left behind their dust storms while we began jogging west to our position above Karameh about six miles away. Our plan said to be there by five-thirty, just as the air show began.

But barely a dozen strides into the hour's run, carrying full gear across the wadis of the Rift east of Karameh, we ran into the enemy.

I don't know who was more surprised, us or the armed Palestinians in their raggedy collection of mismatched surplus uniforms from Arab and Soviet-bloc armies, in sneakers and sandals as well as army boots. None seemed to have helmets, and most wore the black-and-white checkered *keffiyot* that identified them as Fatah, loyal to Arafat's majority faction of the PLO.

Some tried to fight. Most looked for hiding places in the crumbly sandstone gullies of the wadis.

We chased them down into the dry riverbeds and over the ridges, killing about twenty-five who resisted and taking about a dozen more prisoner. All the while, we kept pushing to Karameh under annoying mortar fire from Jordanian Army positions in the foothills to the east behind us. It surprised us as much as the unexpected encounter with the enemy.

In the months after the Six-Day War, our intelligence experts scoffed at the idea that the Jordanian Army would help the Palestinians, or even challenge our temporary occupation of their country while we dealt the PLO a punishing blow. After all, since the end of the '67 war, the PLO under Arafat had challenged King Hussein's authority throughout the country and completely subverted it in places like Karameh. But as so often happens, intelligence estimates proved to be wrong. Luckily, the Jordanians were not very accurate with their mortar fire.

It took almost five hours to move five miles, instead of the hour we planned. Because of that, I knew something was very amiss in the operation. At eleven in the morning we finally reached a bluff overlooking Karameh, giving us a panoramic view of the war in the village below.

About a mile to our west, tanks, armored personnel carriers (APCs), half-tracks (rear-axled tank-treads), and jeeps zigzagged through the village, blasting at resisters holed up inside the dried-mud and tin-walled houses. Planes roared out of Israel in the west, looping in and out of the scene, diving to drop their bombs. Helicopters carrying wounded flew back and forth. From the foothills of the Edom mountain range, Jordanian artillery shelled the battlefield while our artillery shot back.

South, north, and due west, I saw tanks bogged down in the mud of the Jordan River's winter overflow. Towers of smoke rose from burning equipment in the fields and the buildings of the village. The clear, clean air of the desert gave way to the awful smell of war—flaming fuel and oil, burning machinery, and charred bodies.

The IDF was in trouble.

And so was Matan. My communications sergeant, carrying the radio on his back, tuned into Matan's frequency to report our position. I heard General Uzi Narkiss, commanding officer of the central command, in charge of the operation, shouting orders at Matan. "Get your forces organized and get out of the area."

"Impossible," Matan answered, in a voice much cooler than the general's. "I have wounded," he explained.

"Helicopters can take them out," said Narkiss.

"I'm having problems getting to them," Matan explained.

The IDF is not supposed to leave casualties behind. We are a small country, and have no unknown soldiers.

I broke in on the channel. "Matan," I asked, "where are you?"

He gave me his position. "I'm coming to help you," I announced, not waiting for a response. He probably would have said he did not need help, but I distinctly heard him say "problems." I started my fighters on the mile-and-a-half run to Matan's position north of us, handing over our prisoners to another infantry force we encountered in the field.

As soon as we reached Matan, I understood the problem. A soldier lay wounded about a hundred feet away, under intense fire from snipers. It would not be easy to get him out of there alive. But Matan's problems did not stop there. "Another squad is in trouble," he told me. "Their officer was wounded, so we evacuated him. Alexander took over."

"Alexander's a good sergeant," I pointed out. "He can handle things."

"I know," Matan admitted. "But we're getting strange reports from them. They say they are lost, and want help getting out."

I knew Alexander, a good field soldier. Getting lost did not sound like him. The back-packed radios of the time were the best available to the IDF, but not perfect. Frustrating minutes passed until, finally, I got a response to my own calls.

"We're not pinned down," the voice on the radio said. "But maneuvering is difficult."

From what he described, I placed him on the map two wadis away to the north. I told them to stay put and asked Yisrael Arazi, a good friend and my best platoon commander, to pick a dozen fighters for the rescue force. In minutes, we reached the first wadi, where we encountered a little resistance that we quickly dispatched.

Entering the second wadi, I saw Nissim, the air force lieutenant who came along as a tagalong, and immediately understood what happened.

With the platoon's officer wounded, Alexander had taken command. But Nissim pulled rank on the sergeant and looked for what he thought would be a shortcut to the safety of the concentration of IDF forces closer to Karameh.

He tried cutting across the desert on a straight line up and down the wadis. He didn't know it's safer to stick to the high ground rather than down in the riverbeds, where caves, boulders, and brush make easy ambush cover and the slippery banks of crumbly sand and stone are difficult to scale on the run.

Alexander knew how to lead the squad along the ridges, where, if they encountered enemy fire, it would be easier to identify its source—and take it out. The lieutenant, ignorant of basic tactics and believing that rank, not knowledge, gave him authority, endangered my men. Nissim thought it would be a picnic. When it turned into a real firefight, he wanted out. There is nothing more dangerous in combat than a fool.

Always a little hot-blooded, Arazi hissed, "Let's kill him now," making sure Nissim heard. Alexander smiled weakly behind the tagalong's back. I swallowed back my own anger, hushing my angry platoon commander with a wave of my hand.

The air force lieutenant tried stammering an explanation. I cut him off with a glare. "We'll straighten this out when we get back to the base," I vowed, and ordered the soldiers into formation for the hike back.

I took the center, keeping an eye on our flanks, while the platoon fanned out with about five meters between each soldier. We worked our way over the first ridge, alert for any enemy movement, sweating under the midday sun in the desert.

Heading down into the wadi from the ridge, I left behind a three-man squad to provide cover from the cliff top as we slipped and slid down into the riverbed. We slalom-dashed across the dusty wadi floor and climbed the crumbly limestone wall up to the next ridge. Reaching the plateau, I called over the squad left behind. Now we gave them cover in case of enemy fire erupting in our footsteps. They made it across without any shooting, and we started down the second wadi. With me in the center, Arazi took the point.

Just as we reached the most dangerous part of the move down into the wadi, exposed on the slope, fierce, effective fire burst at us from up the wadi's path. I hit the ground, about halfway down the slope, aware of my men doing the same around me.

"I'm hit," Arazi shouted, about thirty yards below me in the wadi bed. He collapsed beside a rock jutting from the wadi floor, clutching at his stomach. Bullets raced across the riverbed, kicking up the dust in tiny cyclones around him—and us.

Above, the three fighters on the top of the ridge returned the enemy fire coming at us in bursts and singles, a constant attack from more than one source. Well hidden, the enemy caught us with nowhere to hide. We were pinned to the ground by hot lead screaming overhead and smacking into the ground around us.

I scanned the scene. We could make it across the wadi to an outcrop of boulders a couple of dozen yards ahead, on the other side of the wadi. But it would mean abandoning Arazi. I could not do that. Seriously wounded and fully exposed to the enemy's withering fire, he was my first priority.

"Get him to cover," I snapped at the squad to my left. They had practiced for this situation hundreds of times. One soldier lofted a smoke grenade. It toppled through the air, exploding into a billowing cloud. Three ran into the smoke screen, racing to rescue their stricken officer, knowing the thick smoke only hid them, but did not protect them from the bullets.

They knew the drill: to get Arazi to cover before anything else. But when the smoke cleared, I saw my soldiers frozen by panic. They forgot everything. One soldier knelt by Arazi's side, a second fumbled with a packet of bandages, and a third stood, fully exposed to the incessant enemy fire.

Bullets stormed across the wadi at us all. I shot back with my AK-47, my Klatch, as we nicknamed the Kalashnikovs captured from the Egyptian Army in Sinai the year before.

Prone, at an odd angle created by the slope of the wadi's bank, I noticed a tiny cloud of dust rise from the ground where a bullet struck just beside me. I ignored it, concentrating on Arazi and the three paralyzed soldiers.

"Get him to cover!" I shouted.

I heard a soft moan beside me. I looked to my right. "Betser, I'm hit," said Engel, a redheaded kibbutznik lying a few meters away. I looked him up and down. Blood darkened his green fatigues above the knee.

"It's your leg," I told him, offering a reassuring smile. "Not your shooting hand." He winced back a smile at me. "Keep firing," I said. He did.

For the third time I shouted for the soldiers around Arazi to get him across the wadi to safety. But just then, one of the three fell soundlessly to the ground beside his wounded commander.

Only a few minutes had passed since the shooting began and we had already lost two good fighters, not counting wounded like Engel, still shooting beside me. If we did not get out of there, we would all die.

"Hanegbi," I called to a soldier about halfway between Arazi and me. "Get down there and tell them to move him to cover."

"No way I'm going down there," Hanegbi answered.

"Hanegbi . . . " I repeated slowly and sternly. More afraid of me, perhaps, than the enemy bullets, he started running toward Arazi. But after a few strides, Hanegbi flung himself to the ground, under heavy fire.

With nothing left to do but go myself, I plucked a smoke grenade from my web-belt and flung it into the wadi. Red smoke streamed from the can. As soon as it began billowing, I dashed down the slope toward Arazi. Firing over my Kalashnikov's sights toward the enemy, aware of my soldiers behind me doing the same, I raced to save my soldiers.

A freak gust blew the red smoke the wrong way, exposing me fully as I zigzagged across the wadi toward Arazi. Bending for my last strides, I saw the shock in his blanched face. Concentrating on his web-belt's canvas strap, I reached for it on the run. I planned to grab it and pull him to the safety of a boulder jutting from the far bank of the wadi. My action would resolve the will of the soldiers who had panicked. Indeed, bursting into their view, lead whistling in the air around us all, I became aware of my soldiers around me beginning to move. I reached for Arazi's belt.

And when I touched it, a blast exploded inside my head.

As if struck by a huge ax, my head felt like it had burst open. The impact jerked me upright, while teeth flew out of my mouth. Blood cascaded from my face, a thick red waterfall pouring over my torso.

Instinctively, I grabbed my throat where the bullet had ripped into my head. But as the blood poured out of me, so did my strength.

Still on my feet, I realized I was dying. The thought echoed inside me, reverberating into a singular serenity that quickly overcame all my other thoughts.

A soldier goes into battle thinking it won't happen to him. That makes it possible to face death. It should not happen to anyone. "But if it does, at least it won't be me." That's what I thought. Now I knew better.

As the officer in charge, I was the last person there who should have been wounded. But as my strength ebbed away and the sensations of my body diminished, I let go of those thoughts. The shooting around me continued, but nothing mattered anymore. I said farewell to the world, ready to die. Still on my feet, I let my hand finally drop the futile effort to stem the bleeding at my throat.

A hot blast of desert air seared my throat, surprising me as it filled my lungs, shocking me with the realization I would live—if I survived the swarm of bullets around me.

Even if I reached cover, I intuitively knew that I should not lie down, certain that if I did, I would drown in my own blood. I must stay on my feet, I thought. Not dead—at least not yet—and still the officer, responsible for my men; getting help for them became my primary concern.

I walked straight ahead, dimly aware of the shooting behind me, and started up the slope leading out of the wadi, knowing that only a few hundred meters away, Matan and his soldiers waited for us, oblivious to our predicament.

Gunshots snapped in the air like a crazed drumming. "Betser, get down! Muki! Get down!" Soldiers shouted around me. But I marched on, alone, directly up the slope.

A warm, familiar feeling in my boots made me think of home, of the fields of Nahalal, pulling irrigation pipes up a field after a night of watering. Then I realized that blood, not water, filled my boots. It soaked down through my uniform, into my socks, filling my laced-up paratrooper boots.

I do not know how long it took to reach Matan's position, but as I marched alone, a tall target in the battle zone, I waited for the enemy bullet that would kill me and thought about all that had gone wrong.

Somehow I managed to make it all the way. No enemy bullet struck me down from behind. Ahead of me familiar faces, soldiers I trained and led, stared at me, the horror of my appearance reflected in their eyes. To my right, someone told me to lie down. I waved a hand, to say no. Every movement of my head turned into an excruciating pain reverberating through my entire body. I tried to speak, but only gurgling gasps came out.

Dr. Assa, our unit doctor, led me to a rock to sit down. Beyond his face peering at my wound, I saw Matan sending a rescue team in the direction of my soldiers in the wadi. While Assa studied my face, not knowing where to start, a medic cut open my trouser leg. For the first time I discovered a wound in my thigh. The bullet reached all the way to the bone.

"Do you want some water?" someone asked. I reached for the canteen with a steady hand. But when I tried to drink, the water only spilled down over the remains of my destroyed jaw. I looked down at the wound in my thigh and poured some water on the bleeding gash.

The wait for the medevac helicopter seemed endless. The memory of the serenity I felt in those moments when death tried to seduce me kept coming back, telling me to close my eyes. But I refused to give up living. I thought of home, of Nahalal, of Nurit and Shaul. I thought of my parents, of my family, and of my oldest brother, Udi, somewhere back in Karameh in the battle. An officer in a battalion from the paratroops brigade fighting inside the village, I wondered if he was also hurt in the operation.

A few minutes went by and the casualty who had first slowed down Matan lay on a stretcher beside me, unconscious. A few more minutes went by and Yisrael Arazi, white as the desert limestone, lay alongside him, still breathing. But when Shoham, who fell so soundlessly in the midst of the fight beside Arazi, came in, I saw he was already dead. Then Engel came in on a stretcher. He smiled weakly at me. With my lower jaw gone, my own smile in return must have been a horrifying sight.

When the medevac chopper finally landed nearby, I waited until they loaded all the other wounded before I climbed aboard, finding a seat in the rear. Doctors used hand signals to communicate with each other as the helicopter's whirring blades lifted us into the air. They cut away Arazi's uniform and filled his arms with needles for blood transfusions. But nobody knew what to do with my problem. I breathed through the hole in my throat. The blood stopped cascading, but it kept dripping from my face onto my soaked uniform.

I caught the eye of one of the doctors and signaled a question with my hand, shifting my eyes back and forth between him and Arazi. The doctor looked down at my friend and then back up at me. He shook his head. I glared back. He went back to work on Arazi.

We flew low, due west, through the towers of smoke from the destroyed tanks, over the green oasis of ancient Jericho, the oldest town in the world, over the bare ancient hills of Judea, until finally we were above the forested hills around Jerusalem, racing toward Hadassah Hospital.

I looked out the window. Below us, I saw an Arab peasant working in a field, using a cow to pull a wooden plow. He did not even look up at the helicopter flying so low overhead. Unaware of us, dead and dying on board, oblivious of the battle raging only a few miles away.

I stayed conscious all the way into the operating room at Jerusalem's Hadassah Hospital. Only the anesthesia finally closed my eyes. I opened them eight hours later.

My brother Udi stood at my bedside. Three years older than me, he is as stocky as I am tall. In my eyes, he is a strong, quiet rock of responsibility and integrity.

With my mouth and jaw wired and bandaged, I could not speak. He passed me a pad of paper. I scrawled my first thought. "Arazi?" I wrote, holding it up to show Udi. He shook his head. Arazi was dead.

I lay in the hospital for a month. My jaw was wired closed, so I used a straw for my liquid diet and was barely able to speak. A dozen of us from Karameh lay in our beds in the ward—paratroopers, sappers, tank drivers, engineers, and infantrymen. The VIPs came to visit with their questions prepared in advance, never really listening to what the wounded said, not really knowing what to say to the wounded, as if embarrassed by the whole situation.

President Zalman Shazar came by the beds to ask his questions. "What's your name?" the elderly man asked me.

"He can't talk!" shouted my comrades. The president kept peering at me, a crowd of hospital personnel and reporters gawking from behind.

"I see," said the president. "So, where are you from?"

Another time, Yaffa Yarkoni, a singer who had entertained Israeli troops since the days of Palmach, came to visit. She sang a few songs, and then noticed me, my jaw all wired up, the bandages covering the stitches in my throat. She reached a line in a song about a loved one, and came over to me to give me a big kiss. I must have looked pretty bad, getting all that attention.

Mostly, we talked in the ward about what had happened – the best debriefing of all, the survivors' dialogue. We all knew what went wrong, but the politicians and generals did not want to know our versions of Karameh. The cover-up began, with combined interests at stake.

Both military and political decision makers responsible for the operation worked to make sure that the public never knew of the debacle. Instead, in newspaper interviews and speeches, the politicians and generals made Karameh sound like a smashing success.

Then-Chief of Staff Haim Bar-Lev gave interviews about how the raid fulfilled all our goals. The politicians and generals could not admit that the IDF had failed to meet its objectives. As far as they were concerned, more casualties meant greater heroism. Uzi Narkiss, the general in charge of the operation, quietly paid the price. A few months later he gave up his uniform for a cushy job with the politicians.

The PLO said Arafat escaped on a motorcycle on the road heading east. I did not see him. But if the *sayeret* had reached our place on time, we might have caught him and the rest of the PLO, and changed history.

I do know that the IDF lost nearly thirty soldiers that day, with seventy wounded. The IDF disgracefully left three bodies behind in the field, and the Jordanians paraded them along with the abandoned tanks in downtown Amman.

For the PLO, Karameh became known as a great victory, despite the fact we killed hundreds of them and destroyed their base. Attacked by the vaunted IDF, they survived less than a year after the IDF humiliated the combined armies of the Arab world.

Walking back to Matan alone from the firefight, waiting for the bullet that would end my life, I had thought about the great big Israel Defense Forces, the army that beat back all the Arab world less than a year before but went into battle without planning, certain that Arab irregulars were no match for them.

I thought about how soldiers without commanders, like those three around Arazi, can panic. And I thought about my own sense of shock at being wounded, not only because of the pain, but because it meant leaving my soldiers behind, in trouble. And, of course, I thought about how I had died—and was given the chance to live.

Victory can be measured by the balance between plan and action. If you win, you planned well. Defeat provides an opportunity to learn. Where did you make mistakes? Did you underestimate or overestimate the opposition? Were there gaps in the intelligence? Was the approach wrong? The timing off? The right means chosen? Who faltered? Who panicked?

But no harmony existed between plan and action. We did not meet our goals. Karameh could have become a textbook case of how not to integrate an organization made up of many parts. But the IDF never asked what went wrong at Karameh. No summaries or formal conclusions were written up, no recommendations made for further inquiry.

In a single stroke, my perceptions of the IDF and its strength, and of my own invincibility, had changed forever. At Karameh I understood my own vulnerability, as well as the IDF's. Since then, before every battle, every operation, and every project I began, I have seen Karameh in my mind's eye, where I learned to learn, and the first thing I learned was that if the IDF could fail so badly, peace was still a long way away.

They reached me at the hospital about a month after the battle, sending a junior officer who had not seen the battle and did not understand anything I talked about. Nobody gave the order for a full investigation with teams to debrief everyone within two weeks, while the events remained fresh in the minds of the participants.

Moshe Dayan came to visit with Nurit one day. I would have told him about what I saw and learned, but by then new medical problems plagued me. I was infected with jaundice from one of the blood transfusions during my operation. I could only sleep and drink water, which I immediately vomited back up through the horrible wires holding my jaw together. Worse than the wound itself, the jaundice left me in no condition to discuss much at all, let alone Karameh.

Six months of recuperation lay ahead of me, said the doctors. But I would not lose touch with my unit. The brigade command picked my brother Udi to replace me as deputy commander of the *sayeret*. "Betsers go and Betsers come" became a motto in the brigade while I went home to the Jezreel Valley to recuperate in Nahalal, my birthplace, where the story of my life really begins.

Basic Values, Basic Training

One of my earliest memories is the sweet-and-sour smell of cow dung and damp straw, mixed with the sound of steaming milk spraying into metal buckets as my grandparents milked the cows in the little barn behind their house, my birthplace.

Russian revolutionaries and social experimenters, my grandparents rejected religion for the sake of farming, and gave up schooling to work with their hands. They believed in action, not words, an ethos that dominated the original settlement movement of the Jezreel Valley.

But they loved ideas. Radical democrats, they planned to turn the Jewish world they knew on its head. In their revolution, Jews became farmers, workers, and artisans instead of intellectuals, merchants, or beggars. Their revolution led them to Zionism, the national liberation movement of the Jewish people, and to the Land of Israel, a sparsely populated corner of the decaying Ottoman empire at the very beginning of the twentieth century.

Born in Russia, my grandfather Yisrael Betser came to the Land via Argentina. His parents started him on his revolutionary course by moving their household from Russia to northern Argentina. A nineteenth-century German-Jewish philanthropist, Baron Maurice Hirsch, had established a self-sufficient Jewish farming colony there.

But living in Moisesville, as Hirsch called his Argentine settlement, did not satisfy Yisrael's aspirations for Jewish self-determination. In

1907, after a year in Moisesville, at the age of twenty-four he traveled alone, halfway around the world, to join the Zionists in the Land of Israel.

Two years later, he met my grandmother, Shifra Shturman, the oldest of three Russian sisters who had arrived in the country calling themselves "workers in the revolutionary movement" and seeking work alongside the men.

Yisrael and Shifra met at Umm Juni, south of the Sea of Galilee, along the banks of the Jordan River, where the Zionist movement sent them to create a settlement. Neighbors to a few tribes of Bedouin, they eked out a living off the banks of the river. Shifra was the only woman with the six men—including Moshe Dayan's father—in the first years at Umm Juni.

The seven young people—all in their early twenties—created the first kibbutz, Degania. And at the end of their first year in the commune, Yisrael Betser and Shifra Shturman married, and then moved southwest to Merhavia, in the Jezreel Valley, where they helped found the second kibbutz.

My aunt Yardena was born there, and so was my father's oldest brother, my uncle Moshe, whom I never knew and for whom I am named. He died early in World War II, a volunteer in the British Army. According to everyone in Nahalal, my uncle Moshe stood out among all the youth of Nahalal for his wisdom, modesty, humor, and diligence. But most of all, they told me, my uncle Moshe stood for honesty.

My grandparents moved several more times, and had five more children—Nahman, my father; my uncles Ya'akov and Zvi; and my aunts Sarah and Havah. But finally they decided against the kibbutz as a way of life, envisioning instead a settlement that combined their individualistic spirit with the science of collectivism. Thus they reached Nahalal, a hill surrounded by a malaria-ridden swamp in the Jezreel Valley.

Their moshav, as they called their experimental farming community, would not be as communal as the kibbutz, where the fields belonged to everyone and nobody had private possessions. Instead of collectively owning the land, each family received an equal share of land and the same means to make the land produce food. They did not have to worry about marketing their produce—the moshav movement created an organization to handle marketing—and the settlement included artisans and craftspeople whose skills earned them a place in the community.

As a scientifically planned community, Nahalal's very architecture served as a symbol as well as a function of the society's organization. They laid out the settlement in a circle, putting a ring of houses around the perimeter and slicing the land around the circle like a pie, with each family getting the same amount of land. Every season, the farmers met to plan what to grow in the coming year, and everyone received the same supply of seeds and equipment. Nobody would own a tractor unless everyone owned a tractor. Until then, they shared. And in 1921, the moshav elected my grandfather Yisrael Betser as its first *mukhtar,* the mayor of Nahalal.

My mother, Sarah Hurvitz, whose family was already five generations in the country (she was born and raised in Tel Aviv), met my father, Nahman, in Kibbutz Haim in the Jezreel Valley, and gave birth to me in my grandparents' house in Nahalal in 1945.

I spent my first four years there, until the end of the War of Independence. Then, answering David Ben-Gurion's call for experienced workers to help build the country, my father took us to Haifa, where he worked as a contractor on major construction sites.

But he preferred the Jezreel Valley—and so did I. Moving back to the valley, just before my eighth birthday, became one of the happiest days of my life. Though we moved to Bet She'arim, it was only a ten-minute gallop on a horse across the fields to my grandparents' home in Nahalal.

I grew up barefoot—not because we could not afford shoes, but because we learned to love the feel of the ground beneath our feet. Like my uncles and aunts and my brothers and sisters, I inherited Yisrael Betser's genes, which gave me height, and Shifra Shturman's genes, which gave me strength. By sixteen I was the tallest of my friends—six-foot-three. And though I weighed only a hundred and sixty pounds, it was all muscle, and remained my constant weight throughout all my years in and out of the army.

I swam, played basketball, rode horses, and most of all, I ran. My greatest pleasure, running, gave me a feeling of freedom. Later, when I went to the army, it would be one of the first things the officers noticed about me. I always came in first, second, or third in the long double-time marches or in the platoon punishments that taught us the discipline of soldiering.

Raised to believe in farming the land to develop it, and soldiering to defend it, army service was more than duty for me; it was a responsibility. But in our family, indeed throughout the Jezreel Valley, war stories were nothing to relish or brag about, indeed were rarely told.

For many years, a rifle hung on the wall of my grandparents' dining room, which also served as their living room. It was not there as decoration or nostalgia. A few years before my birth, an Arab threw a hand grenade into a Nahalal house one night, killing a baby. It could happen again. The *fedayeen* continued coming across the borders to terrorize the Jews of the Land of Israel.

By the age of ten I knew how to use a rifle, an old Lee Enfield my father kept at home. But along with my father's practical lessons in the weapon's handling came a much more profound one. Only if we proved our readiness for self-defense would the Arabs ever accept us in the country. Peace, not war, was the goal. To reach it, we needed to be strong.

Though he was wounded twice as a fighter—once with Wingate, and then later in the War of Independence—I never heard a war story from my father. In the Jezreel Valley, his friends and neighbors admired his farmer's abilities, his readiness to help anyone who needed it, and his preference for deeds over words.

So, like most of the kids of Nahalal—and indeed the rest of the farming settlements of the Jezreel Valley—we learned of our own families' historic heroism through hearsay and the schoolbooks of our country's modern history.

Growing up in Nahalal, even with all the reticence about talking about war and combat, my roots included the Haganah and the Palmach. A self-defense organization, created in the underground during the days of the British occupation of the country, the Haganah provided protection from the Arabs when the British did little to help.

As its strike force, the Palmach became the model for all the special operations forces in the IDF. A combination of British military tactics and kibbutz and moshav values made the Palmach an extraordinary military force, in which young men and women fought together. Using creativity and improvisation to counter the overwhelming numbers of Arab enemies, their guerrilla tactics made the most out of meager resources. Imbued with a profound camaraderie amongst its few hundred members, the Palmach's fighters came from the farms and the labor movement, the elite of the country's youth, recruited by friends and sworn to secrecy.

For me, the best stories I heard from the old-timers in the village gave me clues and hints where to find forgotten arms caches, hidden in the valley during the years of the British Mandate, when it was illegal for a Jew to have a gun—even while under constant attack from Arabs.

Following those clues, I led my friends to caves in the hills above Nahalal or to underground caches hidden beneath the floorboards of old barns. Once, I dug up an old septic tank to find an arms cache that included a Sten gun. My father had built that cache—not that he ever told me about it.

When I turned fifteen, my brother Udi went to the army—to the famed paratroops brigade. Like me, he had sought out old arms caches and tried out the guns he found in the old quarry in the hills north of Nahalal. But suddenly, when he went into the army, he changed. Soldiering stopped being a game for him.

Now, when he came home from the army, he went into the hills with his friends, other new soldiers. I spied on them when they told stories about the army. Combat soldiers all, they complained about tough sergeants and laughed about moments of fear that they overcame. I listened eagerly to their stories—not because I looked forward to war or combat, but because I looked forward to the challenges they described: the long marches and sleepless nights, the exhilaration of parachuting, and the sense of satisfaction that comes from shooting accurately.

Never much interested in school—I attended an agricultural high school not far from Haifa—I preferred hiking the land to reading about it in schoolbooks. Often my girlfriend, Nurit, and I took off for a few days or even weeks to go hiking and camping, whether in the Galilee's hills or in the Negev's desert. For us, no greater pleasure existed than tracing the course of a wadi we visited for the first time.

Indeed, field navigation using only a map and the stars became my favorite pastime, and one of the reasons I wanted to go to a *sayeret*, an IDF special force, where field navigation is a key to the craft of soldiering.

I loved maps, and matching the terrain to the lines drawn on the paper. The North Star, hanging above the Galilee, became a beacon for me wherever I found myself in the countryside I loved, finding signs of seasonal changes, recognizing winter's end by the sprouting of wild lilies in the Galilee's foothills above Nahalal.

And I knew that in the army, especially in the kind of unit I wanted to join—the paratroops *sayeret*, the most elite of the reconnaissance forces, which specialized in special operations—I would learn much more about fieldcraft.

I did not want an army career. I knew the army required discipline. Raised to believe in earned, moral authority, not the authority of rank for rank's sake, I expected to find army life rankling. Medals for heroism or bravery had less appeal than the challenges I would find in a unit where I could bring to full expression my natural talents as an athlete and my love for the land.

Nonetheless, I knew I had talents for soldiering—as an athlete, as a field navigator, and perhaps most of all as a leader of my peers. But I left it unsaid amongst my friends from the valley, where bragging is frowned upon and modesty admired.

So, I spent my last summer before the November draft of 1964 honing my body through the hard work of the farm and athletic competitions. Nurit and I traveled the country, sometimes only the two of us, sometimes with other friends from the valley. We knew we would one day be married—it went almost as unspoken between us as the fact that we knew I would be a good soldier. We would have children and live in Nahalal, in the Dayan family house that she would inherit when she married. The tradition in Nahalal is that the youngest child inherits the farm, after the older children help to build it.

In the fall of 1964, my turn came to stop playing at being a soldier and get ready to become one for real. In those days only four elite reconnaissance units that the IDF calls a *sayeret*—Hebrew for "scouts"—existed.

The Southern Command called its *sayeret* Shaked, meaning almond. Famous for, among other reasons, its Bedouin Moslem commander, Amos Yarkoni (born Abed al-Majid), one of the unit's founders in the fifties, Shaked tracked infiltrators in the Negev coming out of Egypt and Jordan.

The Northern Command also had a *sayeret*, drawn from the Golani Brigade, an infantry unit that specialized in the northern border's defense.

The third *sayeret* was brand-new in 1964, and so secret that I knew nothing of its existence at the time of my draft. Run directly by the general staff, its very name only became public knowledge in the late 1980s, and then only because its successes made it impossible to keep its existence a secret.

So the fourth *sayeret*, the most famous on the eve of my draft, belonged to the paratroops brigade. Famous for its special operations and surprise raids against the enemy, the IDF considered the paratroops *sayeret* the unofficial heir to the 101st Unit, a legendary force established in 1952.

The 101st had struck back at the Arab *fedayeen*, the infiltrators who came across the borders as saboteurs and terrorists. They crossed borders into enemy territory to seek out the culprits and punish them. Ariel "Arik" Sharon, who went on to become a general and a politician, and Meir Har-Zion, who to this day is considered the most legendary of Israel's fighters, led the fifty fighters in the unit.

The stories about the 101st describe them as wild and uncontrollable, soldiers who made rules for themselves. Wounded so many times—including once when he personally took revenge on a Bedouin family for his sister's rape—Meir Har-Zion finally gave up soldiering to build a ranch on a Galilee hilltop.

The unit's radical methods forced the politicians to dismantle the unit after only six months. But the 101st proved to the IDF that a very small number of fighters could deliver a very powerful message. It established traditions for using essentially guerrilla tactics in the strategic fight against terrorism. With the dispersal of the 101st's officers and soldiers into the rest of the army at the end of 1952, those traditions spread throughout all the special warfare units in the army. The spirit of their personal heroism—and the skills they developed as trackers and fighters—remained embedded in the consciousness of the army.

The paratroops brigade, which Sharon commanded after the dismantling of the 101st, claimed the legendary unit's mantle as the tip of the IDF spear, and the brigade's scouts—the *sayeret*—drew its inspiration from the 101st.

My parents took me to the Haifa recruiting station on a brisk November day, knowing the paratroops *sayeret* was my goal. We parted in the manner of people from the Jezreel Valley. I clenched my father's thick, hard hand and we shook once. "To your success," he said.

"Goodbye, *Abba*," I said, then turned to my mother. "Goodbye, *Ima*."

She handed me a bag with a sandwich for the bus ride to the induction center. I towered over her, and bent over to give her a peck on the cheek. She gripped my biceps with her own strong hands and, in a whisper into my ear, wished me luck and asked me to take care of myself before letting me get on the bus to the induction center. That is the way of the Jezreel Valley—laconic and under-stated, never sentimental.

Nowadays, the induction process to the IDF is computerized and before new draftees reach the center, they pretty much know where the army will send them. In those days, neither computers nor advanced registration existed.

But some things never change. A sprawling mass of wooden barracks, sheds, and dozens of tents set into clearings among the wooded groves and open fields of Tel Hashomer, east of Tel Aviv, the center draws all the new recruits to the IDF. Three times a year— February, August, and November—buses bring the eighteen-year-olds recruited in that season's round of the draft.

It is a herding process that begins with chaos and confusion but very quickly turns into the strict organization of the army—even if that army is the IDF, which, as a people's army based on a universal draft, has a degree of informality intolerable to any other professional army.

And like new recruits nowadays into the IDF, those of us arriv-ing at Tel Hashomer that day in November 1964 knew that in addi-tion to the two and a half years we would give to the country in enlisted service, another month in reserves would follow every year until we reached our forties. Most of the IDF is not even in uniform at any given time—it is the reserve force.

This has been part of life in Israel for as long as the country has existed. I wish now, just as I truly wished then, that for my grandchildren—it is probably too late for my children—it will not be necessary. But for all the years Israel and the Arabs have warred, one of the real secrets of the IDF's strength is that almost every family in our tiny country knows what it's like to have someone in the army.

I'm sure induction centers everywhere in the world share the same thing—shouting sergeants. In those days, the most famous sergeant in the IDF was a strict handlebar-mustachioed Yemenite-born tyrant named Hezi, who wore a sharp-pressed uniform and had a whistle hanging at the end of a braided lanyard that draped over his chest.

He rushed us through a series of barracks where it seemed we were given as many shots as a porcupine has needles, then led us into a huge storeroom. Clerks threw uniforms, duffel bags, helmets, and boots at us. Then we were rushed back to the main hall, where they told us where to find the recruiters for various units in the army.

The recruiters all promised the sky—adventure, excitement, professional interest—if we met their criteria. Those who did not meet the standards for combat units ended up as desk clerks and drivers, cooks and adjutants of the rear. To be a *"jobnik"*—a non-combat soldier—was worst of the worst for someone from Nahalal.

From the navy to the air force, they all tried to entice me into their basic training. But I knew where I wanted to go: the paratroops brigade, and specifically to the paratroops *sayeret,* the most elite force in the brigade. Its appeal to me went beyond the fact my brother Udi had served in the unit before going on to become an officer in the brigade. From everything I knew about the *sayeret,* it looked like it would be the most fun.

The tests for the paratroops *sayeret* began a few days after my arrival at the induction center. In one day, the recruiting sergeants from the unit put us through long- and short-distance races, obstacle courses, wrestling matches, and some intense games of basketball. We all tried to impress the recruiters. Only a couple of years older than us, they seemed much, much older, and a lot wiser. Seventy tried out that first day. They picked twenty. I came in first, second, or third in every foot race. Though I had never experienced any real violence among my friends in the valley, we often wrestled for fun.

At six-foot-three, weighing a hundred and sixty pounds of wiry farm-bred muscle, I could get leverage on even the heaviest of my opponents. Because of my height, basketball was always my favorite team sport.

Over the coming four days, the routine repeated itself daily as they tried out new recruits, cutting away those who did not make the grade. Finally, when there were forty who met their standards, they told us to heave our duffel bags onto the roof of a bus to Tel Nof, the air force base that served as brigade headquarters for the paratroopers.

And the coddling stopped. Move this, move that, scrub this, clean that—it went on endlessly. They took us out for twelve-mile marches, and just as the base came into view, they sent us marching in the other direction for another dozen.

We learned about stretcher drills, an IDF favorite for turning a platoon of recruits into a cohesive unit. Soldiers take turns carrying each other on stretchers. It is unpleasant to be one of the four carrying the stretcher, and even worse to be bounced around on top. We did dozens of those, double time around the base, over and over again, learning to work together, learning who shirked and who could be trusted, who had endurance and who merely had bravado. When the sergeants tired of stretcher drills, they made us carry our cots over our heads on ten-kilometer runs, to punish us all for a single soldier's dirty rifle. They let us have two or three hours of sleep in twenty-four hours. But nobody counted; we were too busy learning the rudiments of soldierly discipline.

My love of running came in handy. Because I ran fast I could usually grab a few minutes of shut-eye, waiting for my buddies from the platoon. I ran everywhere, able to maintain a natural loping gait that found a rhythm and kept it over long periods of time. So, I stood out both as the tallest member of the platoon and as one of its fastest, always leading the pack or right on the heels of its leader—usually our commanding officer.

About two weeks after we arrived at Tel Nof, they sent us to Bet Lid, in the center of the country, near Netanya. They combined our platoon with two regular platoons of paratroops recruits, creating a company to go through the three-month basic training together. At the end of three months we faced parachute training, and then another three months learning to command a squad. Only when we finished that course did we become full-fledged soldiers, qualified to wear the red beret and red boots of the paratroopers, silver wings above the left shirt pocket of our green uniforms. By the end of the process, nearly 50 percent of us would be gone, winnowed out and sent to easier outfits.

As trainees for a *sayeret,* we worked harder in our platoon than the two other platoons of trainees. While they did a six-mile march, we hiked a dozen. When they finished twelve miles, we did another fifteen. All our platoon officers and trainers came from the *sayeret,* not the regular battalion. From the start, they gave us the feeling that those who lasted through the course would belong to a very special family of soldiers and officers.

Soldiers everywhere say their basic training was much harder than whatever is given nowadays. In my day nothing in army regulations limited the powers of anyone above the rank of sergeant. An hour of sleep and then three hours of running with our beds over our heads; a twenty-minute catnap, then two hours to build a three-meter-high stone pyramid from rocks we found in the fields. They prepared us for the reality of our work as soldiers, when we'd have to go with very little sleep for days and sometimes weeks at a time, racing around the clock to prepare an operation or fighting constantly in a full-scale war.

At Bet Lid we began to learn about all the platoon weapons. We carried a pair of 7.62 mm machine guns, as well as a mortar and a bazooka. Our first rifles were heavy, cumbersome FNs, made in Israel under Belgian license. As paratroopers, they expected us to know how to handle it all, and we felt grateful when, after we mastered the FNs, they gave us Uzis for our personal weapons. After the 1967 war, Kalashnikovs captured from Arab troops equipped by the Soviets were issued to combat soldiers, and I learned the Kalashnikov is the best all-around assault weapon available. (I used the same one for the next eighteen years of active service and reserve duty.)

But I never found any great pleasure in the handling of guns, though throughout my years in IDF special forces my job often included trying out new weapons. I found the lessons in field tactics, topography, and navigation much more interesting than weapons-training. My love of the geography of the Land of Israel gave me an advantage over the city kids—and sometimes the instructors—when it came time to learn the intricacies of maps and navigation across the land.

But as in any army, mostly we practiced, over and over, until we did it right. Around the clock, day in and day out, we learned to stretch our abilities to our very best, for only the very best would finish the course. Except for two twenty-four-hour weekend leaves toward the end of the first three months of basic training, when I went home to visit with family, friends, and Nurit, we lived inside our platoon and company, barely aware of the rest of the brigade, let alone the rest of the world.

The central theme of basic training is to turn civilians into disciplined soldiers, and the simple principle says that a soldier has to follow orders automatically, without thinking, unless of course it is highly illegal—shooting an unarmed prisoner, for example. That is why there are punishments for every little thing out of place.

Rust on your weapon? Dig an eight-cubic-meter hole. The tent is untidy? Move it fifty times tonight until you get it right. All the punishments have one single goal: whatever you are told to do, do it, because one day in battle, in a moment of sheer confusion and chaos, survival will depend on a clear head—and the ability to perform.

It surprised me at first how easily I took to the army. I never had much respect for authority unless I regarded it as having a fair and moral basis. But the sergeants and officers never found anything to complain about with me. In all the weeks of my basic training, they never singled me out for a punishment. Of course, as a member of the platoon I participated in all the group punishments meted out for whatever fault the officers found in our general performance or in the performance of any individual member of the team.

A *sayeret*'s soldiers—even new recruits—are encouraged to speak their minds about ways to improve the unit's performance, even if it means challenging the commanding officer. In a *sayeret*, there is no place for blind admiration of senior officers. That suited me fine. My parents raised me to believe in myself, to stand up for what I believed. Throughout my career, officers earned my respect because of what they knew and what they taught me. But I learned there are different kinds of leaders.

Some earn respect from their soldiers by drilling so hard that the soldiers know the job as well as the officer. Others create respect through fear of their authority, whether sending soldiers out on a twenty-mile march on a freezing winter night, just because a soldier was late for an assembly, or adding another ten miles to a march because a soldier complained.

The best officers are naturals—combining distance and friendship, an aloofness with intimacy, to inspire the soldiers. I wanted to be that kind of officer like my first company commander, Giora Eitan. The nephew of Rafael "Raful" Eitan—our brigade commander, who rose to become chief of staff and go on to politics—Giora died on the Golan Heights during the Six-Day War.

Most of the other soldiers in the platoon came from the kibbutz and moshav farms of Israel, where the values of settling the land are inseparable from the values of defending it. The city boys often knew more about fighting, and in a way seemed tougher than us at first. But many of them had a hard time with the hard work, tending to complain, especially about the repetition of the drilling.

Maybe one of the many reasons farmers make such good soldiers is that we learn to be patient, whether it is waiting for the seasons or understanding that the weather is beyond control. Just as we knew that we sowed in one season in order to harvest in another, we understood that what we learned in basic training would serve us well in the reality of combat. But the grand finale of the first three months of basic training, a full-scale exercise in the Negev, shook my belief in that simple proposition.

We trucked south, then hiked into the desert, reaching our position just before dawn. The company captain gave us a rousing speech. The platoon commanders briefed us on our assignment.

I looked forward to seeing our platoons form into companies and the companies combine into battalions until the entire force of the paratroops brigade combined with other brigades into an army on the move. Now, I looked up at the row of old oil barrels at the top of a cliff. Enemy positions cannot look like this, I decided. With no minefields to cross, no barbed wire to cut, no trenches to traverse, and nobody shooting back, our company's assignment to take the hill after a pair of air force jets hit it with napalm seemed silly. The whole thing looked fake to me. A lot of hurried night movement, then waiting for hours for nothing, did not make it any better.

It all combined with a problem that began gnawing at me throughout basic training. As far as I could tell, the army had a lot more problems than fake enemies in exercises. Our equipment was terrible. My web-belt became an obsession. It was too tight, too small, inefficient. I kept looking for ways to improve the canvas straps that I needed to carry my equipment.

On my first leave home, a month after the start of basic training, I spent hours in the tailor's shop at Nahalal, finding new ways to sew the canvas belts to fit my long torso. I told the Nahalal tailor my problem, but instead of leaving the web-belt with him, I stayed to watch and learn. From then on, I did my own sewing, learning to baste pouches together so they would not flap against my body when I ran, wiring hooks into the canvas for more clips to hang equipment from.

The web-belts were not the only equipment problem. The small, light Uzis, with their short range and low velocity, made a good tool for house-to-house combat. But at longer distances they lost their accuracy and punch. All during the exercises, aware of the generals watching from the top of a hill in the distance, I wondered if they knew about these problems and others, like the faulty equipment, like stretchers that fell apart.

Finally, at the end of the exercise, company commanders and then regimental commanders and finally the brigade commander gave speeches summing it all up, saying how it worked perfectly. It sounded like a lot of crap to me.

But I had hopes for the second stage of our training. The officers announced that new equipment waited for us when we started the second stage of the course—parachuting. I decided to keep the faith, and at the end of the exercise I felt optimistic setting off on the unit's traditional twenty-four-hour hundred-kilometer (sixty-mile) march through the hills and canyons of the Negev to a small air field at Sde Boker, where a plane waited to take us back to Tel Nof—and a week's leave.

I spent the week with my friends and family at home, helping my father on the farm in the mornings and during the rest of the day hanging out with friends on home leave that week. Nurit was also in the army, and I missed her that weekend. Meanwhile, I did exactly what my brother Udi did with his friends three years before when they came home from the army—we talked about our experiences. And my younger brother Eyal spied on me and my friends, just the way I had spied on Udi.

When I returned to Tel Nof at the end of the leave, disappointment struck. The officers had not exactly lied. They issued new equipment, from uniforms to Uzis—but the same old models we already knew. On my next visit home, I realized I needed to start all over again in the sewing shop, getting my new web-belt to fit properly.

The Night of the Wells

After the airplane takes off, after the release rings are clipped, after standing up, after shuffling down the cabin to the open door with the wind blasting past, after the thump of heartbeat as you fall into the turbulence, after the first few seconds before the chute opens comes the silence.

More than anything else, it is that sweet quiet above the earth that I loved in parachuting. I'm not a great lover of flying. My feet belong on the ground. But I always looked forward to the quiet that comes from being inside the wind itself.

After learning to parachute, we went to the squad commanders' course, where sergeants are picked and future officers spotted. Thirty percent of us had already fallen out, dropped into the regular paratroops or transferred to even easier infantry units. Beginning to feel like real soldiers, we knew how to work in concerted action, aware of our skills and the force we wielded as an organized combat unit.

One day they assigned us to put on a demonstration for Prime Minister Levi Eshkol. We trucked to Palmachim, to check out the landing zone, and a huge sand dune selected as an enemy position, before climbing aboard the planes for the show.

As a boy I read newspaper accounts about such demonstrations. Usually the papers said something like "the paratroopers showed extraordinary combat ability." I imagined all sorts of exciting things—

jumps, racing jeeps, soldiers leaping into the air. Now I looked forward to being in the real thing.

We practiced a few times, but then a senior officer decided that it took too long. So the company commanders planned a little bluff. Instead of jumping with all our equipment, we left the bazookas, mortars, and heavy machine guns on the ground, hidden from the audience full of dignitaries. We jumped with light equipment—mostly Uzis—and picked up the heavy stuff when we hit the ground.

Sure enough, the next day the papers reported that "the para-troopers demonstrated top-notch ability" for the ministers. It became a joke for us. But it also worried me that the army cheated. My feelings about the army reached an all-time low.

But then they picked me as a bazooka operator for my first mission across enemy lines, a first taste of real action. Palestinian *fedayeen* from Kalkiliya, just over the border of the West Bank, when it was still Jordan, disrupted life almost daily in the Kfar Saba area, a few miles northeast of Tel Aviv.

The infiltrators planted mines against car traffic and attacked farmhouses in the middle of the night. Innocent people died daily. The generals above decided to attack water-pumping stations that served the villagers around Kalkiliya, as well as the only gas station in the area. We wanted to force the Jordanian authorities to crack down on the Palestinian *fedayeen*.

I felt lucky to be chosen, one of only three from our platoon attached to a more veteran platoon for the mission. In four months of carrying around the bazooka tube, drilled to conserve ammunition, I had only used four live missiles to practice firing. Now the envy of the other young soldiers in our platoon, I practiced with four live missiles a day, readying for the big day when we would attack the pumping stations.

Euphoric with the assignment, we spent the next two and a half days practicing with the rest of the task force. On the morning of the operation, a final parade drill ended with rousing speeches by the senior commanders. In another few minutes, we would board the trucks taking us to the staging ground in an orange grove near the border. But right after the speeches, one of the older fighters from the task force approached me with a peculiar request.

"Listen," said the sergeant. "My platoon commander says I should trade bazookas with you."

I used a French-made 82 mm bazooka that I knew like the back of my hand. He offered me his 73 mm Belgian-made bazooka. I made a face, pretending not to understand what he wanted. A soldier never gives up his personal weapons.

The sergeant knew that. But he had an explanation. "Yours has more firepower," he said, "and for this mission the platoon commander says I need something stronger than what I've got."

I loved my bazooka. I never missed the bull's-eye in all our practices. But if I argued with him, I might end up missing the mission. Warily, I asked if his worked perfectly.

"Of course," he said.

"Did you try it out? Fire it?" I asked.

"Of course."

There's a control light on a bazooka with which to check whether the trigger mechanism makes the electrical contact that sets off the missile. It is a safety mechanism for the soldier loading the tube to be sure to get out of the way. I took his bazooka, and checked the control switch. It worked.

A new soldier, eager for combat and assigned to his first real mission, does not argue with a sergeant. I did something no soldier should ever do—I traded my personal weapon for someone else's. A few minutes later, we boarded the trucks.

Crossing the border that night, every little noise seemed to reach all the way to Amman. I hugged my bazooka close as we moved silently through the groves, careful to avoid brushing any branches or startling any animals. A single barking dog could awaken the villagers on the outskirts of Kalkiliya, and raise the alarm.

The paranoia of crossing the border passed as I recognized the landscape as identical to Israel's. Farmers on the Jordanian side grew the same kinds of crops that season—even if they did not have our technologies. The fragrance of the orange groves could not be divided by the line that cut the country. The recognition that the border did not divide nature gave me confidence and the paranoia quickly passed.

We heard the pumping station's rhythmic thump as we approached quietly through the groves. The signal went down the line, and I crouched, my loader behind me, ready to slip a missile into the tube when the order came.

I raised my right hand away from the trigger, waiting for his pat on my helmet to let me know he had cleared the bazooka's rear exhaust. I stared down the barrel at the thick walls of the cement building, waiting for the slap on the helmet, the order to fire.

It came. I lowered my hand to the trigger mechanism, made sure of my aim, and fired.

Nothing happened. "Open!" I barked, going through the drill. "Release!" I snapped. He slapped my helmet and I pulled the trigger. Nothing.

"Change rocket," I tried. He did. Nothing. "Try another one!" Nothing.

I had never felt such frustration. I unslung the bazooka and pulled up my Uzi, pouring an angry magazine of bullets into the cement walls of the building. If the sergeant who made me change bazookas had come by right then, I probably would have shot him.

The cease-fire order came down the line while the explosives teams went into action, setting their devices. We began our retreat, the blast from the demolished pumps behind us ripping through the night with a fireball that quickly turned into a thick column of smoke even darker than the starry night. We double-timed it out of the area, heading home before the smell of the smoke could reach our nostrils.

That night, at the debriefing with our platoon commander, I reported what happened to my bazooka. The next morning, the whole company met for a debriefing. The commanders of each of the attacking forces reported on what happened. After the task force commanders spoke, the platoon commanders stepped up to give their speeches, reviewing the operation. My platoon commander mentioned my bazooka's failure.

I jumped to my feet from the center of the crowd of soldiers and faced the officers at the front. "Sir," I said directly to the senior company commander, a captain. "A very serious thing happened." A lowly corporal, I chose my words carefully, speaking in an even voice. I left no doubt about my feelings.

"Go on," the company commander said.

"A sergeant took advantage of the fact that I am a young soldier," I went on. "He knew I did not want to lose my place in the mission. He knew that my bazooka worked and he knew his bazooka had problems."

I paused to make sure they understood, thinking carefully about what I wanted to say. "He cheated me and he lied to me about an order from the platoon commander. And," I summed up, "he created a situation that prevented the proper use of my training at the critical moment of the operation."

Afterward, one of my friends from the platoon told me I sounded like a company commander, not a corporal.

But meanwhile, the sergeant turned red. I looked at his company commander, fully expecting him to immediately dismiss the sergeant from the *sayeret*. Cheating a fellow fighter from the unit seemed to me the worst thing a soldier in the unit could do.

But Tzimel, the company commander—the same Tzimel who would one day tag along at Karameh—said nothing to the sergeant.

Thus, even after my first mission, my doubts about the army remained. I took part in an operation, over the border, with all the elements of combat—preparation, briefing, order, movement, target location, work at the target, return, and performance of the task. I enjoyed that. But the fact that a sergeant cheated another soldier—and that I gave in to him—bothered me.

A few weeks after what we called the Night of the Wells, Tzimel was replaced and our new company commander, Giora Haika, called me to his office with four other soldiers from our platoon, to offer us an officers' training course.

The truth is that I never considered the army as a professional career. I regarded it as my duty as a citizen, and my responsibility as a bearer of the traditions of my family. While in the army, I wanted to do my best. I believed I did. The dilemma chased me during my entire life in the army. As deep in my heart as my love of Nahalal and home, I loved the spirit of special operations, and now, faced with the question of going home or more time in the army, I knew that I wanted to be an officer.

I knew that I enjoyed being the leader. In the squad commanders' course, through which everyone in a *sayeret* must pass, I learned that I enjoyed my natural ability to organize and control a force effectively. From the squad commanders' course, I already learned that 80 percent of the work of a combat officer is training and educating soldiers, and I enjoyed that as much as the self-discovery of leadership.

I asked Giora how much more time the army wanted me for. An extra six months, he said. I did the calculation in my head. It meant serving until June 1967. Okay, I decided on the spot, unable to know then that it would be the first time—but not the last—that the army would ask me to change my personal plans only to have far greater, historic forces change the army's plans for me.

THREE STUBBORN FIGHTERS

A hundred-and-twenty-kilometer non-stop march is long and exhausting, a round-the-clock journey to the limits of endurance. But properly prepared, a soldier can easily handle the seventy-four-mile march.

To build up to a 120 kilometers, you start with a thirty, a fifty, an eighty, until finally, you can do a 120. Between each of the major hikes, you stay in shape with fast marches of five, ten, fifteen kilometers. In the beginning a quick dozen kilometers does not seem like much, but thirty seems like a lot. Once you've done a thirty, a fifty seems possible. The most important thing is that each soldier feel great, not broken, at the end of the 120-kilometer journey.

There are short rests, of five to ten minutes, and longer, twenty-minute breaks to eat. You carry your combat gear—your gun, your web-belt weighed down with supplies, a little food that you can carry in a pack. Nothing special.

The biggest problem is the monotony. The first ten or twenty are easy. After thirty kilometers you begin to get tired, and around forty the realization begins to sink in that it is endless. It is a meditative experience, one of the most personal experiences a person can go through. You learn to know yourself, your physical fitness, your body.

And your head. It is a tremendous emotional effort. At first the soldiers chatter. But very quickly everyone settles into their private rhythm, deep in their own thoughts, knowing nobody can help.

It goes on around the clock. I learned to think of my family and what they were doing while I walked. At four-thirty in the morning, my father rose to milk the cows. At seven, my young brother went to school. At seven in the evening, they sat down to the evening meal of salads and cheese, eggs and fruits. And we continued walking, along the soft sandy Mediterranean beaches, up and down Galilee's hills, across the Negev Desert.

Gradually, people begin to complain. Suddenly, a soldier starts running—he wants it to be over already. The idea is to disconnect your head from your body, not to think of your body. Let your body find its rhythm and it will take care of itself.

I heard people groaning for kilometers, and admired them, knowing they continued despite their pain. The journey is difficult enough when nothing hurts. If something hurts, it is a nightmare. Growing up barefoot made the soles of my feet callused and strong. I never suffered blisters.

On my first 120, at the end of basic training, I noticed something strange. I watched the platoon commanders and the company commander. It always looked easier for them. They made the same physical effort and were not necessarily in better shape than us, but it looked so easy for them.

Only when I reached the officers' training course did I learn the secret—the psychological advantage built into the responsibility of command. When you lead people under great duress, you have to be a model of behavior. The more complaints you hear, the more agile you become. When you serve as a model, you're a commander and not a soldier. The responsibility of leadership makes you forget all the pain, effort, and monotony.

I met infantry soldiers from all over the army at the officers' training course. Supposedly the cream of the crop, the best from every branch of the army, it quickly became apparent that those of us who came from the paratroops brigade, especially the five of us from the *sayeret*, out-soldiered them all. Our combat experience set us apart from all the other cadets, and in fieldcraft we even bettered our instructors.

About three months into the course, an adjutant from the paratroops brigade arrived at the base to see the five of us from the *sayeret*. Waiting for him on the lawn outside his office, we wondered why they sent an adjutant. As combat fighters from the *sayeret*, we never spoke to adjutants, the desk jockeys who worked far from the field.

Moshe went in first, and came out after a few minutes. "This guy is crazy," he said. "If we refuse to sign up for at least another eighteen months at the end of the officer course, we don't go back to the brigade. It's an order straight from Raful."

Some cadets had come to the course from the regular paratroops brigade. I decided that the adjutant had made a mistake. "It's probably for those other guys," I said. "He can't mean us."

"I don't think so," Moshe said. I still did not believe it. I waited for the others to come out. They all heard the same message.

I went in knowing exactly what I would do. I saluted. The adjutant offered me a chair. "How's it going?" he started casually.

"Okay," I grunted. He waited for me to add something. But I stayed silent, waiting to hear what he wanted to tell me.

"Listen," he said, turning officious. "There's an order from Raful. Whoever wants to return to the brigade after the course has to sign up for one additional year, in addition to the extra six months that you already committed to as part of the officers' course."

"Wait a minute, I'm from the *sayeret*," I tried.

"Doesn't matter," said the adjutant, studying the papers in front of him.

"Okay," I said, knowing exactly what I wanted. I used my most formal tone. "I hereby resign from officers' school." That made him raise his head, astonished. Nobody resigns from officers' training. I went on. "I hereby request a transfer back to my unit, where I'll continue my service as a sergeant, as a soldier, not an officer." His mouth dropped open. And to drive the point home, I added, "In fact, I can leave right now."

He gasped, looking for words. Finally he said, "Impossible."

"What do you mean impossible?" I demanded angrily. "What you're doing right now is deception. If someone had told me before this course that I'd have to sign up for another two years . . ."

"Eighteen months," he corrected me.

"You don't get it, do you?" I shot back. "I'm not talking about how much time is involved. I'm talking about the principle of the issue. The deception. If they told me it meant another year, maybe I would have signed up. But they didn't. Now you tell me? In the middle of the course? Forget it. I'm quitting the course and going back to Tel Nof. On principle," I snapped at him.

"Look, this is an order from the brigade commander," he tried, in that defensive desk-jockey manner that always refuses to fight for itself. "And I'll tell him that his order did not go down well here," he added, trying to threaten me.

"You tell him exactly what I told you," I shot back, then stood up and walked out to join my buddies on the lawn.

I told them what I had said, and then each of them went back in and told the adjutant that none of us would sign up for the extra time. It became a matter of principle.

The next day Giora Haika, our company commander, showed up and summoned all five of us for a meeting.

"Are you guys out of your minds?" he began.

I put up my hand. "First of all, they brought us up in the *sayeret* to believe that as fighters, we don't talk to adjutants. Why didn't you or one of our platoon commanders come and talk to us?"

That threw Giora. "I didn't know about it," he admitted ruefully. "It surprised me as much as it surprised you."

He stayed loyal to both sides—us and Raful. He did not say what he thought about the order—good or bad—or even comment on the way it came to us, via an adjutant rather than an officer. But he promised to look into it. Three days later he came back with bad news. "It's more complicated than I thought," he said. "You all know Raful. He's stubborn. And he's brigade commander. You guys think about it, and let me know what you decide."

We discussed it that night, but I had already decided not to let my principles affect their lives. Some planned army careers. If they followed my lead, it could ruin their chances. Too stubborn to admit that he made a mistake, there was no point trying to fight Raful. I suggested that the best thing would be for each of us to decide what we wanted. But Betsers are also stubborn—especially about matters of principle. I made my own plans.

In those years, the next best unit in the IDF after the paratroops *sayeret* was Shaked, the Southern Command's elite reconnaissance force.

Based in the Negev, Shaked saw a lot of action, dealing with border infiltration from both Egypt and Jordan. Almost daily, it faced terrorists from Gaza, Egyptian Army intelligence officers on reconnaissance missions, Jordanian and Palestinian infiltrators from the Jordan Rift, and Bedouin smugglers on ancient routes from Africa to the Persian Gulf through the Sinai and Negev into Jordan and, from there, to Saudi Arabia.

Shaked's legendary commanding officer, Amos Yarkoni, the Bedouin-born former Abed al-Majid, came from the Jezreel Valley. He knew my family. As a child he herded his family's sheep, grazing them in the rich fields that my grandparents and their friends made from the swamps of the valley. My father and Moshe Dayan patrolled the fields on horseback, chasing off the Bedouin ruining the moshav crops with their sheep. The fights with sticks and stones over the fields of Nahalal and the Bedouin grazing lands eventually turned into a strong friendship between my father and Yarkoni.

The War of Independence interrupted that friendship, when pan-Arab rhetoric united all the Arabs against us. But the Bedouin—like the Druze and the Circassians, two other ancient, stateless peoples of the Middle East—have an ancient tradition that serves them well for their survival. Stateless, they know to side with the stronger side in a dispute, and in the country where they live, they are loyal to the state.

In 1948, at the outbreak of the War of Independence, when the Arab world declared war on the newborn Jewish state, the Bedouin, Druze, and Circassians sided with the attempted Arab invasion. Abed al-Majid became a leader of one of the irregular Arab militias that raided Jewish settlements in the area.

But as soon as the IDF began to win in 1948 and it became clear that Israel would survive, many of the Bedouin living inside the borders of the state began to have second thoughts about their loyalties. Moshe Dayan met with Abed al-Majid, his boyhood friend, and talked him into siding with Israel, indeed into joining the IDF. Since then, the Bedouin, the Druze, and the Circassians—ethnic minorities in Israel—are drafted into Israel's security forces. And for the same reason, the Druze of Syria join the Syrian Army.

As soon as my friends from Nahalal in Shaked told Amos that Nahman Betser's son wanted to join his unit, Amos pulled all the necessary strings to get me into his unit as soon as I finished the officers' course. Amos wanted me to train a new Shaked platoon. I wanted to see Shaked action in the Negev, catching armed Palestinians who slipped across the borders of Egypt and Jordan, from Gaza and the West Bank.

The weeks went by in the officers' course. I loved being in the paratroops and did not want to lose the chance to do my reserves in the brigade's *sayeret*. I kept up an unlikely hope to see Raful show up one day to explain the order to us. When he didn't, I decided to go see him myself.

A few weeks before the end of the officers' course, while on weekend leave at home, I went to see him at Tel Adashim, the moshav where he lived a few kilometers up the Jezreel Valley from Nahalal. He knew my family, and welcomed me warmly as both a neighbor and one of his soldiers.

Raful took a lot of pride in his paratroopers. To this day, he always picks up hitchhiking soldiers. But when he sees a hitch-hiking paratrooper, he drops off the soldier already in his car, in order to take the paratrooper. If the surprised soldier complains, Raful says simply, "Next time, be a paratrooper."

We sat in the small carpentry shop in his yard. I went right to the point. "I volunteered for the paratroops *sayeret*," I began, "because it is the best commando unit in the army. You're our brigade com-mander. But because of an arbitrary order that you gave, I'm leaving the paratroops to go to Shaked."

I thought I gave him the opportunity to explain his decision—or reverse it. Instead, he tried to convince me to sign up for another two years in the brigade.

"Raful, it is more than a question of time," I interrupted. "We felt deceived. By the brigade. We were told we'd finish the course and have another six months, and then, in the middle, you told us to do another eighteen months. It was my idea that we all refuse to return to the brigade. The others can decide what they want to do. But there's no way I'm going to break my word—and I believe the brigade broke its word to us."

Raful admired principles, and loyalty to fellow soldiers. But he did not rescind the order. And as I left, he vowed to get me trans-ferred back to the paratroops.

Raful was stubborn. Amos Yarkoni was no less stubborn. He lost a hand in one battle, and part of a leg in another. But the most loving of his soldiers of any commander I have known, he never lost his head.

He beat back Raful's efforts to bring me back to the paratroops brigade. "I saw Raful," Amos said many times over the coming years, coming back to headquarters from Southern Command or the general staff's headquarters in Tel Aviv, "and he's still asking for you."

Their dispute over me went all the way to Shaike Gavish, the general in charge of the Southern Command. Shaked was the apple of Shaike's eye, and he stuck by Amos when Raful complained that he wanted Betser back. But for Amos it became a matter of honor to keep me, and I think it gave him as much pleasure to rebuff Raful's demand for my return to the paratroops as it did to train and lead the sons of the Jezreel Valley's pioneers.

"You are the children of the roots of the valley," he said at every graduation ceremony of soldiers finishing their basic training in his regiment, "sons of the farmers." He told the new soldiers, "You make me proud."

Already past forty when I reached Shaked, Amos was in his last year as its commander, a wise, experienced veteran who taught me secrets of the desert. He spoke a fluent Hebrew, with an Arabic accent, and wore a carefully trimmed black mustache and a black fist at the end of his wrist where he had lost his hand. He came up with his own methods for handling weapons, as fast as anyone with two hands, clutching the weapon in his armpit while using his good hand to reload, then using his forearm to stabilize the gun barrel.

Most of our work involved chasing the infiltrators who came over the Gazan border. They usually crossed at night, cutting through the fence the IDF had installed around Gaza. Our morning patrols picked up the tracks and we gave chase. Sometimes the tracks went back into Gaza. Often they ended in captures. Sometimes they ended with a firefight. Our prey included Egyptian spies, Palestinian terrorists, and smugglers and thieves.

Amos taught us to read all their tracks, as well as the codes of the deserts, fields, and groves of the south. He taught me to look at a withered leaf and know how long ago someone had stepped on it. He taught me the difference between a runner's footstep and an ambusher's crouch marks, between the prints left behind by an Egyptian soldier's boots and a Palestinian terrorist's shoes.

For Bedouin, tracks in the desert are like street signs for someone who grew up in the city. A stranger in the desert can mean a thief or a smuggler, an enemy scout or an ambush. Just as city people watch traffic lights, so Bedouin watch for footprints in the land.

Amos taught it all. "The night has everything," he taught. "Quiet and sound. People moving, cars, a tractor across a field. Anything that has the element of animals in it—always listen, and learn. Turtles, frogs, anything that makes noise—listen. A turtle's path or a frog's bellow means water, and water means people."

All new for the city boys, Amos's lessons made the landscape come alive for the country boys in ways I had only dreamt about. Within a few weeks I read my soldiers' footprints, knowing how tired they became on a long march from the tracks, recognizing a limp in a footstep left in the sand. I've known many Bedouin scouts over the years, but Amos stood head and shoulders above them all in his understanding of the land, in his leadership, in his integrity as a family man, and in his loyalty to Shaked.

He did not give orders. He taught by using example, not theory. Tracking, he taught us, is all about putting yourself in the other person's shoes. One night we chased a terrorist crew that came over from Gaza, tracking four men to a supply shed in a kibbutz orange grove near the border. But on their way out of the grove, a fifth set of tracks joined the party. It confused us all. Where did the fifth man come from? Who was he?

Amos showed up and crouched beside the tracks, studying them for a few moments before suddenly getting up and walking off into the grove. He came back a minute later, astonishing us by holding out an Egyptian commando's knife.

"Simple," he said. "One of the four dropped something or forgot something," Amos explained. "He backtracked, and rejoined the trail where he had already walked. I went back, to search for what he lost," he said, indeed making it sound simple.

The kings of the Negev, from Beer Sheva to Eilat, we chased down Gazan thieves who stole farm supplies; we went after Egyptian intelligence crews who needed to steal something from an Israeli settlement to prove they had made it over the border; and we trapped Palestinian *fedayeen* coming into Israel to wreak their havoc. We even caught a few Israelis—Arabs, Druze, and even a few Jews—trying to escape personal problems by slipping out of the country. We set up our ambushes to capture people coming over from Gaza, but we always kept someone on guard at the rear in case an Israeli appeared out of nowhere.

Despite the importance of the daily routines of border security, the function of any army is to prepare for war. From the start, Amos gave me a platoon to train, as well as my duties as a participant in chases after terrorists.

Every soldier, every officer, no matter how young, knew that notwithstanding cease-fire agreements with Egypt, Syria, Jordan, and Lebanon, war could break out. In January 1967, it might be a year away or five years away. The Arab states made no secret of their intentions to continue fighting our presence in the Land. The first priority of any army unit is to be ready for war.

Amos gave me fifty good soldiers and I winnowed them down to thirty excellent fighters, keeping only those who kept up. The key to any *sayeret* success is fieldcraft—especially navigation. In war, a reconnaissance force moves ahead of advancing armor to scout out the enemy's positions and either overcome them or send back the intelligence needed for the armor to come in and do the job.

I wanted my soldiers to know how to move quickly but thoughtfully. I wanted them aware of their own tracks as well as the tracks of others. They needed to know how to survive on their own, whether finding sustenance in the desert or using the natural routes of the landscape: crannies that provided hiding, cover, and camouflaged shelter, points from which to ambush an enemy or from where an enemy might be watching.

Once they knew the basics, I divided them into squads of two or three, sending them on long-distance navigation routes that took up to a week to complete. I went alone, crisscrossing between the various squads scattered out across the Negev, meeting up with them on the move or when they reached a resting point. I always made sure to surprise them—shooting a round or two in their vicinity, to check their reaction. I remembered the fake drills of my own training and how they disappointed me. I wanted them to understand real-life situations, the reality of soldiering, and how the key to survival is staying alert at all times. Unconventional but effective, my methods kept them alert at all times. Whether training in the heart of the Negev or at the front line of combat, they were soldiers twenty-four hours a day, and must know how to stay alert.

When I came across teams that did not have their weapons handy or I caught them all napping, my ambushes of a few shots over their heads made sure they would never drop their guard again.

That platoon stayed together as a reserve unit for almost twenty years. To this day I hear from soldiers who went through that harsh—but loving—training. The refrain is always the same. "Muki, your training kept us alive through all the wars." And they saw plenty—from the Six-Day War in 1967 to the Lebanon War of 1982, they stayed together as a reserve outfit through all the wars.

In February of 1967, Nurit and I finally married, inheriting the Dayan homestead. We moved to the little three-room house with its two tall palms that Moshe's father planted in the garden when they founded Nahalal. As an officer, I could get home from the south almost every weekend—and sometimes in the middle of the week—except when the unit went operational for a specific mission.

In April, I had a month's leave coming to me before I finished my compulsory service. Then I would be assigned a reserve unit, where I'd serve a month per year until I was no longer fit.

I wanted to go back into the paratroops for my reserve duty. I belonged there, more than any other unit.

But Amos wanted me in Shaked. Nobody—not even Amos—knew the old Bedouin's exact age, but that year he decided the time had come to retire from field command. His deputy, Binyamin "Fuad" Ben-Eliezer, a burly colonel with thin lips that widened into an infectious grin whenever he smiled, came into the force to replace Amos as Shaked's commander. Fuad would go on to become a general and then a politician. Meanwhile, Amos wanted me to stay on, to help Fuad take over.

He made me an extraordinary offer one night sitting over glasses of black tea in his spartan office. "You're going to be a general one day," he said to me in his matter-of-fact tone. "Stay with us in the Southern Command and I'll give you a company," he promised. It would make me one of the youngest company commanders in the IDF. But it meant signing up for another two years. And my plans did not include a full-time professional career in the army.

I shook my head. "I belong in the paratroops," I told him. "You know that. No matter how much I've enjoyed my time with Shaked, the paratroops is my first choice. You know why I came to Shaked—

because of my argument with Raful. But I've fulfilled my duty, and kept to my principles."

"Think about it," he asked. "Promise you'll think about it."

"I will," I promised. "But you know me. I'm not going to change my mind."

At the end of April 1967, my platoon finished its basic training. On the last night of a long field exercise, around a campfire in the Negev under the stars, some of the soldiers pulled out a bottle of wine to pass around to celebrate their graduation from trainees to fighters. I don't drink—and never subject friends to my singing—but I enjoyed their happiness.

After a while I went off into the desert, away from the fire, to look up at the stars and consider my own future. In another few weeks I'd be a civilian again, after two and a half years of compulsory service plus the six months I put in after the officers' training course.

Nurit was pregnant, and the farm waited for me at Nahalal. We talked about traveling to foreign countries. As a teenager, Nurit lived in Tanzania when her father served in a military delegation to that country. Africa sounded interesting. And though I never took school very seriously before the army, the idea of studying geography at university began to appeal to me.

I felt good. Though I had not seen war, I knew that I would do well when the time came. And I knew it would come one day in the future. The Arabs still refused to accept us in the Land of Israel. And when war came, I wanted to experience it as a paratrooper at the tip of the spear of the IDF's defense of the Land.

Few people can surprise me in the desert. Amos could. "Muki, I want to talk with you," said Amos softly, coming up on me from behind, Fuad in his wake.

"I've made up my mind, Amos," I said, knowing what they wanted. "I'm going home. And I want my reserves in the paratroops."

Amos sighed. "I know. But if you're not going to stick around to help Fuad take over the unit," he said softly, "then do something else for me. Go to Tel Hashomer to the induction center. Take over the Shaked recruiting station. I want him," Yarkoni said, using his black fist to point toward Fuad, "to have the best recruits you can find."

I owed Amos for taking me into Shaked after the argument with Raful. It was only a month, and I could spend a lot of it at Nahalal, only a couple of hours north of Tel Hashomer. None of us knew that war would change all my plans. Instead of mustering out in June 1967, I would see my first war.

FIGHTING FOR HONOR

———

Maybe it was our upbringing in a cooperative settlement, maybe because we were so close-knit as a community, maybe because as children we worked out our aggressions in the hard work of farm chores; whatever the reason, the kids from the Jezreel Valley of my youth had no experience with the raw violence of hatred or intentionally inflicting pain on another person.

In great physical shape and motivated by patriotism, like youth anywhere we considered ourselves brave. But while we grew up knowing full well that we would go to the army—and hoped to be among those who would face the enemy, making him die for his country rather than us for ours—we knew nothing about real violence. Raised to understand the necessity of violence for self-defense, we forswore the expression of hatred that gives rise to irrational violence. I hated terrorists, not Arabs. I hated war, not the army.

I went camping every year as a boy with Noar Ha-Oved, a scouts-like movement affiliated to the moshav settlement movement to which my parents belonged. Each year we went to a different campsite for a couple of weeks of living under the stars, hiking the countryside, and visiting historic sites. One year we went to Jerusalem, another to the Negev, a third to Galilee. Our counselors were also teenagers, two or three years older than the campers.

The year I turned fourteen, we went to a woods near Hadera, halfway between Haifa and Tel Aviv. We camped in a wooded grove at the far edges of the town. At the far end of our camp field, a field faucet much like the one in the back of the house at Nahalal provided water. Five of us went over one afternoon with our canteens to fill up.

But, reaching the tap, we encountered something we never saw before: kids from the town and city. They dressed differently, they spoke differently, they behaved differently. We wore sandals and shorts. They wore shoes and long pants. To us farm kids from the Jezreel Valley, they seemed to exude a mysterious threat that made no sense.

"What do you want?" asked their leader, a little taller than the others, just as I was taller than my friends.

"We're from the camp down the field," I explained, speaking for the five of us. "We have permission to use this tap," I added, taking a step toward the faucet.

He sidestepped, blocking my access to the tap. "You can't have any," he said. "Beat it."

It astonished me. I wondered what gave him the right to deny anyone water. But even more confusing was our fear.

I remember those seconds clearly. Nobody had ever challenged me so forcefully. The showdown became a matter of honor. My grandparents and parents taught me never to back down. To give in to the threat, to run back to camp to report to the counselors instead of taking command of the situation, would be shameful. But the other option, to face down their challenge, seemed beyond any of us. None of us ever fought for real, with the intention of causing pain to the other. At most, we wrestled. "We're here to get water," I repeated, as leader of my friends. "We have permission."

"Beat it," their leader scoffed at me again.

The tension rose. I knew I had the right to take the water, and I understood in that moment that, ready or not, I would stand up for my rights even if it meant a fight. They looked like they knew about fighting. That turned into a second shock for me. All I knew about fighting came from the outdoor movies at Nahalal in summer, and I knew *that* was not for real.

Innocent and ignorant of fighting, throwing a punch or slapping someone was outside the realm of my experience. I saw the experience of violence in their eyes. Yet, behind the aggression and the threats, I also saw a nervous fear. In that instant I realized that fear is as much present in the enemy's mind as it is in your own, and the winner is the one who can conquer his fear.

It all boiled down to a decision. Either we fight or we ignore them, try to take some water and see if they challenged us further. Their leader took a step forward. My body tensed as I realized that we had reached the point of no return. I did not know how, but I knew I would fight.

Just then, one of the counselors from our camp came running. He flew into the tense scene without stopping to ask questions and did what needed to be done. He went for the biggest kid, punching him once in the face. The gang leader reeled backward, falling to the ground. His friends ran. A moment later, the city kid jumped to his feet and ran after his friends.

I stood there, open-mouthed, watching the city kids' retreat, for the first time in my life understanding the nature of fighting.

I carried that memory for years, until it gave birth to one of the tests I conceived to grade the new Shaked recruits. In addition to the usual tests of physical endurance and team spirit, I wanted to judge the candidates on their ability to use violence.

I lined them up in two rows facing each other. "Now, take turns hitting each other," I commanded.

From their expressions I could tell that most did not understand the order.

"Slap your partner. Across the face," I explained. Nobody would get really hurt. But I would quickly see who held back and who hit with too much pleasure, who still did not understand the order and who tried but did not follow through.

"Is that how you slap someone?" I asked, approaching one of the hesitant recruits, using my most pleasant voice. I learned a long time ago that the only reason to raise my voice is to be heard over noise, not to impress anyone with my authority.

The soldier shrugged. I walloped him with an open-handed slap on the cheek, sending him flying. "Now you hit me," I said as he recovered. But he was afraid—after all, I was an officer.

"Hit me," I ordered. He threw something too soft to count. Again I walloped him. Again he climbed back to his feet. And again I gave the order for him to slap me.

By then he became mad. But I could take care of that later, teaching that anger is a good motive but a terrible tactic. When he hit me as hard as I hit him, I knew I could make a soldier out of him.

I wanted to see if they overcame the psychological barrier resulting from inexperience. After all, it is always better to experience conflict on the drill field before getting to the real thing in combat. I did not want soldiers who enjoyed inflicting pain. I did want soldiers unafraid to use force.

NOT THE SIX-DAY WAR,
THE THREE-HOUR WAR

I thought I would recruit the new Shaked class and then go back to Nahalal. But Gamal Abdel Nasser, president of Egypt, made other plans for me—and Israel—in mid-May of 1967.

Barely a week after my arrival at Tel Hashomer, Nasser suddenly blockaded the Red Sea, preventing ships from reaching Eilat, our southernmost port. The threat of war turned even more serious when he evicted the UN peacekeeping troops posted in Sinai since the 1956 Suez campaign and began massing troops and armor on the border between the Negev and the Sinai.

Television broadcasts from Cairo and the rest of the Arab world showed millions of people in the streets screaming support for *jihad*, an Islamic holy war against us. They planned to drive us into the sea, said the Arab leaders, mobilizing their armies.

Nasser sent his entire army up to our borders. The IDF mobilized its reserves. War looked inevitable. And I felt I belonged in the paratroops when it broke out.

Shaked was a great outfit for daily security work guarding the borders, but in a war, I reckoned, the paratroops would get to the most important battlefields. Believing the army bureaucracy might overlook me because of the overlap between the end of my active service and my assignment to a reserve unit, I decided to take matters into my own hands.

I gave the recruiting station command to the Shaked sergeant and headed to the paratroops brigade, where they welcomed me with open arms. They planned a drop into Sharm al-Sheikh, at the southern tip of the Sinai, far behind enemy lines. I joined the planning.

It took Amos less than twenty-four hours to find me. "You're the best tracker in the country." I sighed, recognizing his voice and knowing what he wanted—for me to return to Shaked.

"I didn't have to track," Amos said with a soft chuckle. "I know you, and I know where you're from," he said.

Maybe as a son of the Jezreel Valley he meant that he would have done the same. It is too late now to ask him—he passed away in the late eighties. But to his credit, he never gave me the feeling I needed to apologize, and never said anything more about the incident.

He gave me back the troops I had just finished training, plus dozens of additional soldiers called up from the reserves. Just as he promised, I was leading a company-size force at the age of twenty-three.

Beefed up by reservists, Shaked split up into several forces spread out along the Egyptian front lines forming rapidly in front of our eyes on the long line dividing the Negev from Sinai.

Assigned the lead reconnaissance position for the First Battalion of the Ninth Brigade under Arik Sharon's divisional command, my battle orders were clear and simple. As the advance reconnaissance unit for the battalion, we would move into Sinai ahead of Sharon's armor, seeking out enemy positions to attack. If we could take them on our own, we would. If not, patched into a radio network with Fuad and Amos, we would pass the intelligence back to brigade headquarters, for the artillery or our own armor to handle the enemy position. We were going to be the first Israeli soldiers over the line into Sinai, with the entire strength of Arik Sharon's division behind us.

It meant two weeks of excruciating waiting. In the city, on the home front, they dug bomb shelters and worried. At least we kept busy.

Every night we patrolled the Egyptian lines, a fifteen-minute drive away across a desert plain broken by gravely dunes and wide mouths of ancient wadis that had not seen rain for millennia. Every night, more Egyptian tanks and artillery lined up against us.

Daytime, we dug in and prepared our own attack. Israel is much too small to allow any enemy penetration of the country. The basic principle of combat is to assault. Ambushed, assault. Under fire, assault. Not blindly, of course, not without thinking. Think, plan, but then assault. It might cost a life, but if you don't assault, you'll lose everything as the enemy closes in. The principle of combat for a single unit, it is also the general principle for the entire army. We cannot afford to let a single enemy tank cross our lines.

Indeed, while they announced their intentions to invade our country, we planned to fight back by invading theirs. Tens of thousands of Israeli soldiers arrived in the south to face the hundreds of thousands of Egyptian soldiers lining up a few miles away to the west.

Those of us on the line felt confident, especially in combat units like mine, where we planned on taking the initiative in the war. But the government hesitated. And public self-confidence drained away day by day. Meanwhile, the Arab frenzy for war mounted. History appeared to make it a life-and-death battle for us. With the Holocaust less than a generation away, once again the lives of millions of Jews were in danger, simply because they were Jews.

For two weeks, the politicians tried to avoid war, while we worked to prepare for it. The economy came to a halt, with the full-scale call-up that put all the able-bodied men in the country into the trenches. And on the front lines we prepared: daily parades—morning, noon, and evening. Daily maintenance of vehicles—jeeps, command cars, and half-tracks; physical training every day, including running, weapons practice, and hand-to-hand combat. Sweat dries fast in the dry heat, and at night stiff breezes swept across the plain. We worked hard, waiting for the war to begin.

We barely slept those two weeks. I kept the soldiers busy in daytime, keeping equipment in shape, learning maps, and drilling. At night I patrolled by jeep and on foot, bringing eyewitness reports on enemy troop formations to command headquarters, where they updated the aerial photographs and other intelligence reports arriving from headquarters.

The radio and daily newspapers only told us that the government met or the UN met, that Jerusalem appealed for a peaceful resolution, and the foreign minister spoke with his counterparts from the superpowers. Meanwhile, Nasser's speeches to a million enthusiastic followers in Cairo promised the Arab world a victory as great as Saladin's victory over the Crusaders.

In the Night of the Wells I learned that a soldier's first border crossing is a primal experience. You live all your life in a country with an enemy on the other side of the border. You cross the border expecting an ambush. But when you cross the border and see that the enemy's side is just like yours, with the same vegetation, the same orange groves, the same sand and stone, you realize that on both sides there are simply peaceful citizens who want to live quietly, working their fields or living their lives.

Nonetheless, in special operations like the Night of the Wells, you know how you're going in and how you're coming out. It is your initiative, based on your plan. That moment of paranoia crossing the border—and the alert serenity that follows—is almost a luxury compared to the feeling on the eve of war. In war, all you know is how to go in. You can never know how you will come out.

Just before dawn on June 5, 1967, the orders came down to get ready. Up and down the line, engines rumbled in the darkness that gradually gave way to the brilliant light of the sun rising in the east behind us.

The first wave of planes, weighed down by bombs and flying low against radar, flew overhead just as the sun came over the horizon. They flew away from the rising sun, westward into the enemy's eyes. And we raced after them.

It took fifteen minutes to reach our first encounter with the enemy. A gravelly dune loomed ahead. I raised a hand, and the three jeeps and three armored personnel carriers behind me came to a halt.

With the sun directly behind me, my shadow carved a slender black line down the middle of the dune as I made my way up. Just below the ridge, I fell to a crawl. The latest intelligence—indeed, my own eyewitness observations from only two nights before—made me expect twenty or thirty tanks laid out in formations in the flat plain of a wadi's mouth gaping open to the mazes of mountains in Sinai, where the Children of Israel wandered for forty years.

Already crawling up the ridge, I sensed something wrong in the air. The sky darkened, with thick black smoke rising in columns.

Now, as I lifted my head over the ridge to look down on the enemy, expecting to see dozens of tanks moving into action, I saw the source of those black, smoky clouds. I raised my binoculars. Behind me, soldiers whispered, wondering about the delay. And at first even I did not understand what had happened.

The towers of smoke rose from more than a dozen tanks burning like torches in the morning sun. Other tanks stood motionless in the sheer white plain of the wadi mouth. Dozens of jeeps and trucks lay scattered across the landscape like broken toys.

"Someone has already been here," I murmured to myself, looking down on the strange scene, knowing it was impossible. *We* were supposed to be the first over the line. Shocked—and thrilled, as the meaning of what I saw sank in—I scanned the horizon from north to south, trying to make sense of the scene, realizing that the air force had indeed preceded us.

And in the distance, the most amazing sight of all: thousands of Egyptian soldiers trudging west, escaping the battlefield, trying to walk home far across the Sinai Peninsula to the Suez Canal and Egypt, beyond.

I called my observations back to Amos and Fuad in the Shaked command car, elsewhere in Sharon's advancing army.

"I want to take my force down to investigate," I summed up.

Fuad responded with a refrain that I would hear over and over again during the coming hours and days. "Okay, Betser," he said, "but go slow and safe."

Our anticipation quickly turned into astonishment as we sped into the smoke blowing across the plain. Then, as we drove directly into the center of the first flanking camp, our amazement at the destruction of the tanks turned to horror.

From the distance, the war looked like an angry giant had broken his toys. Here we saw the real cost of war: as the smoke swirled around us, the broken toys turned into broken people. A severed arm pointed nowhere. A head, its mouth open, looked surprised that the rest of its body was gone. The wind carried the thick stink of burning flesh.

I stood up in the jeep, raising a hand to call for a halt. Below me, an Egyptian soldier lay on his back, the flies already gathering in the open cavity of his charred chest. His smooth face was too young to need to shave daily. Where did he come from, I wondered. Cairo? Alexandria? Or a peasants' village on the banks of the Nile? I felt sorry for him, so far from home. I thought of my home, and how close it felt.

A moaning Egyptian soldier broke the quiet. I signaled the medics to look for survivors and treat them. Looking back at my soldiers, I saw my own shock reflected in the eyes of the young soldiers I finished training only a month before. But in the eyes of the older reservists, who went through the '56 campaign in the Sinai, I saw something else—an understanding of the pain experienced by those of us who never before saw such destruction coping with the initially overwhelming feelings of horrified awe at the result of war.

And the war continued.

It did not take long for the tanks to catch up and remind us to get moving again. As the tanks came to a halt, we pulled out after a few words with the commanders, then headed west to the heart of the Sinai.

Our jeeps quickly caught up with the Egyptian soldiers walking away from the battle that never took place. We drove through them like a car making its way down a street crowded with pedestrians. But these shell-shocked pedestrians wore the pale, sand-colored uniforms of the Egyptian Army, a defeated army broken to its core.

Sometimes we shot a burst into the air—but only as a siren, to get them out of the way. Other times we saw them across the wide plain of the desert: hundreds of helpless, frightened soldiers, with no weapons and abandoned by officers who managed to grab working vehicles to drive home, leaving their soldiers to fend for themselves.

Rarely did we come across an Egyptian still carrying a weapon.

We had expected battles from hill to hill, ridge to ridge, and valley to valley. Instead, our biggest problem seemed to be getting through the crowds of Egyptians trying to get home.

For two days and nights we moved through those crowds across Sinai, heading west across the center of the Sinai desert. Nights, we rested—another luxury of that war in 1967. In the chill of the desert night, and because of the rules of field security—

though we obviously had won, the war was not over—we used blankets instead of campfires to keep warm. We ate cold rations and caught a few hours' sleep before rising before dawn to continue.

On the third day, we reached the outskirts of Tamad, a small Egyptian fortress at an oasis where the Bedouin kept a working waterwell. For the first time, we reached a defended Egyptian position. But even that barely counted as a fight. The Egyptians gave up quickly, after a few rounds of mortar fire and a jeep raid into their camp.

We made camp at Tamad, where the rest of Shaked's forces joined us. The next morning, when we woke in our camp, hundreds of Egyptians surrounded us—not to fight, but to surrender. They wanted food. They wanted to go home.

Fuad called together the force for a briefing. Starting his talk, he suddenly stopped. "Who's that?" He squinted, pointing toward the edge of the crowd of dust-covered fighters. An Egyptian soldier, just as dust-covered as any of us, sat amidst the soldiers, hoping for food. We gave him a tin of rations and some water, then sent him on his way.

Fuad's briefing thrilled us all. The IDF controlled Sinai, he announced. But in the north, he continued, battles raged for the Golan Heights.

For nearly twenty years, since the end of the War of Independence, Syrian artillery and cannons on the high ground of the Golan plateau above the Sea of Galilee had shelled our settlements below the Heights. Over the years, dozens died in the indiscriminate shelling of the farming settlements in the foothills of the Golan Heights.

But when we gathered at the pickup point for the helicopters to take us to the Golan, Fuad announced another change in plans. In el-Arish, a beach town on the Mediterranean coast of northern Sinai, Egyptian commando forces harassed our forces, who took the town in the first days of the war. Later, I learned my brother Udi fought in that sector, in battles much tougher than anything I had seen so far during the war.

"They're hiding out during the day and operating at night," said Fuad. "And they've caused casualties. Dead and wounded." It sounded exactly like the kind of job Shaked knew best how to handle.

We reached the soft dunes of northern Sinai in late afternoon, taking positions near the el-Arish airport. That night, staff officers from the armored corps brigade showed up to brief us on the situation. Jumpy and nervous from non-stop fighting holding the town after its quick capture, they described "swarms" of Egyptian commandos hitting the supply lines on the road through town from Gaza to Kantara at the northern tip of the Suez Canal.

Fuad and Amos questioned locals in the area, but either too scared to tell us what they knew or truly ignorant, the locals gave us little. I suggested that aerial surveillance might help, and the air force provided a two-seated Piper.

I asked the pilot, Elisha, for "low to mid-level recon over the town and beach." Instead, he began sweeping the dunes as if he could turn the Piper into a Mirage, coming in a few meters off the tops of dunes, diving and skimming the surface of the beach. To make matters worse, he occasionally let off a burst from the machine gun mounted in the plane's nose.

"Hey, Elisha," I shouted over the noise of the propeller and engine, "drive carefully," deliberately choosing the term for our trip, to make the point that he should take it easy. I tried to make light of his reckless flying, which took us much too fast over the town for me to spot anything of value in the search for the commandos. But he ignored me. Up and down, over and over, he dove toward the sand dunes, leveling off and then veering to the right or left, seeking another target. I can handle danger. But I have no patience for recklessness. "Put me down," I finally ordered, not hiding the anger in my voice. He obeyed.

A few minutes later, Elisha took off with a blast of wind, leaving me on the tarmac beside Fuad and Amos, who waited for my return. "That boy's endangering himself for no good reason," I told them.

A few minutes later, the radio squawked a report that Elisha had crashed and was killed. Shivers raced up and down my spine as I realized that a miracle saved me from ending up dead in a fiery crash in the dunes.

We hovered in a chopper over the beaches of el-Arish. Despite clear packs of footsteps on the soft white sand, none ended anywhere except amidst others. It made no sense. We figured they probably hid out in town disguised as civilians during the day and at night gathered their equipment from caches hidden in the area. We decided to go in by jeep and on foot for a closer look for the caches.

The beaches of el-Arish are a fine white sand that slips and slides in tiny avalanches with every step. We hiked up and down the sand, spread out across the beach from the water's edge all the way to the narrow broken road dividing the beach from the town.

Nothing appeared extraordinary to me as I studied the terrain—except the palm branches, I realized, about halfway down the beach.

Any grove of palms has fallen branches. But these branches seemed too neatly arranged, and too green to be dead wood. I looked up. From what I saw so far of el-Arish—salt-eaten single-story villas facing the beach, a dusty main street flanked by two-story buildings, and a shantytown of refugee camps around it, I doubted the el-Arish municipality made a point of pruning its wild trees.

The tall palms grew out of a depression between two dunes, in what the Arabs call a *tmila*, where underground fresh water and seawater meet, forcing the fresh water up closer to the surface. With the underground water barely a meter and a half (five feet) below the surface, and the fronds as a roof, I realized a *tmila* can make a perfect underground cave for hiding.

I caught the eye of some nearby soldiers and waved, backing away from the frond roof, warning the soldiers running toward me to be quiet as they approached. I hand-signaled them into formation, and we carefully approached the basin where the long branches seemed too neatly organized to be natural.

We had walked by those palm branches half a dozen times in the last hour, and nothing had happened. I only made an educated guess. But I wanted to be careful, just in case. Ready? I silently signaled my fighters. They nodded and aimed their Uzis at the palm branches.

Carefully, almost delicately, I lifted one of the dry fronds. Ten Egyptian commandos, guns ready, waited for us. We shot first. They all died in those bare seconds it takes to empty a magazine.

Up and down the beach, we stopped everywhere we found stands of palms. We shot at the edges of each *tmila*, calling for them to surrender. If they refused, we assaulted. Some surrendered; some did not. It was war.

I had an easy war—Israel had an easy war—but war is no picnic. In the Rafiah area, where my brother Udi fought under Raful, tough tank battles ended in the town with house-to-house combat against Egyptian soldiers refusing to retreat or surrender. Some 650 Israeli soldiers died in the war, fighting in the Sinai, on the Golan, and in Jerusalem and the West Bank.

One of my best friends at the time, Ranny Marx, died in Sinai. Ranny and I served together as platoon commanders in Shaked, but his release from the army came three months earlier than mine. He went home to Kibbutz Hazorea, and when war broke out, they gave him a reconnaissance platoon attached to an armored brigade.

Giora Eitan, Raful's nephew and my first company commander when I joined the army, died on the Golan.

No matter how great the victory of the war, funerals are full of sorrow. I went to dozens in the weeks after the war. But we needed to put aside our emotions.

The rest of the world might think the war ended in six days. For us, the fighting continued, postponing my release. Shaked moved to Kantara on the Suez Canal, part of the new IDF deployment along the banks of the famous waterway.

In places, the Canal is barely a couple of football fields wide, flanked by undulating banks of dunes and hard sand creating natural cover—and long stretches of exposed territory. It stopped tanks—but not artillery, mortar fire, or even a sniper's bullets. Shaked worked along the Canal, ferrying supplies to isolated positions up and down the Canal and chasing down occasional Egyptian commando attempts to harass our new lines.

Late one afternoon, a strange request came to Shaked. A platoon from the armored corps *sayeret* under Brigadier General Shmuel "Gorodish" Gonen, lost three jeeps about ten kilometers south of Kantara. Hit by fire from the opposite banks, the patrol abandoned their jeeps and equipment in the attack.

"Gorodish wants us to get the jeeps back," Fuad said.

"That's strange," I said, perturbed by the mission. "A *sayeret* wants someone else to do their job? They should be able to get the stuff themselves. And why does Gorodish want to risk lives for three jeeps?"

Fuad scowled. "I bet they left behind the coded maps for the entire zone."

"I'd be embarrassed to ask for help if I were Gorodish," I said.

Fuad, who would go on to become a politician, stayed silent on that point. Gorodish came out of the Six-Day War a hero, the general who made a point of riding into battle standing exposed in the turret of his tank. I thought about Raful as I followed Fuad to the semi-trailer that carried the mobile headquarters of the Southern Command. Raful would never ask for a force from outside his direct command to fix a mistake by his own men.

Famous for his capricious temper, Gorodish surprised me with a polite, respectful attitude toward us. He ordered coffee and tea brought in, and then explained the situation, starting by pointing at the map on the long table in the trailer, to show us where to find the jeeps.

Fuad had guessed right. "I don't care about the jeeps," Gorodish explained from the start. "It's the maps and equipment." He worried that the Egyptians, spotting the abandoned jeeps, would send commandos across to investigate and find the coded maps outlining the full deployment of our forces on the canal.

I could see his dilemma. What would be more disgraceful to a famous hero of the Six-Day War—to ask Shaked to handle something that his own men screwed up, or to tell the general staff to change all the codes on all the maps in the army?

"Please get the maps, codes, and radios back," he pleaded, adding, "tonight," almost sheepishly.

Three basic scenarios faced us: either nobody had touched the jeeps, or the Egyptians had already stolen it all and booby-trapped what they left behind, or they still waited in ambush for the IDF to send someone back.

By eight that night, I worked out a plan based on a ten-kilometer hike across the dunes to the canal, rather than a jeep ride on the road that could be seen from the other side.

Gorodish okayed the plan, and I picked a dozen of my fighters for the mission. The general insisted on sending along three soldiers from the squad that had abandoned the jeeps. "They'll show you where to find them," he said.

He already showed us on the map where to find the jeeps. I did not need them, or want them. But I think Gorodish wanted them to see how the job should be done. I saw no point in arguing it with him. But setting off, with the three soldiers from his *sayeret* in tow,

I decided not to count on them for any significant aspect of the assignment.

It took two and a half hours across the dunes to reach the last few hundred meters to the jeeps. Three forces would approach the target—two flanking squads from north and south, and the third squad, which I led, would approach the jeeps from the east. I left Gorodish's soldiers behind. "To protect our rear," I said, not expecting any trouble from there, but wanting them out of our way. "Just stay alert and watch for our signal," I instructed them one last time as my three squads went into action.

We crawled the last two hundred meters, over the ridge of a dune and then down into the clearing. It took almost as long to cross those last two hundred meters as it took to make the ten-kilometer hike. We could see across the canal to the Egyptian position on the other side, marked by a tall tower that gave them a view over the dunes and ramparts on the east bank. We crawled all the way to the jeeps, careful not to let our profiles show in the stark, treeless landscape of the moonlit night.

Before trying to take anything, we needed to check that no booby traps waited for us when we opened the glove compartment or tried moving the radio set. One by one we checked each vehicle, then just as slowly and carefully loaded two stretchers with the equipment—radio sets and weapons. I collected all the maps to put them in my pack, for safekeeping.

We left as quietly as we came, crawling. I used a flashlight to blink the signal to the other two forces—and the three soldiers from the armored corps *sayeret*—to rejoin us.

My two flanking squads crossed low against the horizon, approaching in minutes. But no response came from Gorodish's three soldiers. We crept carefully toward them, all the while blinking my flashlight, worried an enemy commando ambush had got them and now waited for us to walk into their trap. Finally, close enough to see them, the sight shocked me.

They had simply fallen asleep. I leapt to my feet and ran the last few meters. Enraged, I kicked the first one I reached in the shoulder. A second jumped to his feet, fumbling for his rifle. My foot rose to give another kick.

"Stop!" cried one of my soldiers behind me.

I paused, foot in mid-air, speechless at the three soldiers' audacity —and my own loss of control. Finally, I snarled, "I'll settle this later," ignoring their attempts to make excuses. Turning my back on them, I began the march back to the base, my platoon in formation behind me, Gorodish's soldiers following sheepishly.

For the entire ten-kilometer (six-mile) march I walked in silence, knowing they worried about what would happen when I told Gorodish about their dereliction. A few hundred meters before we reached camp, one of the three approached, stumbling as he tried to match my stride in the sand. "Sir?" he tried. I ignored him.

"Sir, I just want to tell you that we screwed up." His voice trembled. I stonewalled.

"If you tell Gorodish what happened," he said, "it will mean prison for us."

I knew that. But more than anything, I wanted to finish the mission. I finally spoke. "You'll hear what I have to say when we get to camp."

About a hundred meters before camp, I called the soldiers together for a debriefing, to discuss their performance. For an elite special force, a debriefing right after an operation is critical, while the details are still fresh in the mind and mistakes can be remembered and corrected for the future.

"You did excellent work," I began, believing that praise is as important as criticism for a leader. Though I was only a few years older than them, I was their officer, which meant being a teacher as much as a commander.

The three armored corps soldiers, afraid to look me in the eye, sat with their heads bowed at the edges of the pack of fighters at my feet. "An excellent maneuver, with a good stealthy approach. Nobody could have noticed us. You found good cover; unloading the jeeps went smoothly. A first-class operation.

"But we all know the reason for this mission," I continued. "Another force abandoned those vehicles. They gave us the problem instead of solving it themselves. I left them behind because I did not trust them in the first place. I did not ask them to set up an ambush or a covering-fire position. I asked for nothing except for them to sit there quietly and wait. 'Just keep your eyes open,' I told them. And they fell asleep."

"I know exactly what's coming to you," I said, for the first time speaking directly to the three soldiers from the armored corps *sayeret*. "And I'm sure that right now you're feeling something that you won't forget for many years." I paused, letting my words sink in.

With sunrise minutes away, the light was bright enough to read the lines of dust across my soldiers' faces, dark enough to see the lights on at the brigadier general's command trailer. I wanted the whole affair to be over. "Dismissed," I finally said, releasing them.

I don't know what became of those three soldiers, but I'm sure that even now, more than twenty years later, they must still occasionally remember with shame the events of that night. I know I have never forgiven them—but I also never said a word about it to Gorodish.

The air force won the war in three hours. The armored corps and infantry finished it in six days. On the seventh day, the people of Israel celebrated—but a new war began. None of us—except for a very few visionaries, like David Ben-Gurion, then an old man living in the Negev and long out of power—understood that our new, presumably safer, borders imprisoned us along with the Palestinians of the West Bank and Gaza.

Inside Israel, many saw the war as a miracle, a divinely inspired liberation of the biblical homelands called Judea and Samaria in the West Bank. Most—including almost the entire political leadership of Israel—were blind to the fact that to hold those lands, we would need to maintain a military occupation. It would take nearly a generation before the Palestinians inside those territories rebelled against that occupation, and then almost another ten years for us to realize that we could not hold the territories by force, suppressing their aspirations forever.

Nobody conducted any soul-searching about what really happened in the Six-Day War. The celebrations overshadowed the funerals of more than 650 of our young men, and women too, who died. Tough tank battles around Rafiah, where Gorodish's unit and Raful's paratroops brigade—including my brother Udi—took many casualties. So did the house-to-house fighting in East Jerusalem, reuniting the city that was left divided by the cease-fire lines at the end of the War of Independence. Getting up to the Golan plateau, where the Syrians held the high ground, cost hundreds of lives.

But the people preferred euphoria to reality. Hero worship—an instant industry of victory albums, books, and records—developed within hours of the last shots fired. Public opinion-makers, politicians, and generals, the chief of staff and the newspapers, the foreign correspondents and the rabbis—everyone analyzed the results of the war on the assumption it was a great victory.

We repaired border problems left over after the War of Independence, widening the country's borders at its center, where, until 1967, barely ten miles separated the Jordanian border from the Mediterranean Sea.

We reunited Jerusalem, which the cease-fire lines of 1949 left divided down the middle by tin and cement walls, from which Jordanian soldiers sniped at citizens in the streets of Jewish Jerusalem and denied religious Jews access to the Western Wall, the last remnant of the Jewish Temple of the ancient Jewish commonwealths.

On the Golan, we eliminated the Syrian artillery threat over our settlements in the lowlands of eastern Galilee, while in the south, the capture of the Sinai Peninsula more than tripled the physical area under Israel's control. Everyone regarded the new borders as safer.

The whole world treated Israelis like heroes, especially the Americans, who seem to worship efficiency. In June 1967, we gave them a model of efficiency, while they sank deeper into the morass of Vietnam.

Worse—we regarded the enemy as weak and primitive. The barefoot Egyptian soldiers, abandoned by their officers and escaping home across the sands of Sinai, inscribed an indelible image in our minds.

It all felt wrong to me, but like everyone else I fell into the trap of believing that the IDF was invincible, with the best commanders, the best air force, the best everything.

So, despite voices like David Ben-Gurion's, warning that we had swallowed the enemy alive inside those new borders, the vast majority refused to listen. In fact, the vast majority figured that the IDF could conquer Arab capitals with the same ease with which we had captured the Sinai.

For years to come after the Six-Day War, all we heard from the Arabs was "no recognition of Israel, no negotiations with Israel, no peace with Israel." We interpreted that to mean we could do whatever we wanted. One day, we said to ourselves, the Arabs will come to their senses and sue for peace.

Meanwhile, despite all the talk of pan-Arab brotherhood, they let the Palestinians rot in refugee camps instead of absorbing them into their societies.

By winning the Six-Day War, we won territories that appeared to give us security, emphasized our link to the biblical lands of our ancestors, and created the impression we could do whatever we wanted. Successive governments called the territories a card to trade for peace but settled the areas with civilians, arguing that Zionism regarded settlement as the way to defend the country's borders. Many were blinded to the facts of the military occupation because they were so enthralled with messianic visions.

Right after the war, the Labor government ran down to Ofira in Sharm al-Sheikh, laying a road down the Sinai coast just to build a town at the end of the peninsula. In northern Sinai they developed Rafiah; on the West Bank they established the farming settlements in the Jordan Rift Valley and, inspired by the Bible, put up Kiryat Arba near Hebron. (Later, from the late seventies to the end of the eighties, the Likud emphasized Israel's biblical ties to the territories and, using tax breaks to get people to move there, increased the Jewish population from three thousand families to ten times that many—about 150,000 people.)

I must confess that I also fell for the belief that our strength and Arab weakness made the need for compromise irrelevant. Moshe Dayan said, "It's better to have Sharm al-Sheikh without peace than peace without Sharm al-Sheikh." Only a decade later, in perhaps his greatest act of bravery, Dayan changed his mind as one of the architects of the Camp David agreement, the first peace treaty between Israel and one of its Arab neighbors.

But meanwhile, an unrealistic assessment of our capabilities led inexorably to the Yom Kippur War, when Egypt and Syria caught us completely by surprise and we would learn that force has limits, that euphoria is no response to war, and that our enemies can also learn the lessons of one war to prepare for the next.

HOME—TO THE PARATROOPS

The war postponed my departure from the army. I stayed with Shaked through the establishment of its new headquarters in Sinai, at Rafiah, an abandoned UN field station that became one of the IDF's biggest bases in Sinai. But by August, two months after the Six-Day War, I looked forward to being at home for good by the Rosh Hashanah New Year holiday in September.

One hot evening, I sat on the steps of the Shaked office, thinking about the future, watching the vast desert sky for shooting stars. A popular Tel Aviv rock-and-roll band entertained the troops. The music wafted across the camp. I prefer an acoustic guitar or accordion and quiet singing around a campfire. But I took pleasure in the happiness of the soldiers, and my own anticipation about mustering out of the army and going back to Nahalal.

"There you are!" Matan Vilnai strode toward me across the packed sand of the camp. "I've been looking all over for you." The son of Zev Vilnai, one of Israel's most famous historians and guides to the Land of Israel, Matan graduated from a military high school near Haifa and, like me, went straight to the paratroops. A few years older than me, in his mid-twenties—one of the youngest captains in the army at the time—he wanted a career in the army. On the eve of the war he won the appointment as commander of the paratroops *sayeret*, my original unit. Nearly thirty years later, in 1995, he would become deputy chief of staff.

"I hear you're leaving Shaked," he said, taking a seat beside me on the cement steps.

"And going home," I added.

"But you applied to the paratroops brigade for reserve duty," he pointed out.

"Of course."

"I saw Fuad's letter," he said. "Not that I needed to see your file to know I wanted you."

"Fuad really went overboard in that letter," I pointed out.

Fuad wrote a letter for the Southern Command's adjutant to attach to my personal file. He gave it to me when I began the process of finishing my service, a much longer procedure than the one involved on induction day. On my way to Southern Command headquarters in the Negev, I sneaked a look at the contents, quickly closing it after reading its embarrassing shower of compliments. People from the Jezreel Valley only use language like that in eulogies at cemeteries—and, even there, sparingly.

At Southern Command headquarters, however, they wanted to keep good officers in their service. My formal request for a transfer to the paratroops brigade did not please the adjutant at command headquarters when I handed over Fuad's letter.

" 'To Whom It May Concern,' " the senior Southern Command adjutant read aloud from Fuad's letter, not realizing I already knew what it said. " 'The officer finished his service in a satisfactory manner,' " he began, inventing a totally different text for Fuad's letter, the upshot of which said that the adjutant could decide where I would best serve the IDF. And since regional commands hate losing good officers, he naturally wanted to keep me in the Southern Command and not let me go to the paratroops brigade.

I did not let him get away with it, but I did not tell him I knew what Fuad's letter really said. "Look," I said firmly. "I don't even know why I'm talking to you, a desk jockey. You work against our own side, not the enemy. Give me my file. I'm going to the paratroops." I reached out for the file. "Don't worry," I told him. "They'll take me."

No lieutenant had ever spoke to him that way before. He folded the letter back into the envelope and handed it over to me, along with the brown folder that I'd carry to the desk jockey for the paratroops brigade. At least in the paratroops brigade, even the clerks, male or female—including my little sister Tami, who served as a company clerk in the paratroops *sayeret*—have all jumped at least once.

So, that night in Rafiah, I reassured Matan that come September he would find me ready for reserve duty in the paratroops brigade. "You're getting me for reserves," I promised him.

"No," he broke in. "I want you as my deputy."

"I'm going back home," I reiterated. "Back to Nahalal."

"I want you," Matan said.

I shook my head, no. I had made up my mind.

"Listen," he said softly. "We had a terrible war."

I knew. I had wanted to be with the brigade, and particularly its *sayeret*, rushing to the brigade headquarters with the first signs of war in mid-May. But Amos had grabbed me back for Shaked. Later, I heard the paratroops *sayeret* began the war sitting in a plane on a runway, waiting to fly over Sinai and parachute into Sharm al-Sheikh, at the peninsula's southernmost tip. But the air force's success made the jump unnecessary. From then on, the unit chased after battles they never reached in time to see action. They went through the entire war barely firing a single shot.

"I need you," he said. "You have the experience of the *sayeret* as a new recruit, plus skills from Shaked. There's a lot of tracking ahead. Intelligence predicts a buildup of terrorists along the borders. We're going to be busy chasing them down. You turn out the best soldiers."

Matan can be very persuasive. The performers on the flatbed truck had long since gone to sleep while we still talked it over. I finally admitted that it appealed to me. But at the end of our talk I only conceded that I needed time to think.

"How much time?" he wanted to know.

The next day was Friday, and I had already planned a trip home for the weekend with another soldier going home to the Jezreel Valley. In another few weeks I would be home for good, but meanwhile, whenever I found the opportunity, I went for a visit to see Nurit, pregnant with Shaul, and my folks and friends. "A couple of days," I promised Matan.

Though Israel is small, the roads in those days were not very good, especially from the heart of Sinai, far in the south, to the Galilee. By car, coming out of Sinai, the trip to Nahalal could take as long as eight hours. With Nurit pregnant at home, I didn't want to waste any time waiting for a bus or hitchhiking. But my parents always taught that where there's a will, there's a way.

When Nasser evicted them, the UN troops left behind some Citroën Deux Cheveauxes, frog-eyed two-horsepower cars, like a French version of the Volkswagen Beetle. The IDF also had Deux Cheveauxes. The UN cars were painted white-and-blue, ours gray.

I got hold of some gray paint, and painted one of the Deux Cheveauxes, changing the license plate to the white on black of the army instead of the black on white of the UN, and we started home to Nahalal. The Military Police set up checkpoints at roadblocks out of Sinai and Gaza to catch looters. One stopped us. They searched the trunk and the backseat and all the while I sat there smiling at them. They never realized the car itself was booty. We laughed about it most of the way back to the Galilee.

All weekend, I considered Matan's offer. I walked in the fields and worked in the barn, my mind and heart like two sets of scales, each in turn weighing the values I held dear.

I loved being at home with Nurit, now in her final weeks of pregnancy. I also loved the action of the army. Yet I had no interest in an army career, to become a general like Amos Yarkoni had predicted. Generals watched battles from the distance and spent more time behind desks than in the field.

I loved being in the fields of the Jezreel Valley. But I also loved being in the field with my soldiers, an officer teaching the self-reliance they needed to survive on the battlefield.

Indeed, I loved the heightened awareness that comes in an operation, when all the senses are at work and you feel 110 percent alive. I loved the mental and physical challenges that come with being in a special forces unit. I loved going up to the edges of my abilities, and derived pleasure in knowing I stayed calm at the height of confusion.

But Nurit and I had made plans. We wanted to travel, and I surprised myself by realizing that I wanted to go to school, to study the geography of the Land of Israel. It was the subject I loved most, for it combined zoology and botany as well as geology and history.

I wanted my own life, but the values instilled in me from childhood told me to answer the call of service in my country's defense.

* * *

79

Though the war ended in six days, non-stop conflict followed. Day and night, Egyptian MiGs and artillery hit our new positions on the east banks of the Suez Canal. At Ras al-Ash, near the northern end of the Canal, an infantry platoon holding the position ran out of supplies and asked headquarters for help. I took a platoon in jeeps and half-tracks, carrying ammunition and medical supplies.

Under fire the entire way, it took almost three hours to travel the twenty kilometers, stopping wherever the Egyptians could see us across the Canal, putting up our own covering fire, and then racing vehicle by vehicle across the open stretch.

But the most frightening moment on the trip to Ras al-Ash came on our arrival. I had never seen frightened Israeli soldiers. And these soldiers literally shivered with fear, hunkering in their underground bunkers. They continued shaking long after the ground stopped after a MiG attack.

They begged us to take them out of there. We stayed a few hours. Our presence helped calm them down. I had almost decided to chalk up their fear to their specific circumstances, but when we returned to Kantara, I was in for another shock.

Hit by artillery, Shaked's command moved to a position a few kilometers north, perfectly normal military behavior considering the circumstances. But nobody radioed us with the news. I suddenly realized then that maybe we beat the Egyptian Army in the war, but as an enemy, they could still hurt us.

Eventually, that long three-year static-line war that developed after the Six-Day War became known as the War of Attrition. It cost more than five hundred of our soldiers' lives before it ended in August 1970. But few people in the summer of 1967 wanted to let signs of a new war disrupt the euphoria over the war just won.

Maybe the big wars are over, I thought—not knowing how wrong I would be proven in only six years—but the little wars remained, especially against the terrorists. More than any other IDF unit that I knew of at the time, the paratroopers in the brigade's *sayeret* would be the front-line fighters in those little wars. And I knew I had the ability to contribute, and therefore the responsibility.

As deputy commander of the *sayeret*, Matan wanted me to train the next generation of fighters. With my experiences from the war, from Shaked, and from the *sayeret* itself, I could make a difference, he said. At home, friends from the unit, unable to hide their envy that I saw action in the war while they sat on a runway, confirmed that morale in the paratroops *sayeret* fell low after the war passed them by.

That Saturday night after dinner, I went for a walk into the darkness of the field behind our house, listening to the sounds of night that had once frightened me so much as a child and now were so familiar.

I could remember when only Nahalal's lights graced our corner of the valley, and how Bet She'arim began to grow after my parents moved there from Haifa.

Now, settlements filled the valley, and their far-off lights twinkled like bracelets in the night in every direction I looked. Nahalal was safe. My family was safe. Nurit and our baby would not be alone in Nahalal, surrounded by family and friends, hers and mine both. I could get home often, both for short day visits and weekends— except when an operation required me. Matan was right, I realized. He did need me.

But in less than a year I would be home again—recuperating from wounds suffered in a military defeat resulting from underestimating the enemy at Karameh.

UNFRIENDLY SKIES

"**D**isability claim," said the Defense Ministry clerk from the rehabilitation department, stacking a sheaf of forms on my bedside night table in the hospital in Afula, the main town of the Jezreel Valley.

The doctors took off all the bandages except a large white square covering the wound on my throat. But steel wires still held my rebuilt jaw together, forcing me to learn to groan a whisper, and even that hurt. I shook my head no. The last thing I wanted was to be listed as an invalid.

"You have to sign to get your disability . . ." he repeated.

I interrupted him. "Forget it. I have no intention of signing."

"Huh?"

"I'm not disabled," I rasped. "I'm wounded. But I'm going to be healthy. I'm not suing anybody."

"It is procedure," he tried.

"I'm recovering."

"Fine," said the clerk. "Sign here." He leaned over the folder of papers he shoved in my hands and turned a page. "And here."

Weak but not incapacitated, I grabbed his shirt and wheezed "Get out of here" into his astonished face.

He came back a second time, a few days after I got home. I threw him out. The third time they sent a friend of mine, also wounded in battle, to explain the procedure.

"You sign now, and in a year's time they give you a permanent disability percentage and you get all kinds of benefits," explained my friend. "Money, Muki. They give you money."

"I do not want to lower my combat-fitness profile," I insisted. The last thing I wanted was for the IDF doctors to decide I was no longer fit for combat anymore. "I'm not taking money if it means lowering my profile."

I still did not know if I wanted to go back to the army full-time. But I wanted reserve duty in a combat unit. If they lowered my profile, it meant reserves behind a desk. Nothing was worse.

"There's no connection between the two," my friend promised. The disability forms go to the Defense Ministry, not the army, he said. "There's no connection."

But I do not trust bureaucracies. I ignored the letter the army sent asking me to appear in front of a medical panel. I ignored a second letter as well. So when I ignored the third summons, they closed the file, never changing my medical records. As far as the big, official army knew, I never caught the bullet at Karameh.

At home, Nurit had her hands full with our year-old baby boy, Shaul, and nursing me back to health. I began working on the farm, regaining my strength. I started by gardening in the shade of the two palm trees that stood at the entrance to our garden. At first I tired quickly. But nonetheless, I worked every day, learning to recognize my new face after the plastic surgery that repaired the lower half of my face. It widened my jaw slightly, just enough to surprise me the first few times I caught a glance of myself in the mirror.

By summer, the jaundice faded to a memory while I reached full strength, able to toss bales like in the old days. As strong as ever, I handled all the jobs on the farm.

Life was good. Shaul crawled freely in the backyard, which led to a barn and a chicken coop, just like at my grandparents'. Nurit was happy. We looked forward to a good harvest in the fall.

But I began itching to get back to the action. The Six-Day War did not put an end to Arab refusal to let us live in peace. The Jordanians lost control on their side of the border in the Jordan Rift, especially after Karameh, when we failed to nip the PLO in the bud.

Now, the PLO ran the Jordan Rift on the Jordanian side of the Jordan River and Nahal Arava south of the Dead Sea. Another kind

83

of war of attrition raged in the Jordan Rift. Instead of the artillery and snipers firing across the Suez Canal on the Egyptian front, nightly hunts for armed infiltrators making their way over the Jordan River lit up the sky with flares. It meant action for a *sayeret*. A lot of action. And I missed it.

I kept in touch with the unit. My brother had replaced me as the *sayeret's* deputy commander, so he brought stories, as did friends who came to visit. But I did not need any stories to know what I missed: the cool nights under the stars, alert to all the nature of the desert, aware of its harmony, and listening for the enemy's arrival, the sound that disrupted the quiet. I missed keeping my eye on the tracks, I missed watching the horizon, I missed leading my soldiers into position for attack, and I missed outwitting the enemy. But most of all, I felt absurd, worrying about harvests while my friends fought.

Then, in July 1968, the Arabs surprised us with a new form of warfare—state-supported terror. They grabbed an El Al plane heading to Tel Aviv out of Rome, forcing the pilot to take it to Algeria. The Algerian government welcomed the hijackers as heroes. Our citizens sat helpless in Algerian hands for more than two weeks. In the end, Jerusalem gave in to the terrorists' demands, releasing Palestinian prisoners, captured and tried for terrorism, in exchange for the hostages held by the Algerians.

Disgusted by the tactic of attacking innocent civilians, it appalled me, indeed shocked me, that the government gave into the terrorists' demands. I asked friends from the security services why El Al did not have an appropriate security mechanism to prevent hijackings. "We're working on it," they promised.

"As soon as you have something, let me know," I asked. I wanted in on *that* action.

In January of 1969, I received a letter at home. Only two lines long, but embossed with the seal of the state, it asked me to attend an interview at an office in Tel Aviv not far from the defense ministry.

They knew nothing about my injury, but the scar on my throat still blazed red. I told them what had happened—they said it should not be a hindrance to taking the course, which started in another month.

But two weeks later, a phone call woke me at home in the middle of the night. "There's been another attack on an El Al plane," said the voice. "We're moving up the schedule. We start training tomorrow."

* * *

"Who here has ever used a pistol?" The old man in the front of the classroom spoke Hebrew with a thick American accent that made me want to smile. A few of the fellows around me grinned, raising their hands. Though I did know about pistols, something in his voice made me keep my hand down. I'm glad I did.

"None of you know shit," he snarled at us. "What do you guys know about it? Have you ever walked down Amsterdam Ave. at two in the morning and have somebody pull a blade on you?" Out of nowhere, it seemed, a Beretta appeared in his hand, cocked and ready to fire. "Call me Dave," he said, beginning a three-week immersion in the use of a Beretta in close quarters.

His Hebrew was so bad it became infectious. By the end of the first week, the dozen of us he did not throw out—with a tear in his eye, because he wanted us all to pass, but "if you can't cut it, I got to cut you"—all spoke Hebrew with the flat *r*'s and *l*'s of his funny accent.

A master of the handgun, Dave covered all aspects of hand-to-hand combat in tight quarters, emphasizing accuracy. "The idea is to hit the terrorist, not the airplane," he pointed out over and over again with a shake of his head, making us repeat every move until we got it right.

He chose the .22 Beretta as the weapon for the job because the small caliber, combined with the low bullet velocity, would be less dangerous in the confines of an airplane, where a punctured window means disaster at 35,000 feet inside a pressurized cabin.

However, the relative weakness of the Beretta meant that two shots would probably be necessary to stop an enemy. Dave called it the "bang-bang." We worked with moving targets, inside a cabin mock-up, until we knew all the moves Dave taught—and new ones we invented as we learned.

We learned every commercial passenger plane, from El Al's small fleet to all the other commercial lines that flew into Israel. The Arabs made no secret of their plans to hijack more planes. But we kept our plans secret.

Boarding the plane like regular passengers, wearing business suits or sport jackets with ties, we carried an attaché case or carry-on bag as part of our disguise as innocent business travelers.

Usually, intelligence reports indicated whether a flight might be a likely target because of VIPs on board—or potentially suspicious passengers, like Arabs, or students from countries in the West or Japan, where the PLO made strong inroads in far-leftist circles.

Our strategically located seats gave us views of the entire cabin. As soon as the plane took off, we used the opportunity to move down the aisle, matching faces to the names on the passenger list. When the plane landed we disembarked just like regular passengers.

Suddenly, cities like Paris, London, and New York became routine for me, a farm boy in the great big world. But I never made it to the right place.

Terrorists grabbed an El Al plane on the tarmac at Zurich, killing the pilot, Yoram Peres, from Ma'ayan Zvi. One of my friends from Dave's course, Mordechai Rahamim, managed to stop the terrorist. The Swiss police arrested Rahamim, blowing our cover.

A few weeks later, I was in New York on the job when terrorists hijacked an El Al plane leaving Amsterdam. One of our marshals screwed that one up. He knew the pilot from home, and the terrorists struck while he visited his friend in the cockpit.

A firefight broke out, ending with a dead terrorist and two wounded—a terrorist woman named Leila Haled, and one of the El Al stewards. The British arrested the terrorists. Haled, a black-haired beauty, quickly became the darling of the British tabloids, a celebrity for the radical new left. Tried and convicted, she did not spend much time in jail. The British, like every other European country, preferred to negotiate with terrorists. When the PLO hijacked a British plane demanding Haled's release, London gave in. They never did that with the Irish Republican Army's terrorists, not comprehending that terrorism is a worldwide phenomenon, and that only a united front can beat it.

In Munich, I missed another attack on a bus carrying El Al passengers from the terminal to the plane. Uri Cohen, the pilot, fought off one of the terrorists, making him drop one of his grenades, which exploded and killed the terrorist.

I spent a year and a half on the road, every week in a different city, and not once did I see any action. But once, right after takeoff from Paris, I came very close to putting into practice what Dave taught so well.

Nothing in the intelligence report that morning said anything about an Arab on board. But while the plane still climbed, the NO SMOKING and SEAT BELT signs still flashing, I sensed movement behind my seat, which was in a strategic position near the cockpit door.

Turning, I saw a young man in a suit, with the swarthy complexion of an Arab. He stood in the passageway between the first class and tourist sections of the Boeing. I looked around for the stewardess to shoo him back to his seat, but she disappeared into the kitchen right after takeoff.

I reached into my jacket, touching the gun in the custom-fit holster beneath my left armpit. The suspect stood by the curtain, looking in the direction of the cockpit door. If I spoke to him, it would break my cover. I tensed, ready to draw and give him the "bang-bang," as Dave called the two-shot move. The cockpit door flung open—something that never should happen during takeoff—and the steward came out, taking a seat beside the cockpit door. I pulled the gun out of the holster far enough to get my finger into the trigger guard.

The suspected terrorist took a step forward, brushing aside the curtain between the two cabins. I pulled the gun another few inches out of its holster, ready to swing and aim if the suspect made one more move.

Just then, the stewardess came out of the kitchen. "What are you doing?" she asked my suspect. "Don't you see the SEAT BELT sign?"

"I needed the toilet," said the young man sheepishly.

"You're from tourist section," the stewardess brusquely told him. "Back there," she added, pointing toward the rear of the plane.

That wayward traveler never knew how close he came to dying. But an American tourist sitting across the aisle from me watched the whole thing. He grinned at me, raising a thumb in a gesture of approval before going back to his magazine.

After Mordechai Rahamim killed the terrorist in Zurich, the whole world knew that El Al planes carried armed marshals. It put the Swiss in an uncomfortable position, to arrest Mordechai and put him on trial. Afterward, they let him go—but the public revelation of our work made it even more difficult. Suddenly, the national sport of traveling Israelis became trying to pick us out in the crowd. We were trained to ignore the staring and never to respond to the guesses. If passengers tried to fraternize, we brushed them off with a smile or a frown but did not get involved in conversations. In the air, we needed to remain alert at all times.

Of course, wherever we landed, we came under the scrutiny of law enforcement agencies and secret intelligence services. With most of the European countries quiet agreements for cooperation prevailed. But Americans are particularly zealous about armed foreign agents on their soil. And our cover as businessmen could not succeed for long—how many twenty-four- or twenty-five-year-old businessmen travel in and out of international airports without any luggage for stays of two or three days at most?

But after the incident in Zurich, when Mordechai Rahamim pulled out his gun, our operators decided that the best policy vis-à-vis the Americans would be telling the truth.

By then, my trips to Manhattan were routine. No questions at customs. Cab to the hotel, rest, and some sightseeing for the two or three day layover before making the trip back in the other direction.

My next flight into Manhattan came a week or so after the Zurich incident. I went through passport control without any problems. But as I moved into the arrivals terminal, a black guy approached me and flashed something shiny at me. A peddler? I thought. "No thanks," I said, walking past.

"What do you mean 'no thanks,' " the man snapped, slapping a hand on my shoulder. "FBI."

My English is not very good—just good enough to identify myself as a businessman, tell a taxi driver an address, and ask for steak, salad, and potatoes at a restaurant. But even in Nahalal we had seen Hollywood movies. I understood "FBI."

"You come with me," he said, holding my arm and leading me to a side room. Three American special agents waited to question me. "Empty your pockets," said the black agent.

I pulled out a short club from under my jacket and a canister of Mace from a pocket. "I am security for El Al," I admitted, just as our operators back home had instructed us after the Zurich incident.

Until then, we had denied any connection to El Al security. The Americans suspected us, but never knew for sure. But Zurich changed everything. The agents fell speechless. Indeed, for a moment I thought they did not understand my bad English with its thick Hebrew accent. I repeated myself. "Yes, I am El Al security," I said to their astonished faces.

Until that moment they had treated me with a sullen, brusque attitude. Suddenly, they turned respectful, full of questions and curiosity. They wanted to know about my training and my military background. I did not understand everything they asked. But I also had my instructions: I could admit to being an El Al security officer—nothing more.

They made some phone calls—to Washington, I guess—and a little while later let me go.

"Have a good time in New York," said the black federal agent whom I first mistook for a petty thief. He slapped me on the back like an old friend. "And stay out of trouble," he said as we parted, not realizing that I had been looking for trouble for eighteen months— and never found it in the air marshal job.

In fact, the job bored me. The excitement of foreign cities wore off quickly. Cities are stifling, noisy places that hold little magic for me. Three days home, then three days on the road, made it even worse.

But then I flew to Africa.

The first time I landed in Nairobi, I teamed up with another air marshal for a four-day trip into the nature reserves of Kenya and Tanzania. A hundred trips to New York, London, and Paris paled compared to four days in the African bush.

Everything enchanted me. It was a totally different world, where nature dominated everything. Africa spoke to me in ways that America or Europe never could. I loved the colors and smells, the dignified way people carried themselves in the villages and even in the city. I loved the dark brown soil and its mysterious fruits and vegetables. I loved the wild herds and flocks in the game reserves, themselves much larger than all of Israel. I loved everything about the place.

I already knew a little about Africa. At sixteen, just as our romance began to blossom, Nurit moved to Tanzania when her father joined the military delegation there. For six months we corresponded weekly, until she and her younger brother came home, wanting to finish high school in Israel. Back in Israel, Nurit became as excited as me about finding a way to return to Africa, together.

Almost every African country, except for the Arab nations of North Africa, wanted an Israeli military legation to train army units.

Brigadier General Yitzhak Bar-On commanded the special unit inside Military Intelligence specializing in foreign aid. I was only a lieutenant, and a reservist at that, so it took a bit of chutzpah for me to call a brigadier in Tel Aviv to ask for an appointment.

We met in a nondescript office building not far from the defense ministry compound in downtown Tel Aviv, and I told him about my background and how Africa appealed to me. He said very little, and the short meeting came to an end. "If there's something to talk about," he told me, "we'll call you."

That weekend I flew to Rome, one of my last trips for El Al. The whole trip I wondered if I would ever hear from Bar-On again. But when I returned home Nurit's first news was that the brigadier's office had called.

"I checked you out," he said when I phoned him back, "and we have things to talk about."

"I'm ready," I said eagerly.

"We need young people, and especially paratroopers," he explained. "For a particular African country."

"That's me," I jumped in.

"But there's one problem," he said ominously, pausing before adding, "You'll have to go to school. For a course," he said. "You need to learn English. And African geography and culture, and . . ." I figured he had looked into my background all the way back to high school, where I had never found much enthusiasm for academics.

"No problem," I interrupted. "I can do that, if it means getting to Africa."

"And the course will not start for a few months," he added, probably worried that my youth made me impatient.

But as a farmer—and as an officer who had spent many a night waiting for an ambush to work—I knew patience as both tactic and strategy. And I had a strategy.

As I left his office that morning, I realized that I knew a perfect solution to fill at least part of the time before I went back to school to learn English and about Africa. There was a forty-day company commanders' course starting in the fall. Because I was automatically eligible as a deputy commander of a *sayeret*, the course would give me captain's bars and make me even more valuable to Bar-On's military missions to Africa.

So, in September 1970, I hung up my El Al Beretta .22 and began the course at a West Bank training base near Shechem, the biblical city the Arabs call Nablus. It covered theoretical and practical elements of running a company. My experience of the Six-Day War with Shaked, when my platoon grew to company size with all the reservists, made much of the material familiar to me.

But far more important than what I learned in the course, I met Uri Simhoni, one of the instructors and commander-designate for Sayeret Egoz, the Northern Command's new special operations and reconnaissance force. Uri wanted me as a staff officer for Egoz, which was then spearheading operations against the PLO in Lebanon, where their terrorists had established themselves after being evicted from Jordan.

That same month in 1970, King Hussein of Jordan finally took action against the PLO's state-within-a-state in the Jordan Rift and in the Palestinian refugee camps around Amman. The showdown between Hussein and Arafat turned into a month-long bloody civil war. Called Black September, the 1970 civil war in Jordan ended with the PLO's eviction from the Hashemite kingdom.

But it did not put an end to PLO attacks on Israeli settlements and roads. Taking advantage of Lebanon's relatively free political climate, Arafat moved his organization to Beirut from Jordan, and quickly established an armed presence in southern Lebanon, right over the border from Israel.

Instead of infiltrating across the Jordan River, the PLO cells came across the mountainous border in the north on their way to terror attacks in the villages and towns of the Galilee. As Northern Command's *sayeret*, Egoz was another tip of the spear in the fight against those incursions.

But I would not give up my dreams of Africa. "I appreciate the offer," I told Uri, "but I'm scheduled for a course in six months, and then two years in Africa. I can't commit to anything longer than six months."

He considered the problem—and came up with a solution. "I'll give you the reconnaissance company," he suggested, "and a free hand to train them as you see fit."

It would work, I realized. A *sayeret*'s reconnaissance company trains new recruits. A six-month course in Egoz dovetailed perfectly with Yitzhak Bar-On's schedule for me. But I wanted something more from Uri.

"What?" Uri asked. "You'll be a staff officer. I'll give you a secretary, a car, what else do you want?"

"If there's an operation," I told Uri, "I'm in. No matter what." I needed the action. I knew it from the moment I began recuperating after Karameh. I wanted to know if Karameh ruined the psychological mechanism that enables every soldier to go into battle with the feeling that it can't happen to him.

I had spent a year and a half flying around the world as an El Al marshal, looking for action, but never getting the chance to find out if psychologically I survived Karameh. With Yasser Arafat and his Fatah, the largest of the organizations in the PLO, taking over southern Lebanon, my being with Egoz would put me back in the thick of things.

I did not have to explain any of that to Uri. He promised me a place in any operation Egoz planned.

So, in October 1970, I went straight from the company commanders' course to Egoz. My officers and soldiers arrived a few days after I started. As soon as they got off the bus we put them in formation for an eighty-kilometer march, warning them that by the end of the course, half would be gone, sent to other, less demanding units than the Northern Command's *sayeret*.

I drew on all my experience—from the paratroops *sayeret*, from Shaked, the war, and Karameh—to turn the Egoz training course into one of the toughest and smartest in the IDF.

The recruits were the best the sergeants and officers at Tel Hashomer's induction center could find. But the Northern Command's mountainous purview includes some of the toughest terrain our soldiers faced. Physical strength and coordination are important. Mental strength makes the difference. Teamwork, drive, ambition, willpower—these are basic elements.

But I wanted more, I warned them as we set off to trace the length of the mountainous border with Lebanon all the way to Mount Hermon, in the northeast. I wanted the truth. Honesty is the source of reliability, the basic precondition for membership in a *sayeret* under my command.

COMBAT-FIT

T he action I wanted more than anything else came in early 1971, in the heart of a small town in southern Lebanon called el-Hiam, where my father once battled alongside Moshe Dayan in the days of the Palmach.

Field security prevented any mention of the operation to my father. A few days before the operation, I dropped by to see him at Bet She'arim, twenty minutes from the base. As usual, we did not speak much that afternoon. In my green fatigues and combat boots, I helped him load a trailer with bales of hay. I did not tell him that in a few days I would face enemy bullets again. But he understood why I wanted to be in Egoz that winter. "Take care of yourself," he said as we parted.

By the beginning of 1971, the PLO presence gave southeast Lebanon a new name—Fatahland, named for Arafat's organization, the largest of the PLO's groups. His irregulars used the hilly, rocky terrain as a launching ground for terror attacks against Israeli settlements on the border. Arafat learned an important lesson at Karameh —to spread out his forces, instead of concentrating them in one place. Throughout the towns and villages of Fatahland, the PLO—without any interference from the Lebanese government—established an armed presence. From Mount Hermon, in the east, all the way to the Mediterranean, they used southern Lebanon as a safe haven for their hit-and-run attacks across the border.

Terrorists strike where people least expect to be harmed—on a public bus, in a movie theater, shopping in the market, at work in an orchard picking apples. Beating terrorism means putting them on the run, keeping them off-balance, making them fear the places where they feel safest—in short, giving them a taste of their own medicine. No air attack heard coming from afar could be as damaging to the spirit as a face-to-face encounter with combat-proficient soldiers on their own doorstep.

Dusk falls quickly in the mountains. On the last day of January 1971, just as the sun disappeared in the west but even before the purpling sky turned black, thirty-five Egoz soldiers moved quietly across the border near Kibbutz Dan, heading to a little house in the center of el-Hiam.

Uri kept his promise to me, giving me the number-two slot in the five-man force that would make the final assault on the doorstep of Fatah's regional command headquarters for the area north of Metulla, our northernmost town. Again I would be at the tip of the spear.

We kept to a grueling pace to meet the schedule—five hours through the cold, damp mountains to the outskirts of town, then another two hours of quiet movement in ones and twos from shadow to shadow, through el-Hiam to reach the target without detection.

As we drew closer to the target, squads broke off from the formation, taking up flanking positions to safeguard the heart of the operation—the attack—and protect the route of our retreat.

Just as the aerial intelligence maps promised, a small rise overlooked the house from the northeast. The last of the forces broke off to take up a position on the rise. Led by Moshe Kafri, Uri's deputy, the force carried machine guns and rocket-propelled grenades that would soften up the target before the final assault by the five-man team Uri selected for the attack.

Seven of us crept into a small clump of bushes at the edge of a small grove beside the single-story house. Uri Simhoni and one of his staff officers, Baruch, would stay behind while the final five made the last approach. Baruch carried infrared binoculars.

I crawled into position, scanning the dark house and the yard around it. "Uri," I whispered. "I can see the guard. He's sitting on the tractor." Less than twenty meters away, easy for me to take out with my silenced Uzi, the guard sat in the driver's seat of the tractor, a Kalashnikov on his lap.

"He's right," Baruch said softly, peering through the cumbersome binoculars at the guard. "And he's got a Klatch," Baruch added, using the nickname we gave to the Kalashnikov.

Military Intelligence had warned we might find two guards on the job. But none of us spotted anyone else in the yard or its surroundings.

Three clicks on the radio—Moshe Kafri reporting his troops had reached their position—snapped softly over the speaker. The guard took a drag of his cigarette.

"Uri," I whispered again. "I'll crawl over and finish him off quietly."

"Wait," he murmured back.

"Uri, I can get closer," I pleaded. "Let me get closer and I'll finish him off."

"We'll wait a little while longer." Uri decided.

Too late. The guard flicked away the last of his cigarette, stretched, and then climbed down from the tractor, walking to the house and up the stairs to the porch, disappearing into the building.

Finally, Uri gave the order, first signaling us to get ready to run down the lane to the house; then, clicking the walkie-talkie mike, he signaled Kafri to begin.

Bazookas, rocket-propelled grenades, and the heavy fire from machine guns slammed into the house. The fire slashed through wood-and-iron shutters, shattering the glass. The shooting went on for a long full minute. Then there was silence. Uri gave us the nod, and we started the sprint to the house down a narrow lane between bushes into the yard. The narrow lane forced us into a column.

David Agmon, the senior company commander in Egoz, went first. I followed, with Dubi Adar, Michael Sofer, and Udi Kain, three junior officers, behind me. Since we ran in a column, only David Agmon had a clear shot as we sprinted. He let off a burst and then paused, his weapon jammed.

I passed him without stopping, spraying short bursts toward the porch as I ran into the yard, the other four fighters behind me.

Suddenly, from the porch five meters ahead a spray of tracer fire burst out of a Kalashnikov, directly at us. I ran on, into the enemy's flashing fire, my Uzi spewing its own bullets at the Fatah fighter on the porch. A bullet caught him in the chest, hurling him backward against the wall. He slid down, giving me time to reach the wall beneath the porch.

But his Kalashnikov continued firing into the darkness. I pulled a grenade from my web-belt, plucked out the pin, and tossed it over my head onto the porch. Three seconds went by before the grenade's blast silenced the enemy gun. Only then did I turn to look around behind me.

The four other fighters in my group lay on the ground behind me, each wounded in his own way. I used the radio to report on the wounded, then sprinted to the nearest window, tossing two grenades inside. But even before they exploded Michael Sofer appeared by my side. "It was only a crease," he said of the blood trickling down from his forehead, then added one of his own grenades. We took cover leaning side by side against the wall under the window, tensed while we waited for the explosions.

Barely seconds had passed since the shooting stopped, but already the unit doctor was at work on Dubi, trying to save his life under the blurry light of a flashlight. But the young lieutenant died. The bullets had smashed Agmon's wrist and destroyed Udi Kain's foot from the ankle down.

Each of us carried a Gur device, a powerful explosive charge that can be clamped to a wall. While the medics treated the wounded, I cut loose the four Gurs they carried and assigned a couple of soldiers who came running down from Kafri's position to set them just as we had planned. Finally, with the wounded on their way out on the stretchers, I gave the order to set the detonators. The seventeen and a half seconds gave us plenty of time to find cover from the flying debris. We wanted to go back after the explosion to assess the damage. But headquarters told Uri not to take any more chances.

So we headed home, slowed down by a stretcher carrying the crippled Udi and a second carrying Dubi's body. Just before dawn, we finally found a safe field for a medevac chopper to come in and take our wounded. A few hours later, we crossed the border on foot at Kibbutz Dan.

Setting out for battle takes a leap of faith to believe you will survive combat. Every soldier who has been through a firefight knows this psychological mechanism. But after Karameh, I could not be sure that I could still make that leap of faith. Until el-Hiam.

When the shooting started, I kept going. When Agmon's Uzi jammed, I had kept up the assault, running forward into the fire. I had made the leap of faith; I did not flinch. The psychological mechanism still worked.

Yet, despite my personal accomplishment as a soldier and the strategic value of the attack, the mission took a very high price. An officer dead and two wounded is a painful price for a small unit, a small army, a small country.

Nonetheless, our operation, and others like it through the seventies, put pressure on the PLO, making them feel vulnerable deep in their heartland. We struck where they felt safest—at home, on their doorstep. It put them on the defensive, forcing them to protect themselves rather than plot more terror against our people.

Keep terrorists on the run, is the rule. It might make them harder to find, but it preoccupies them with their own safety rather than plotting their crimes.

Military Intelligence was never certain about precisely how many died inside the Fatah house in el-Hiam. Vague reports from the Lebanese press reported two or three dead. We took comfort in the fact that Fatah shut down that headquarters, moving further north, away from the border and our settlements.

As for me, like a rider getting back on after a horse had thrown him, my performance in el-Hiam proved that Karameh did not break my combat spirit.

RED SKIES OVER JINJA

Before the Six-Day War, Israelis taught farming in countries throughout Africa, Asia, and Latin America. After the Six-Day War, those countries still unaligned with the Arabs or the Soviet Union wanted our military aid.

Africa appealed to me for personal reasons. I wanted to drive and hike into its primordial past. I felt an invisible vibration under the huge skies of the continent, and fell in love with the simplicity and mystery of the place. The pure state of nature interested me, not geopolitics. Luckily, my personal interest coincided with the state's, which wanted Africa as a market for exports and political influence.

The Israeli delegations going out still included civilians from institutions like Solel Boneh, Mekorot, and other Israeli companies that won civil engineering contracts in Africa. But the new countries in post-colonialist Africa wanted armies, and the IDF's reputation after the Six-Day War made us their first choice.

The Ministry of Defense and Foreign Ministry ran a joint six-month course for official aid delegations. Held at Beit Berl, the Labor party's college campus north of Tel Aviv, the courses covered language training and regional issues ranging from geography to tribal cultures. I knew just enough English to get in and out of foreign countries as a reticent air marshal. Now I needed enough to teach a course in topography to African officers.

Along with the histories of the major tribes of central Africa and the political economies of the states where Israeli military delegations served, they also taught us proper behavior at cocktail parties and official dinners. As I rarely drink alcohol, I learned to nurse a single glass of wine for toasts and to ask for soda water instead of whiskey.

Halfway through the course, hot news came from Africa. The Ugandan deputy chief of staff had pulled off a coup, becoming chief of staff and head of state. As a graduate of an IDF paratroops course, Idi Amin, the new Ugandan president, referred to Golda Meir and Moshe Dayan as his idols, keeping pictures of them on his desk. Amin is our friend, said the experts from the Foreign and Defense ministries. I was naive.

A few days after the coup, Burka Bar-Lev, the IDF brigadier general who headed Israel's mission to Uganda, came into my life. He wanted me to go to a Ugandan town called Jinja, to build a battalion of paratroopers, starting with a one-hundred-man company. Three other Israeli families lived in Jinja on Defense Ministry assignments: two artillery officers, plus Itzik Bar-Akiva, the IDF officer who officially headed the Israeli mission in the town.

"The Ugandans are fine at parades," Burka told me. "The British, after all, trained most of them. You're going to turn them into paratroopers, starting with Amin's own general staff officers. They're coming here for a three-week course. You have the entire army at your disposal. Anything you want—airplanes, helicopters, and as much shooting as they want."

The generosity astounded me. Even in a *sayeret*, we tried to conserve ammo. But as Burka explained it to me, Israel's business in Uganda was business. "The more ammo they use, the more they'll buy."

A rude awakening from my innocent ideals that said Israel's aid to Third World countries served nobler interests than mere money, Burka's straightforward talk about what to expect in Uganda included something else that made us both laugh. In retrospect, it should have been a warning.

"You've got to understand," he told me about Amin. "He's like an overgrown child playing with outsize toys," he said, and then laughed. "You know what he's asking for now? A submarine. For Lake Victoria."

At the time, it did seem funny. "We'll never give him one, of course," Burka reassured me. But Amin's eccentricities did make for amusing stories. (He made ambassadors from countries out of favor carry him on a throne.) Burka left me with the impression that such things could never happen to us Israelis in Uganda. Amin loved Israel, Burka said. And Israel, in the years after 1967, needed all the friends it could get.

The Soviet Union aligned with the Arabs, using them as proxies against the United States. In Europe, West Germany felt guilty about the Holocaust, but was forbidden by its constitution to sell arms. The French, who sold us arms until 1967, imposed an arms embargo against us after the victory in 1967. I decided not to worry about Amin's eccentricities and Israel's African interests, concentrating on the job I'd do and the pleasures that awaited me and Nurit as we traveled the countryside.

A few days after the Beit Berl course ended, about thirty Ugandan officers showed up in Israel for a three-week paratroopers' course the Defense Ministry had organized for foreign military officers. A Ugandan brigadier in his forties arrived with his deputy, staff officers, and platoon commanders.

I had never met such charming, polite people. Educated by the British, they knew military principles, but nothing about combat. They understood logistics and field strategies, but had never planned an operation.

We gave them an intensive three-week course, a condensed version of what we give our own paratroops recruits: topography, navigation, raids, helicopter-borne raids, parachuting, and working with air support. We began at five in the morning with calisthenics and worked into the night, with three short breaks for food. We treated them like recruits, not generals, colonels, or majors. Everyone did everything. They seemed to love it.

We took them into the hills of Samaria, north of the West Bank town of Nablus, running them through maneuvers that led up to an offensive deployment that included helicopter-borne assaults and parachute raids. We took them to the Golan, where we did house-to-house combat exercises in the abandoned Syrian town of Kuneitra. As usually happens in a course, when the trainers and trainees are working hard and having a good time, a real camaraderie developed amongst us, irrespective of rank.

Only when I reached Uganda, a few weeks after the course, did I realize how strange it must have been to them. In Uganda, company commanders were issued a Mercedes with a driver. Staff headquarters for a brigade commander looked like a palace to me, with white-gloved guards standing all day long at attention. Only then did I realize that just as exotic as their army appeared to me, so must ours have appeared to them.

With their British training, discipline of the ranks meant more than anything else. The rote and ritual of military traditions seemed more important than any other aspect of service. A Ugandan company commander snapped to attention when a battalion commander stepped into view. It made no difference whether the battalion commander noticed — only when the senior officer either gave the order to go to ease or disappeared did the junior officer relax.

The Ugandan Army kept tremendous distance between its ranks. Officers in the Ugandan Army had chauffeurs, personal guards, and servants, something completely foreign to someone who grew up on a moshav, with a strong ideological commitment to respect for work and the equality of people. In the IDF officers eat with their troops, and while distance always exists between a commander and his soldiers, the intimacy of friendship, especially in a special forces unit, overrides the traditional formalities of the military.

One day at Entebbe airport to pick up supplies from Israel, I bumped into one of the battalion commanders we had trained back home. I could not resist asking him whether he felt slighted about our treatment of them during the three-week course. "Here you're gods, but the way we treated you there . . ." I began, curious about his feelings during those three weeks when we made his life miserable.

His answer surprised me. "It was wonderful." He beamed. "One of the greatest experiences in my whole life."

But the greatest shock to me on arrival in Uganda came with the house. A family of servants lived in a shack straight out of *Uncle Tom's Cabin*, at the far end of the large backyard.

In the IDF, officers are not allowed to use soldiers for personal chores. Nobody ever polished my boots. But suddenly in Africa, servants kept my uniforms pressed and my boots shined. They would not let Nurit or me lift a finger to take care of the house. Told to pay the whole family fifty shillings a month, barely a week's wages in Israel, I immediately tripled their pay.

It made me a hero to the servants of the neighborhood and a villain in the eyes of the British colonialists who still lived there. One day in the butcher shop, the price of a steak seemed far too low. I held out twice the amount the butcher asked for. A British woman behind me in line started shouting at me. "You Israelis are spoiling them! You're ruining them for us!" she shrieked at me, turning red in the face with exasperation. I laughed, gave the butcher a wink as I took my meat, and left the money for him on the counter.

The house came with an acre and a half of land, exquisitely gardened by one of the servants, a teenager from the family. I wanted to work in the gorgeous garden. As a farmer, I loved the way the African land's fertility and the sky's abundant rain made everything grow so quickly. But when I asked the gardener where to find the lawn mower, he became very agitated.

Finally, Nurit came out of the house. With English much better than mine and experience with servants from her six months in Tanzania, she finally understood the problem. "He says he takes care of the lawn and it is not right for you, as the master of the house, to do the work." My grandfather must have turned in his grave. It took some explaining, but finally they agreed to let me work in the garden whenever I wanted.

The luxuries that came with the job went beyond the fancy house. They gave me money to buy a car—that became the moment when I finally realized exactly how far from Israel I had traveled. I bought a brand-new Peugeot 404, a car that cost a fortune in Israel, far beyond my means.

Jinja sits on the banks of the White Nile, about eighty kilometers north of Kampala, the Ugandan capital. The countryside is green, lush, wet—everything Israel is not. I made it my habit, every morning on the road to the army base, to stop to admire the view of the lake, constantly astounded that our entire country could fit into a corner of the massive body of fresh water.

The weather, too, astonished me. The sky turns red in minutes, and then suddenly rain, thunder, and lightning swallow everything up for an hour, two, or three. It felt like the world breaking up around me. Terrifyingly close, bolts of lightning filled half the sky, and thunder shook the ground. Then the rain stopped, as suddenly as it had started. Until I reached Jinja, I had never experienced warm rain. In the Galilee, rain comes in winter and is always cold. In Uganda, we only knew heat and humidity. At home, we count every millimeter. In Uganda, they count the rainfall by centimeters.

After I saw the rain the first time, I understood why my house needed a full-time gardener. You pruned a tree and used one of the branches as a sapling, just sticking it in the ground and letting nature take over. Theodor Herzl, the Austrian journalist who founded modern Zionism, once suggested making a deal with the British empire to turn Uganda into the Jewish homeland. Now, in Uganda, I wondered about the wisdom of the Zionist movement's decision to reject the Uganda plan. In Uganda, farming would have been a lot easier than in the Middle East.

I spent the first three days in Jinja getting organized, and then, ready to work, I went to the army base. My arrival made the other Israelis—and the African officers who served on my staff—very nervous.

"This is not Israel," said Itzik Bar-Akiva, the senior Israeli officer in Jinja. "Here you can take your time. They gave you ten days to get organized. Use them."

"I'm organized. I'm ready to go to work," I said.

"Please, Muki," said Bar-Akiva. "Slow down, take it easier."

I realized they worried my pace would force them to change theirs. But I could not sit around twiddling my thumbs. I let two more days pass and then called my staff officers to a meeting. They lined up at attention in front of me, like new recruits in front of a master sergeant. The formality made me uncomfortable. But they insisted on it.

We began with platoon training, including mounted jeeps, recoilless rifles, mortars, bazookas, and other basics for a company of paratroopers. The training went smoothly—though I kept encountering major differences in attitude between my experience from home and theirs, in Africa.

One day a jeep accident required the hospitalization of a couple of soldiers. I asked the staff officers for a report on what had happened.

"It is not important," said the company commander.

"What do you mean, not important?" I asked, not understanding what he meant.

"These things have no importance here," he said apathetically.

"I want a report," I ordered. "Every soldier involved is to be interviewed." Coming from the IDF, where an officer's top priority is his soldiers' safety, I found his attitude about the accident infuriatingly difficult to understand. Personal safety when handling weapons made sense to him. He knew how to punish a soldier careless with a weapon. But he and his fellow officers did not understand the need for self-discipline in handling vehicles as carefully as weapons. Most of all, the Ugandan officers did not regard their soldiers' lives as important.

It took three months of training to reach a full company drill, involving integrated platoon maneuvers. To conduct a proper exercise, we needed some real room for the recoilless rifles and mortars. Nowhere in the immediate vicinity of Jinja seemed appropriate, so I searched the maps, finding an area about four hundred kilometers south.

I called in the Ugandan staff officers. "We're going here," I said, pointing to the map. They looked at me as if I had lost my senses.

"It's four hundred kilometers . . . It's far to drive . . . It's a lot of administrative work to move the entire company . . ." the Ugandans complained. I ignored the bellyaching.

But after the meeting, Bar-Akiva approached me, appalled by my plan. "Muki, you don't understand. People don't work hard here, they don't do things that way here."

"I'm here to train them," I insisted, "and I fully intend to fulfill my assignment to the best of my ability."

Itzik and I compromised by letting Burka decide. As mission chief, the ultimate authority for the Israeli military delegation in Uganda, he lived in Kampala. Close to Amin and in touch with Israel, Burka always knew the gossip from home. "Itzik says you're going overboard with your training," he said.

"We went through a long course," I explained, "and I think we should carry out a proper company drill, emphasizing the use of recoilless files. That's the place to do it. There's no other place. So what if it's four hundred kilometers?" I asked. I leaned forward in my chair, waiting for his response.

"You know what?" he said, laughing, taking a cake from the tray brought in by a servant. "No problem. Go ahead. Do it."

About ten days before the drill, I decided to drive down to scout out the area before finalizing the plan. Itzik Ban-Akiva invited himself along, and so did the two other Israelis posted in the Jinja area.

We left early in the morning, spent a few hours in the field, and then started home. Foreboding feelings that I could not quite pin down bothered me all the way back. Sometimes I get premonitions, and something felt wrong. Certainly, my feelings had something to do with a road accident: I refused to let anyone else drive. But on the way back, after nearly 350 kilometers of driving on the dusty roads of southern Uganda—and after the other guys in the car pestered me quite a bit—I handed over the wheel to Itzik. Since he was a former officer of the 101st and a member of the Egged bus cooperative, I trusted his driving. Twenty kilometers later he braked and swerved to avoid something on the road, losing control of my beautiful Peugeot. We rolled over three times before it came to a stop in the middle of an African field. From what seemed to be out of nowhere, farmers and villagers came to watch the strangers in their fields. Luckily, nobody was hurt, and the car started right up. We used our fists to pound out the dent in the car roof and finished the ride home.

With the accident behind us, I expected the foreboding feeling to go away. It did not—and for good reason, I learned when we returned to Jinja.

During the ten days of preparation for the trip south for the drill, the gossip in Jinja said the Libyans had offered large sums of money to Amin—if he would kick us out of the country.

The day before the drill, the base commander in Jinja invited us into his office. "Mr. Qaddafi says Libyan officers can train us better than Israelis," he said, laughing at the idea. We all joined in. "It is only politics," he added with a sigh, and then dropped a bombshell. "But it is good you'll be away from the base for a few days on your drill. Some Libyan officers are coming to Uganda to visit bases and see for themselves what they might be able to offer us. They'll be visiting our base. So it's actually for the best you're not here when they come."

Back in my office, I called Burka. He confirmed it all. "I sent a cable to Jerusalem today, but there's nothing to worry about. I spoke with Amin. Everything's under control," he promised me.

The next day, I took the entire company south, and the drill went ahead just as we planned. On the last day of the exercise, some of the soldiers became excited about a small herd of elephants and a group of giraffes about a mile away from our camp.

By then, even I had become blasé about seeing such magnificent animals in the wild. But something in the soldiers' manner gave me an uneasy feeling. Watching them, I did not need to understand Swahili to figure out that they wanted to try a rocket-propelled grenade on the animals.

"Do I understand correctly?" I asked the Ugandan company commander. "They think they are going to shoot the elephant? With an RPG?"

The company commander smiled at me. "Yes," he said, "for the ivory."

It shocked me. "Absolutely not," I said. "Nobody is to do any such thing."

"Why not, Captain Betser?" he asked. "It has nothing to do with the drill. It will be after the drill."

"When I'm here," I shot back, "everything has something to do with the drill. Now, give the order. Tell them to stop."

"Why not?" he asked. "There are many of these animals. What difference does one dead elephant make?"

"The law says you're not allowed to shoot them," I pointed out.

"The law is for civilians. We are soldiers," he answered proudly.

I shook my head slowly back and forth. "No," I said softly, my most threatening tone. One of the trainees in the three-week IDF paratroopers' course, he knew I meant business. And training these paratroopers had as much to do with making them good citizens as it did with making them good soldiers. As a guest in his country I never spoke against Amin, but I taught his soldiers that loyalty in a modern army must be to the state and its institutions—including the law—not a personality. Besides, I loved Africa for its nature more than anything else. The idea of using an RPG on the elephant made me sick.

"Not this time," he told his soldiers, his message clear: Wait until Captain Betser was gone. But he would have to be careful. I think he understood that if I caught any one of them using military equipment to shoot animals for fun—or profit—I might shoot them.

Back from the full-company drill, we heard the Libyans had come and gone. I called Burka to ask what had happened. "Amin's playing with the Libyans," he said. "He wants to see how much money they'll offer him."

"Maybe he's playing with us," I suggested.

"No, no, everything's fine. Everything's under control."

I hung up with my foreboding feeling stronger than ever. Nobody in the course at Beit Berl had ever pointed out that the Arabs—particularly Egypt, north of Uganda—might get worried over our involvement in Uganda. They might think that we planned to use the Ugandan air base at Entebbe as a staging ground for Israeli air attacks on Egypt or other Arab states in North Africa. No such plan existed, but the Arabs seemed to believe it. Nobody told us, "Gentlemen, the Arabs will do whatever they can to get us out of Africa."

And since everyone knew about Amin's "eccentricities" but never openly discussed them, nobody dared raise the possibility that he would indeed throw us out of the country. Burka called the Libyan visit "bad manners on Amin's part" but nothing for us to worry about.

But less than a week after I brought my Ugandan paratroopers back to Jinja, Amin surprised us. He gave twenty-four hours to all the non-military Israeli organizations and companies to leave Uganda. Israelis working for Mekorot, the hydrology company; Solel Boneh, the construction company that had built the airport at Entebbe; and other contractors, suddenly saw their personal plans in ruin. Many had brought their families, put their children in school, and planned a life there for more than a couple of years.

I called Burka. "How can he throw them out like this?" I asked.

"Politics," Burka said. "That's all—politics. He'll throw them out and let those of us in the military delegation stay. Don't worry. It's all a show for the Libyans."

Up until then, the Ugandans had treated those of us from the Israeli military delegations with utmost respect. Even when we were in civilian clothes, our identity cards as officers issued by the Ugandan Army got us through roadblocks that held up regular traffic for hours or even days.

That sense of immunity—and the false confidence that we controlled Amin and not the other way around—blinded us to reality. Within forty-eight hours, he would strip away our charter, giving the military legation twenty-four hours to pack and leave.

From our privileged status we suddenly fell to the position of unwanted nobodies. People we knew in Jinja, Kampala, and elsewhere in the country suddenly became unavailable to us.

In Uganda barely three and a half months, Nurit and I and little Shaul had collected little to pack. But other Israeli families, older than us and much longer in Jinja, had collected possessions from over as much as four years of life in Africa. We helped our Israeli neighbors pack. After a while I headed back to our house to load the car. Reaching the yard, I found half a platoon of Ugandan soldiers parading to the front door. An officer I did not know stood on the front walkway, hands on his hips. The old servant, George, the gardener's grandfather, stood watching unhappily from the distance.

In my trouser waistband under my shirt I carried a revolver issued to me at the Israeli embassy when I first arrived in Uganda. All members of the Israeli military delegation in Uganda carried such revolvers, keeping them secret from the Ugandans, for just such an emergency.

I said nothing to the Ugandan platoon commander. He said nothing to me, ignoring my presence. He followed his men into the house. I followed him.

While they raided the refrigerator he used a short fly-stick to flick at objects that interested him. He walked slowly, inspecting each room, as if he planned to take possession. I remained silent, but followed quietly, watching, aware of his soldiers' eyes on me, but his eyes deliberately avoided mine.

Finally, back out the front door, he turned. But instead of looking at me, he called out to his soldiers. They doubled-timed it out of the house, lined up and he marched them off.

Hatred and hostility suddenly replaced the respect and friendship we had felt in the country. The headlines of that morning's newspaper—"GO BACK TO ISRAEL"—gave us only twenty-four hours to

do so. The servants cried, of course, but whether they really loved us or cried because they had just lost their jobs, I will never know.

The newspaper claimed Israel plotted to overthrow Amin's government. He decided to let Egyptians and Libyans train his air force, using Mirage jets they promised to provide. He proved his point with typical Amin logic, by explaining that Israel used Mirages to crush the Arab air forces in 1967.

The Arabs, of course, never supplied the jets, probably because the French would not let them. I did not blame Paris for selling planes to both sides in the Middle East conflict. We more or less did the same in Africa. But in Africa, the only possible threat to Uganda came from Tanzania, where we also trained soldiers. Only once in my three months in Uganda did I hear of any border clashes. I called for a report. The clash was as foolish as the newspaper reports claiming we plotted Amin's overthrow.

But the moral issues of geopolitics were far from our minds that day. We four Israeli families that lived in the same neighborhood gathered in one of the houses to plan our escape to Kampala. The question arose whether we would be safer with or without our guns.

Four Israeli families debating what to do can go on for hours. Some said it would be safer to go unarmed in case a roadblock stopped us for a search. Someone called Burka in Kampala, up to his own ears in the logistics of getting everyone out of the country. Burka left it in our hands. "It's your call," he said. "Just get down here as fast as you can."

Someone had to make a decision. "Folks," I decided, "we're holding on to the guns. We're traveling as tourists, not soldiers, but we keep the guns for our personal safety. Now, let's get going."

We camouflaged our convoy of cars by moving individually down the road, leapfrogging our way and trying not to draw attention. "We are tourists," I reminded everyone as each car left. "Nobody is going to bother us."

But leaving Jinja, I thought of Karameh. Just as in Karameh I had wondered "Where is the great big IDF?" that had won the Six-Day War, now I wondered to myself "Where's your country now?"

For the first time—and may it forever be the last—I felt what it means to be a Jew in exile, a helpless refugee without protection in a foreign country where the authorities are full of hatred for us.

Burka waited for us in Kampala. We stayed overnight in a hotel in the city and left in the morning on a commercial flight to Nairobi. There, the IDF would take us home in a Stratocruiser.

Boarding the commercial flight in Entebbe, I mourned for the beautiful country I would miss, and its people, who deserved much better than Idi Amin. But most of all I mourned for my own country, humiliated by a tin-pot dictator.

I worked hard to get to Uganda, to live in Africa for at least two years. Leaving after four months, I never expected to see Uganda again. Forlorn, I climbed the stairs to the plane, watching four-year-old Shaul climb the stairs clutching Nurit's hand, unaware that I would return one night under circumstances much different than the disgrace we all felt then.

THE UNIT

Nahalal gave me power and strength, because it gave me roots and values that shaped my life, and the freedom to choose between the two ideals of my family—developing the land as a farmer or defending it as a soldier. I loved doing both.

The rude interruption of our adventure in Uganda forced me to choose between the two values. I returned to the country at a time of a new wave of Arab terror attacks on Israel, both inside the country and against Israeli and Jewish institutions overseas. My African experience began for personal reasons, but its ignominious ending made me realize that Israel still had troubles. I felt I could help.

As soon as our tenants in Nahalal heard why we had come home, they let us break their lease. But they needed a few days to get organized. Meanwhile, the Defense Ministry gave us a hotel room in Netanya.

I decided to call Matan Vilnai, now a battalion commander in the paratroops brigade, and one of the youngest in the entire IDF.

"Don't move," he ordered as soon as he recognized my voice. "Where are you?"

I told him, and we met that afternoon in a small restaurant near the beach. For a long hour we told each other stories, catching up. When I mentioned going back to the army, he offered me a company command in his battalion. From there, I figured, I could get to the job I really wanted—commander of the paratroops *sayeret*. I accepted his offer.

But a few days later, I bumped into a friend on the street in Tel Aviv. My plans to go back to the army excited him. "Listen, Muki," he said. "You've got to come to our unit, Sayeret Matkal. It's the greatest unit now. The Unit. We're doing serious stuff. Like Sabena."

The most secret unit in the Israeli army, under the direct command of the chief of staff, Sayeret Matkal was used for only the most special operations. Founded in the sixties by a legendary fighter named Avraham Arnan, it sat out the Six-Day War because, as Arnan always said, "a Sayeret Matkal fighter is much too valuable for the chaos of war."

Instead, Sayeret Matkal, also known as the Unit, only went on missions planned down to the last detail. None of its missions were known to the public—until Ahmed Jibril's Popular Front for the Liberation of Palestine, one of the PLO's member groups, hijacked a Sabena airliner full of passengers to Israel.

The plane sat on the runway at Lod's Ben-Gurion Airport while the country held its breath. Camouflaged as airline technicians and in a perfectly timed assault, the Unit burst into the plane, killing and capturing the hijackers and rescuing the passengers.

Even after the successful rescue, the first ever in airline history, the army spokesman would only confirm the use of a "special unit." The military censor killed any story that went beyond that description of Sayeret Matkal. Every army unit is "the unit" for its members. But when cabinet ministers ask the chief of staff if "the Unit" can be used to solve a particular problem, everyone knows they mean Sayeret Matkal.

"Times are changing," said my friend. "And we have a great commander. Ehud Barak," he added. "Sabena proved the Unit's coming into its own," my friend said. "And, believe me, when Ehud hears you want to go back to the army, he's going to want you."

"I'm already committed," I protested. "I made promises. I gave my word to Matan that I'd go to his battalion."

"Well, you can't stop me from telling Ehud that you're back in the country," my friend warned as we parted.

We are a tiny country, and though the army appears large, it is really very small. In the tiny circle of special forces fighters, we all knew of each other, even if we never worked together. I had heard of Ehud. Raised in the Jezreel Valley on a kibbutz, he played piano and studied physics, read history and philosophy—and led the rescue on the tarmac that spring.

By the time I returned to Netanya that evening, Ehud had left two messages for me to call. It did not surprise me. His reputation as a bulldozer preceded him. "I want to meet you," he began when I finally got through to answer his calls. "Tomorrow. At your hotel. We have a lot to talk about."

"You understand that I've already promised Matan, and . . . " I tried to explain.

"Yes, I know. You promised the paratroops. But I want to come and talk to you. From what I hear about you, the Unit is where you belong."

The usual career ladder for the big army included tours in various branches. It can turn into a thirty-year tour for the very best, from the draft all the way to the chief of staff.

But at twenty-five, I figured life was too short to commit myself to twenty-five years in any one profession. The usual career path—a few years in special forces, then a few more in the armored corps or the intelligence branch, then back to infantry as a brigadier, and on to the competition for a seat on the general staff—bored me with its predictability and its bureaucratic nature. I wanted to be in special forces—my entire life seemed to prepare me for it. From the traditions of my family through my childhood as an adventuring hiker and into my army service until then, it seemed as if I was being prepared for a unit like Sayeret Matkal.

Matan's offer took me back to paratrooping, a basic requirement for every special forces fighter, and my first love in the army. But I knew that if Ehud Barak offered me an interesting job in the general staff's *sayeret*, I truly would be at the tip of the IDF spear.

Short and stocky, Ehud exuded a tremendous energy when he showed up the next day, immediately making a good impression by getting right to the point. He had done his homework, collecting intelligence on me. He knew what I wanted. He came to offer me a job: "I want you as commander of the new recruits, and as a senior staff officer."

We sat in a corner of the hotel lobby. "If you only want to come for a year or two, that's fine," he began. "You'll have a great time, and then you can go back to Nahalal and do reserves with us. But if you want an army career, coming to the Unit will also be good for you. It will give you some ideas, enrich you, give you something for the road to bring to other jobs. I promise you, people will get to know you."

It won me over. But I gave him a problem. "I promised Matan," I told Ehud. "You figure out how to solve it."

"No problem," he said. "I'll take care of Matan."

But after Ehud left, I felt bad. I wanted Matan to hear the news directly from me. I wanted him to know that I did not go behind his back. Ehud came to me, not the other way around.

Between my hotel lobby phone and Matan on a radio in the field up north, communication directly with him became impossible. But I heard through the grapevine that he had already told his staff officers about my arrival. It put my integrity on the line.

I borrowed a car and drove to Tel Nof to see Levi Hofesh, then paratroops brigade commander, to ask for his help in the dilemma.

"Things are getting complicated," I began. "On the one hand I promised Matan. On the other hand Ehud made me an offer. I want you and Matan to know that whatever you decide is fine with me."

"What are you worried about?" Levi smiled at me. "Two commanders are fighting over you!" He laughed. "And between you and me," the paratroops brigade commander added, lowering his voice, "I would pick Sayeret Matkal."

Like Raful and Amos Yarkoni's argument over me, questions of my next job in the army went to a higher authority. Ehud went directly to chief of staff David "Dado" Elazar. Matan never had a chance.

I rented an apartment not far from the Sayeret Matkal base, while Nurit and Shaul went back to Nahalal, where I would go home for weekends, holidays, and vacations. A few days later, the phone rang.

"Muki Betser?"

"Yes?"

"Yonni Netanyahu."

Drafted three months before me, Yonni served in the paratroops regular brigade while I went to the brigade's *sayeret*. Our officers' training courses had overlapped, but we had never worked together. Now Ehud's deputy, Yonni's reputation preceded him. A brave, enthusiastic fighter, he always carried a book of history or philosophy for the hours of waiting in any military operation. "It's settled, Muki," he said. "I'm sending a car for you. We've got something cooking."

When I heard him say "something cooking," it confirmed everything I had expected from the Unit. Twenty minutes later, a car showed up for me. Within the hour, Ehud gave me an office, a car, a secretary, and a new force of recruits to train. Most important, he gave me an operation to help plan.

Two years earlier, at the height of the War of Attrition in 1970, Syrian artillery opened fire onto the Golan and Israel, trying to open a second front in addition to the fighting with Egypt from the banks of the Suez Canal.

Israel fought back with air strikes at the artillery positions inside Syria. An Israeli Air Force Phantom, hit by MiG missiles, fell over Damascus. Gideon Magen, a thirty-two-year-old kibbutznik, and Pini Nahmani, a twenty-six-year-old moshavnik, became the first Israeli POWs in Syria since the end of the Six-Day War.

Their only sign of life came a few days after their capture. Syria's state-run television broadcast pictures of them in a Damascus prison. Pini clearly was badly injured, lying on a stretcher. But the Syrians refused to negotiate for their release with the International Red Cross, indeed denied the IRC access to the two Israelis.

Three months later, the IDF responded. An armored force crossed the Syrian border, capturing thirty-seven Syrian soldiers to take as hostages in a trade. But during the operation, a Mirage flown by Boaz Eitan, a twenty-one-year-old moshavnik, caught a missile from a Syrian MiG.

Now they held three POWs, whom they considered far more valuable than their own thirty-seven soldiers in our hands. For two years, they ignored our appeals to make a trade through diplomatic channels. The Red Cross had not managed to see our boys. We wanted them back.

Going into Damascus to get them might be possible—but getting everyone out alive was not. It left one option: kidnapping someone much more valuable to the enemy than some soldiers.

The intelligence corps came up with reconnaissance tours conducted by high-ranking Syrian intelligence and air force officers along the Lebanese-Israeli border. They usually traveled in a convoy of civilian cars for the officers, escorted by Lebanese forces, including motorcycle-mounted Military Police, jeeps, and Land Rovers. Lebanese Army armored-car escorts passed them off along sectors of the border.

If we grabbed the officers unharmed as they moved along the patrol road on the Lebanese side, we could offer them back to Damascus in exchange for our boys.

From Metulla to Rosh Hanikra on the Mediterranean coast, the parallel border roads on our side and the Lebanese side are separated by only a few hundred meters, except for a few places where the gap narrowed to a few dozen meters.

We wanted to be as close to the border as possible, in an area where vegetation and terrain provided cover. Intelligence decided on the region of Kibbutz Zar'it, where orchards right up to the border road provided good cover before we dashed down a slope into Lebanese territory.

Called the box, the operation maneuvered three forces—one to surprise the targets, and two others to flank them and close escape routes—into a box surrounding the target. Much of the preparation for the mission depended on timing. Intelligence would tip us off twenty-four hours in advance of one of the Syrian patrols.

"With delicacy," Ehud described the operation. If we went in blasting away, dead Syrian officers would be useless in a prisoner exchange. We needed to surprise them with such an overwhelming show of force that they would prefer to surrender than to put up any opposition. But a large force on the border would draw the attention of the Lebanese and scare off the Syrians. We wanted an operation that only the Syrians—and we—knew about. We could let Damascus know that very night that we held the officers, and offer to make the exchange.

The Unit had already tried the maneuver once, just before I arrived. But at the last minute, just as the convoy made its approach, Dado called it off, citing reports of unexpected Lebanese forces in the area.

Just after my arrival, I joined a second attempt. Ehud and his small force hunkered down in camouflage on the Lebanese side of the border, to handle the grab. A second force waited east of Ehud.

"As trainees for a *sayeret*, we worked harder in our platoon than the two other platoons of trainees. While they did a six-mile march, we hiked a dozen. When they finished twelve miles, we did another fifteen. All our platoon officers and trainers came from the *sayeret*, not the regular battalion. From the start, they gave us the feeling that those who lasted through the course would belong to a very special family of soldiers and officers."

I'm the one propped up on my elbow on the ground beside the platoon machine-gun barrel.

THE NIGHT OF THE WELLS

"The truth is that I never considered the army as a professional career. I regarded it as my duty as a citizen, and my responsibility as a bearer of the traditions of my family. While in the army, I wanted to do my best. I believed I did. The dilemma chased me during my entire life in the army. As deep in my heart as my love of Nahalal and home, I loved the spirit of special operations, and now, faced with the question of going home or more time in the army, I knew I wanted to be an officer."

Yitzhak Rabin—then–chief of staff—reviews a graduating class of new officers. As usual, I was the tallest in my unit.

"My life seemed perfect in early March 1968. I was married to my childhood sweetheart, father to a newborn son; my unit was the most famous of all the special reconnaissance forces the IDF calls a *sayeret*. The newspapers called us the 'tip of the spear.'"

The day before Karameh, at brigade headquarters.

"Right then, nobody could have ordered battle-hungry Sayeret Matkal fighters to get down from the half-tracks. Giora told the transport major to file whatever report he wanted. Meanwhile, we had a war to fight."

Aboard our half-tracks on the Golan.

"Just before dawn, we found Baidatch and the rest of the force, just where he had promised. 'Amitai told us to wait behind while he went in with Amiram, Cheetah, and Moshe,' Shlomo began mournfully. 'They figured the Egyptians all ran away. We should have gone building by building.' Although shaken up by what happened, he gave a clear and concise briefing. 'They drove down the runway advancing on the field. That's when the enemy hit. Under fire, we got the wounded out. But we couldn't reach Amitai. He's still lying there.'"

Shlomo briefs me on what happened to Amitai.

On the banks of Egypt's Great Bitter Lake, waiting for our next move during the Yom Kippur War, I found three oranges in my pocket with which to practice my juggling.

DEATH IN THE MANGO GROVES

"Landing, we expected resistance. Instead, it felt like a deluxe trip to a magnificent view. The ragged peaks of Jebel Ataka looked down over a vast territory. Due east was the Eygptian Third Army, blanketing the flatland between the Suez Canal and the Mitla Pass, inside Sinai. To our northeast, Bren's division advanced toward Suez to complete the siege, at the southern mouth of the canal on the Suez Gulf. It all looked like pieces on a vast chessboard."

Right after landing on the strategic peak, we took a short coffee break. By the end of our first day, we needed to share our water and hardtack rations—cakes of protein and nutrients—with forty Egyptian prisoners.

"'Battalion commanders in the Ugandan Army ride around in Mercedeses with chauffeurs and a couple of Land Rovers of soldiers behind them,' I suggested. 'With that disguise, we could drive through into any military installation in the country without stopping. By the time they figure out who we really are, we'll be on the job.'"

We brought the Mercedes home with us from Entebbe. Here I'm standing beside it as the rear doors to the plane open.

They would watch the Syrians pass and then block a U-turn. A third force—mine—waited west of Ehud, to block the Syrians in case they got through.

Heading into Lebanon, my force—mounted on three armored personnel carriers—would pass a small UN position, stationed in south Lebanon since the armistice agreement at the end of the War of Independence. Then, a few dozen meters away, we would pass an even smaller Lebanese police checkpoint, before heading in Ehud's direction.

I briefed my soldiers carefully. "They don't expect us," I told the team I picked for the job. "But it's not unusual for them to see us in the area on patrols. We just don't want them to think we're on our way to action nearby. So, keep your barrels lowered, and look relaxed as we drive by."

Ehud and his fighters crept in by foot during the night, finding camouflage in the natural terrain of shrubbery and boulders along the side of the road where we wanted to catch the convoy. Dado ran the command-and-control center from a grove near the border.

My three APCs waited on our side of the border for the command. Just after noon, I heard Ehud's voice over the network. "They're coming," he said. I signaled my men to be on alert. The APC engines revved.

"Two sedans," I heard Ehud report back to Dado. "One Land Rover . . . two jeeps . . . an armored personnel carrier . . . "

"Halt!" said a voice on the radio network. I recognized it as Motta Gur, commander of the Northern Command, running the operation with Dado from the field headquarters in the grove.

"It's okay," Ehud protested. "It is no problem for us." The radio static clicked on and off for a second. I held my breath waiting for the next voice.

Dado took command from Motta. "No," he decided.

"I request authorization to proceed," Ehud insisted. I heard the tension in his voice. "I see them. A few meters away. I can jump them now."

"No," Dado said emphatically. "No authorization."

I sighed, understanding that Ehud had mentioned the armored personnel carrier because he wanted to portray the events accurately, not because he thought it meant trouble. Less than a minute later, the convoy of Syrian officers and their Lebanese security drove past me on the Lebanese road below. We had practiced for just such a formation. But the generals had decided the Lebanese APC made the operation too risky.

One of the most frustrating moments I have ever experienced, it felt like we betrayed our POWs. We remained in position another few minutes. Then Ehud called us all into the grove, where Dado and Motta waited.

All the force commanders spoke that afternoon, but Ehud led the charge. "I gave a truthful report," he began, containing his anger's tone, but not its message. "I never expected that the presence of an APC would make you decide not to act. We prepared for the presence of an APC. It posed no threat. Your decision made us cancel an operation that might be the last chance we get to free those boys."

Dado and Motta listened like schoolkids being reproached by an angry teacher, and Ehud went on. "But the worst thing about your decision," said Ehud, "is that you created a situation where next time, we might not report all the information we have, worried that you will make a decision like today's."

Motta deferred to Dado, whose scowl showed the conflict inside him. An orphan who had escaped from Yugoslavia as a youngster during the Nazi occupation, he fought in the Palmach and rose in the army. Instead of shutting us up with a reminder of his rank, he let us release the anger, proving his greatness as a commander. His head bowed low, a stick in his hand scratching patterns in the dark hard ground of the grove, he listened to each of the senior officers. We all backed Ehud.

Finally, Dado looked up at us. "Maybe I was wrong," he said. "I just hope we get another chance."

Less than a week later, we did. Ehud called in the staff officers to announce the Syrian reconnaissance was returning the next day. "This time, I'm not taking any chances," he promised. "I'm going to stay with the generals, and if they make any trouble, I'll explain that we can do it."

He gave Yonni command of the main force, and we added an element to the operation—two decoy cars, hoods up, looking like breakdowns, parked by the side of the road. Along with the cars full

of fighters, troops from the Unit lined the road, dug in and camouflaged in the rough terrain.

Again I took the mobile flanking force in front of the Syrian
convoy, while a company from Egoz waited at the back. But we
added a tank to my force, to ease the generals' concerns. Once again,
we planned a three-sided box around the target. Egoz took the east;
my half-company took the west.

Around eleven that morning, the Egoz force reported sighting
an approaching convoy—two Land Rovers and two armored cars,
moving south toward Rameish, the village on the other side of the
Lebanese border road.

But about half a mile north of the village, the convoy stopped.
Yonni's force, both those hidden in the landscape and those waiting
in the two cars ready to zip down to the Lebanese road, went on high
alert. I gave the order to start the engines.

The minutes ticked by slowly. At eleven twenty-five, Ehud sent
the two decoy cars down to the Lebanese road. I could not see them
from my position—only when I reached the road—but according to
the plan they would roll to a stop beside the road, fighters scram-
bling to take cover, joining other fighters who had waited all night in
position. One of Yonni's soldiers, disguised as a civilian, raised the
hood of the first car, to make it look like a breakdown.

But as so often happens in a special operation, the unexpected
changed everything. A VW van appeared on the road, approaching the Syrian convoy. It pulled up beside the two Land Rovers
and two armored cars, and then made a U-turn and sped away.
One of Yonni's fighters ran to him with news of the VW's appearance. The Syrian convoy began to turn around, an arduous process
for four large vehicles like the Land Rovers and armored cars on the
narrow road. The Egoz scouts reported the VW's suspicious movement to Ehud. Disappointment began to well in my chest as the
report of the VW came over the network. The generals would
cancel again, I feared.

But the brilliance of the Unit includes the ability to improvise, a
tradition carried down from the Palmach. Ehud gave the order.
Yonni's force burst into action, some racing in the two decoy cars the
few hundred yards to the Syrian convoy, waiting for its lead armored
car to make the U-turn. As the two cars pulled up to the Syrian convoy,

other fighters popped out of their hiding places on the slope above the road, only a few dozen meters away.

My APCs stormed forward, with the tank lumbering after us in the rear. In thirty seconds we reached the Lebanese road below us. Passing the UN position and the Lebanese policemen, I watched their bored expressions change to shock. But my soldiers kept their barrels down, just as I had told them, and from my position at the front of the open APC I smiled down at the Lebanese.

Ahead of us, I saw one of our Arabic-speaking officers standing on a boulder above the road, shouting, "Freeze! Surrender!" through a loudspeaker at the Syrians and their Lebanese guards. While some of Yonni's troops pulled the Arabs out of the two cars, others held the two Lebanese armored cars at gunpoint.

Just before I came into view, Lebanese soldiers in one of the armored cars tried to shoot back. Yonni's fighters cut them down. But as I appeared on the road, I saw our only casualty in the operation. The officer with the loudspeaker fell, clutching his ankle where a Lebanese bullet had struck him.

As my APC pulled up to the fracas, Yonni's fighters blindfolded the last of the Syrians, who kept shouting "No blood! No blood" as they hustled him and his friends into the two decoy cars to take back to Israel. Meanwhile, my soldiers loaded the five captured Lebanese soldiers onto the APCs.

Suddenly, I noticed a Syrian officer and a Lebanese soldier trying to escape north across a plowed field on the fourth, open, side of the three-sided box we had made around the convoy. I gave the order to chase them down, but they managed to get down a steep slope, away from our clutches. We turned around, heading for the border. As we crossed the border back into Israel, one of the five Lebanese wounded in the firefight died on board my APC.

Ehud, Dado, and Motta, along with other grinning senior officers, watched as we handed over the prisoners to an interrogation force to hold them until their release in exchange for our POWs. Everything had worked so far. Settling down into the standard debriefing that immediately follows every special operation, we waited for Dado to begin, certain that in a few hours or days our POWs would be home.

Beaming, Dado scanned the faces of the soldiers and officers sitting in front of him on the ground. "This cancels last week's mistake," he began. "And now the Syrians have some incentive to return our boys. Our prisoners include a general, and," Dado paused for effect, "two colonels from Syrian Air Force Intelligence."

Syrian dictator Hafez el-Assad began his career in the air force. We immediately understood that capturing two intelligence colonels from his power base inside the Syrian Army held the key to a successful exchange.

By nightfall, Israel made the following secret offer to the Syrians: We will not publicize this humiliation. We will return your people this very night—in a prisoner exchange for our people. Within a few hours I heard Damascus agreed to the trade.

But, very quickly, Golda Meir's government figured that if the Syrians, the most stubborn and obstinate of our enemies, agreed so quickly to our terms, then Damascus could use its influence in Egypt. Cairo held ten of our soldiers, including pilots shot down during the War of Attrition. We held several dozen Egyptian POWs.

Obviously, such a process is long and complex—and the politicians did not know how to keep a secret. The story of the kidnapping leaked. Negotiations as delicate as those do not work well under the limelight of world attention. The Egyptians refused to cooperate. Eight months went by. Finally, our side returned to the original offer made to the Syrians: release our boys, and you'll get yours. The Syrians agreed.

A few weeks later, the air force threw a party for the three freed POWs, and invited us to the celebration. Taking seats at the back of the hall, we wore civilian clothes. It was a very emotional evening.

The former POWs went up onstage to describe their experiences under Syrian torture in the long months of isolation in the dank underground cells of Damascus. They carried Pini Nahmani, in a wheelchair, onto the stage. "While we sat in prison in Damascus, we always hoped the guys from Sayeret Matkal would show up to get us out," he said.

We all squirmed uncomfortably. A nice thing to say; we appreciated the compliment—but it was the last thing in the world we wanted to hear in public. Our strength as a force capable of surprising the enemy relied on the secrecy of our unit. The censor made sure Pini's remarks about our existence never left the room.

THE JOB

No celebrations or treats for special warriors follow a Sayeret Matkal operation. The day after the capture of the five Syrian officers, we went back to work.

Like every unit in the IDF, Sayeret Matkal combines regular soldiers with reservists. But while most Israeli veterans of the universal draft can expect thirty days of reserves a year, Sayeret Matkal fighters can expect to do upward of sixty.

Reservists participate at all levels of the daily activities of the Unit. They train on new weapons, learn new tactics and drills. They help plan new missions, drill for upcoming operations, take courses in their specialties, and help plan new missions.

On a typical day, one team of fighters might be on a combined movement-and-camouflage exercise in the Negev, while a second group is on a security check somewhere in the country. Back at the base, a team might be testing a new method for recapturing a hijacked airplane (Sayeret Maktal's base has its own runway), while another squad is trying out an Israel Military Industries (IMI) prototype of a new assault rifle or a new kind of night-scope, while others study aerial photographs of a terrorist command headquarters the Unit wants to take out. And finally, a standing unit of fighters is always on standby, ready in case of an emergency involving terrorists holding hostages. If necessary, they can be on a chopper within minutes for action anywhere in Israel.

Avraham Arnan founded Sayeret Matkal as a special force capable of responding immediately to emergencies requiring unconventional military solutions, and for highly specialized reconnaissance missions into enemy territory. Inspired by David Stirling, the founder of the British SAS, Arnan established Sayeret Matkal during Yitzhak Rabin's tenure as IDF chief of staff. Arnan made the Hebrew translation of Stirling's book *Who Dares Wins* required reading for new recruits, issued to them along with their weapons in their first days in the Unit.

But as the Formula One of the infantry, where new methods are tried out and developed so they can eventually be transferred to all the infantry units of the army, the chief infantry and paratroops officer carries the Unit's brief in the chief of staff's office. Nonetheless, many career-track officers coming out of Sayeret Matkal chose intelligence as the next step on their professional ladder, supplying their colleagues back at Sayeret Matkal the data we needed to come up with operational plans for the problems we faced.

Every chief of staff knew the names of all the senior officers in Sayeret Matkal, the ultimate small army of the IDF. The Unit's commander, usually a colonel, has direct access to the chief of staff. Arnan's concept gave us an independence that no other unit—except perhaps certain fighter wings—enjoy in the IDF.

With our own budget, we decided what we needed to buy—or pay to have developed. With access to the highest ranks of command for intelligence and full logistical support from other branches of the army, we could initiate operations, as well as take assignments and develop operations, as well as suggest missions.

But of all the differences between Sayeret Matkal and the rest of the army, one thing distinguished it above all else: Sayeret Matkal does not prepare for war. Arnan considered the Unit too valuable for the chaos of warfare. Instead, the Unit's task is threefold: to perfect capabilities; to plan and execute operations; and to develop new fighting doctrines for the tasks created by international terrorism.

Like every *sayeret* in the IDF, the Unit takes its basic recruits from the draft three times a year from the Tel Hashomer induction center. My basic training for the paratroops *sayeret* lasted almost a year. I taught a six-month basic training course in Egoz. The basic training of a Sayeret Matkal fighter is much, much longer.

At the end of their basic training, juniors win Sayeret Matkal pins in a very private ceremony attended only by other members of the Unit. From then on, the fighter is considered combat-ready—but more training lies ahead. If he is lucky, during that period he might get picked to participate in an operation.

Yonni trained new recruits until he became Ehud's deputy. Now, I became responsible for making fighters out of people with the basic combination of high intelligence, technical ability, and physical fitness required of any special forces unit.

But I also looked for integrity in my fighters, as well as native skills that went beyond what could be taught. From driving to shooting, swimming to climbing, everyone learned every skill—but some would always be better than others in their particular talent. It's the toughest regimen in the IDF, and many, if not most, are unable to complete the course.

Familiarity with the IDF's entire arsenal of personal weapons, ranging from those made by the Israel Military Industries (IMI) to those acquired either in the world arms market or as booty from the enemy, is elementary in Sayeret Matkal.

First and foremost, scouts must observe and report accurately. Sayeret Matkal fighters learn to use all the observation and communications instruments available to the IDF. Night-scopes, cameras, binoculars, and radios of all types and sizes—a Sayeret Matkal fighter is proficient with them all.

Maps—reading them and drawing them accurately—as well as aerial photographs, become as easy to decipher as a newspaper. The soldiers learn to move, and hide in, every kind of terrain. In tiny Israel, the topography ranges from the snows of Mount Hermon to the desert canyons of the Negev. Sayeret Matkal is at home everywhere in the country.

They learn camouflage techniques, taking care of their air supply and waste disposal, living on hard, dry compressed tack, proving they know how to stay cool with the enemy walking over their heads. Self-control and presence of mind are as critical as a fighting spirit. At least once during their initial training, they are kidnapped—literally off the street in civilian clothes, sometimes—and taken prisoner to see if they can stand up to the pressures of interrogation, believing that their tormentors truly are Arabs. Sayeret Matkal always makes sure that many, if not most, of its soldiers know Arabic. I don't—except for basic farmer's talk. My specialties lie elsewhere.

One of the many climaxes in the training is a solo four-day personal navigation of more than a hundred miles around the country—which is barely 250 miles long. Not allowed to make contact with any acquaintances, not allowed to use a vehicle, they must leave their mark at dozens of coordinates within certain time limits. They never knew when I might appear, catching them cheating. I trailed them the same way I followed my Shaked recruits.

The last night of the final drill, the new fighters end up not far from Masada. A short live-fire exercise ends with a run up the mountain to the plateau where Jews of the Second Commonwealth, two thousand years ago, committed suicide rather than be taken alive by the Romans. There, with only the stars and their comrades as witnesses, the gold pins of the Unit are handed out, worn inside the shirt lapel, as secret as the Unit itself. It is a moving ceremony for all involved. But from that night on, they are fighters in Sayeret Matkal, the IDF chief of staff's most elite reconnaissance force, the Unit.

SPRING OF YOUTH

I always understood the Palestinian demand for self-determination. The territories we won in 1967 in a war imposed upon us were, according my understanding, supposed to be used as a card to trade for true peace. I supported border corrections in the Jerusalem area, for example, but disagreed with government policies that put Israeli settlers deep into the territories.

As far as I was concerned, the only way to peace lay in dividing the country between us and the Palestinians. It meant compromise with the Palestinians. Not with terrorism. No matter what the cause, terrorism outraged me, and as long as the PLO preferred the battlefield over the negotiations table, I wanted to be in the fight.

By early 1973, we decided to hit them at home, just like in el-Hiam. Only this time, we would end up going beyond the doorstep—to their bedrooms in Beirut.

The most Western city of the Arab world, Beirut, with its casinos and lidos, its boulevards flanked by French and Italian boutiques, and its banks with their bullion in underground cellars, drew the wealthiest of tourists and Arabs seeking political freedom in the Lebanese capital.

That very freedom, the result of a tenuous political balance among Maronite Christians, Sunni and Shiite Moslems, and Druze tribes, also made it possible for the PLO to take over sections of the city and large swaths of the country, especially in southern

Lebanon. They took West Beirut, in the hills above the port. Refugee camps provided foot soldiers. But the leadership lived well—in large part off money from Arab regimes both supporting the Palestinian cause and afraid of their violence.

Indeed, after King Hussein threw the PLO out of Jordan in September 1970, Beirut became the world center for international terrorism. Land-mine factories, arms depots, narcotics smuggling, and PLO training camps became as much a part of Beirut's landscape as the bikinied girls on the beaches. Terror groups like the IRA in Ireland, the Red Brigades in West Germany, the Red Army in Japan, and the Shining Path in Latin America sent their operatives to PLO headquarters in Beirut for training in the latest terror techniques.

In the fall of 1972, a Fatah force, including some Western European terrorists—allegedly including Carlos the Jackal (though our briefings never pinned him down there, and never referred to him by the nickname given him by the popular press)—pulled off the most audacious act of international terrorism until then. Calling themselves Black September, in memory of the Palestinian defeat in Jordan in 1970, they kidnapped our Israeli athletes at the Munich Olympic Games.

The hijacking captured a global audience for the terrorists' message—the eradication of Israel—and immediately put the Unit on alert. As far as we knew at the time, our unit was alone in the world with any capabilities for such rescue operations.

While Sayeret Matkal organized into a task force to fly to Germany, Mossad chief Zvi Zamir flew ahead to make the arrangements. But the Germans turned down Zamir's offer of help, saying their security forces would handle the problem.

They did—botching it badly. Eleven Israeli athletes died in a bloodbath at the Munich airport. After a morning memorial service, the Games went on.*

The trauma of the Munich Olympics Massacre struck deep into the soul of Israel. Many remembered the last Olympics in Germany,

*Only after the massacre did the Germans admit they did not have a counterterror unit like Sayeret Matkal. Indeed, as a result of the massacre, they asked Israel for help in establishing the GSG9, their special operations counterterrorism group.

in 1936, when Hitler used the international sporting event as a tool to gain legitimacy in the eyes of the world. In 1972, Bonn wanted the Olympics to demonstrate Germany's full rehabilitation into a Western democracy with a thriving economy. Every Israeli watching the horror of the drama in Munich in 1972 thought of Germany and the Holocaust. Once again, Jews died in Germany simply because they were Jews.

Obviously, we could only rely on ourselves to bring those responsible for the crime to justice. Prime Minister Golda Meir ordered the entire military and intelligence community to target the people who had planned and executed the attack on our athletes, an extraordinary request for revenge. Mossad agents shot it out with Palestinians in Western Europe all that summer, in a twilight war of espionage and assassinations. And in February of 1973, Ehud came back to base from a meeting at the *kirya,* the Defense Ministry and IDF compound in downtown Tel Aviv, and called in the Unit's top officers. Settling in around the brown Formica-topped T-shaped table in his office, he looked pleased. He opened a brown cardboard folder on his desk and pulled out three grainy photographs.

"Mohammed 'Abu Yusuf' Najar, chief of Black September," he began, laying down the first photo like a playing card.

"Kamal Adouan, in charge of PLO terror attacks inside Israel as PLO chief of operations," he said with the second. "And Kamal Nasser, Arafat's spokesman," he said, slapping the third card onto the table.

These three men had organized almost all the terrorism against Israeli targets since 1968. We knew their names. But Ehud's expression suggested the intelligence brief contained more than pictures. He pulled out a map of Beirut.

"The two Kamals," he said, referring to Adouan and Nasser, "live on the second and third floors of a building on the corner of a side street at the end of Rue Verdun in the neighborhood of A-Sir. Here." He pointed to an area inland from the port. "A pretty fancy neighborhood," he said, and then threw down the clincher: "Abu Yusuf lives across the street."

We all immediately understood. We looked around the table at each other, already knowing what lay ahead. But then Ehud surprised us again—with a trump card. "We have the architectural plans of their apartments," he said, pulling out the next stack of documents from the folder. "So, can we get them?"

Sayeret Matkal never turns down an assignment—or a challenge. We began working that night, starting with a brainstorming session, the first stage in planning any operation. Ehud encouraged new ideas, rejecting nothing out of hand. He created an atmosphere in which everyone felt free to suggest the wildest as well as the safest approaches to an operation.

Hierarchy in Sayeret Matkal is very different from any other unit in the army. Friendly and intimate, candid and open, rank plays no role in a planning session, where inventiveness and originality are more useful than military tradition or conventional doctrine. Gradually, the best ideas are set aside for further development. Eventually, the best idea stands out.

Fueled by black coffee and dark tea, we quickly ruled out helicopters, which would eliminate the element of surprise. Besides, Raful's paratroopers had used that method of arrival in December 1968 when he landed in Beirut's international airport for an hour, to blow up thirteen Arab airliners in retaliation for the bombing of an El Al plane about to take off in Athens. And we never repeat our methods.

"Tourists," said the brief we came up with. We would arrive by sea, riding into the shoreline aboard rubber Zodiacs powered by outboard engines.

From the beach we needed to get to the targets, about ten kilometers away inside the city. The Mossad provided the information about the terrorist leaders' apartments. It also provided cars. How many cars depended on the size of the force, which raised the question of firepower. Disguised as civilian tourists—and limited to whatever vehicles the Mossad arranged—we would have to carry our entire arsenal under our clothes. Explosive charges to open the doors to the targets' apartments had to be compact enough to carry on our body, or in an innocuous bag.

At our request, Israel Military Industries had already begun development of a mini-Uzi. And we needed silencers in case of interference on the way—and the guards we expected to find.

Eventually, we created a three-unit structure under a front field command-and-control position standing guard against interference from Lebanese police—and arriving PLO defenders. Run by Ehud, the command-and-control station in the street below the apartments would maintain contact with the floating operational headquarters in the mother ship that brought us, while three squads hit the three apartments simultaneously.

We marked all the known PLO holdings in the city, to avoid any contact with them on our way in and out of the city. We figured on twenty minutes from the first shots until PLO and Lebanese reinforcements arrived on the scene. By then, we should be back on the beach, getting into the boats for the ride home. By reducing the number of fighters to the absolute minimum, we could reduce the number of cars we needed to three.

After the Munich Massacre at the Olympics, Golda wanted to go after "the heart and brain as well as the feet and hands of the terrorists." Moshe Dayan decided to turn our mission, which a computer called "Operation Spring of Youth," into the centerpiece of a wider operation that night.

A force drawn from the paratroops brigade, led by Amnon Shahak—who would eventually succeed Ehud as chief of staff in 1995—got the assignment to hit the six-story headquarters of the world's airline hijacking experts, George Habash's Popular Front for the Liberation of Palestine. Two other forces, paratroops and the Shayetet (the navy's *sayeret* of commandos), were to raid weapons-manufacturing facilities and fuel dumps that the PLO maintained in the Tyre-Sidon area.

Each unit planned its action independently, and except for a handful of the most senior officers, each unit knew nothing of the other operations planned for the same night. Indeed, to keep field security at its tightest, none of the chosen fighters knew the true identity of their targets until a week before the mission.

Already at the first brainstorming session, I asked Ehud for the toughest of the three assignments on the mission. He gave me a grainy passport-size photo that I carried in my shirt pocket from that first night on. I wanted no doubt in my mind the night I met my prey.

Constantly refining our plans, we quickly realized that if we had already decided to go in as tourists, we should enhance the disguise by making some of us women. The smallest, most baby-faced fighters among us got the job. With a barrel chest and a baby face, Ehud looked perfect as a brunette, while tiny Amiram Levine, and Lonny, a soldier I picked for my team, looked good as bleached blondes.

While they got hold of wigs and dresses—grenades would fill out their chests into ample bosoms—the rest of us went one-by-one to a men's shop on Allenby Street in downtown Tel Aviv. When the fifth big guy in two days came into the shop asking for an oversize jacket, the owner guessed something was cooking. Field security sent around an officer to warn the haberdasher to keep his mouth shut.

We worked with a constant flow of intelligence, starting with the gold mine of the architectural plans. Intelligence reported two or three guards stationed outside the two apartment buildings—unless Arafat visited. Then, they doubled and tripled the guard for the PLO chief's late-night visits. We planned for that as well, hoping for it like a bonus.

Israel Military Industries sent over mini-Uzi prototypes, but they were not ready for the job. We tried some foreign-made, light-weight, and compact submachine guns, but they jammed too often to trust on such a mission, so we decided to go back to the tried-and-true Uzi as the weapon to hide under our sport jackets.

I ran the small-arms drills with silenced nine-millimeter Berettas, instead of the twenty-twos I had learned from Dave during my air marshal training. We all practiced shooting from a moving vehicle, and changing drivers on the wheel, in case something went wrong and we needed to drive ourselves.

For explosives, we decided on a very accurate, lightweight, and flexible explosive developed by a golden-handed Sayeret Matkal gadget-maker to take out a lock with a very concentrated, precise blast. But just in case, a fighter from each team carried an attaché case with extra weapons and combustibles, including quarter-kilo rolls of the explosives.

Learning to move as a group through a residential neighbor-hood—without being noticeable to an outsider—became a top prior-ity. We practiced every night at a construction site in north Tel Aviv's Tochnit Lamed, quite similar to the neighborhood layout and architectural style of A-Sir in Beirut. Four- to eight-story apartment buildings lined the quiet streets. In twos and threes, the "women" matched up in couples with three men, we walked through the neighborhood. Ehud, barely reaching my shoulders, put his arm around my waist and I put my hand on his shoulder, a pair of lovers out for a stroll.

Chief of staff Dado Elazar lived only a few blocks away in Neve Avivim, another apartment complex in north Tel Aviv. Almost every night he showed up to watch us. One night he stopped Ehud and me, walking arm in arm.

"What do you have under there?" Dado asked with a sly smile, and reached for my jacket buttons. I let him search me. I carried four grenades on my waist, the Uzi slung into an underarm holster I had wired to make into a custom fit, a Beretta in a second holster under the other arm, and eight magazines of thirty bullets each in pouches that I had sewed into the sport jacket's inside lining. Dado grinned at my hidden arsenal.

If he asked Ehud, the Sayeret Matkal commander could have shown him a similar armory hanging from a web-belt sewn under the skirt, and an explosive cleavage under the oversize faux-Chanel jacket.

Over and over, we moved through the neighborhood into the two almost-finished apartment buildings standing opposite each other at the end of the short street, breaking off into four separate forces—three for the apartments, and Ehud's force in the street. Over and over, I ran up the stairs with my teammates Lonny and Zvika Livneh, counting each flight to make sure we did not get off at the wrong floor, each time slicing seconds off the time until it worked perfectly.

Our training in the populated neighborhood presented an extraordinary field-security problem. One night, a neighbor from the nearest occupied building about seventy-five meters away called the cops.

Chief paratroops officer Emmanuel "Mano" Shaked, overseeing the entire operation, sent us into hiding when the blue flashing lights of the police car slowly turned into the street where we practiced. Alone in an empty construction site in the middle of the night, Mano probably appeared mighty suspicious to the blue-uniformed patrolmen, who did not recognize him. Luckily, Dado came by. Everyone in Israel recognizes the chief of staff. He swore them to secrecy and told them to forget what they had seen. No report ever appeared in the police logs, though afterward, when the world headlines blared reports of our action, they probably figured out what we were doing there.

One night, after one of those long practice sessions in Tochnit Lamed, a soldier from another force in the mission came to me with a question. "Muki," he began hesitantly. "There is no backup on this mission, is there? I mean, if something goes wrong . . . "

"That's true," I said, right back at him. That unanswerable question gnawed at us all, but none dared voice it. The IDF does not believe in suicide missions.

I decided to call a meeting of the task force. I thought out my speech carefully. "We're going on a very unusual operation," I began, "a civilian target in the heart of a city. The targets will have guards. They also might be armed, themselves. Civilians live all around them, and we have to be extremely careful not to harm them.

"We have a lot of good intelligence. But the best intelligence we have is that these are people with blood on their hands." I paused to let my words sink in. "We are taking a relatively great risk. But we are convinced," I said, knowing I spoke for all the officers who planned the raid, "that the level of risk is logical and reasonable.

"If we do it right, we can get away without any harm. But anything can happen. That's true. If it does, we need to stay cool, take heart, and remain confident that we know how to manage."

I looked around at them, only a couple of years younger than me. I felt confident in all of them, and told them so. "And because I have that confidence, I am convinced we will succeed."

Nobody asked a question. But I wanted to make one more important point. "This is the first time that, as a unit, we are targeting a personal enemy by name and not encountering them as anonymous enemy soldiers. But as far as the government of the State of Israel is concerned, these three people are war criminals. We are deliberately taking revenge for what happened in Munich. We want this enemy to know our anger, and to fear it."

Yonni wanted to take part from the start. But as Ehud's deputy, he filled in as acting commander of the Unit while Ehud focused entirely on the preparations for the mission. On all such operations, there is complete compartmentalization. Indeed, other than those of us on the mission, Yonni was the only person in Sayeret Matkal, aside from the participants, who knew about the operation. Seventy-two hours before the mission, he burst into my office. "Muki, listen, I just spoke to Ehud, and he said that if it is okay with you, I can join your team."

He gave me a look of expectation with a hint of pleading in his eyes, and no time to respond as he went on. "I stayed out of the way for three weeks," he said. "I managed the Unit. But I don't want to miss this operation. I told Ehud that I'm ready to go as a regular soldier. Ehud said okay, so I asked him who had the most complicated and critical target."

"What did he say?" I asked.

He smiled at me. "You do." He paused, waiting for me to say something. But I remained quiet.

"Ehud says it is up to you," he went on. "If you say okay, then it is fine with him."

He knew nothing of the plans except what he had heard during that first session when Ehud laid out the original intelligence. A great fighter, terrifically motivated and powerfully courageous, as long as I did not have to take someone off my team to make room for him, Yonni was one "tagalong" I was always ready to accept on board my team.

"Here's what we've got planned . . . " I began, and Yonni became the fourth man on my team.

The IDF uses enemy role-playing extensively. But in special operations missions, where the entire effort is offensive and planned to the last detail, one of the final and most important steps in the exercises is dismantling the plan at every step, thinking up unexpected events to test our reactions in case of a surprise.

It is called "cases and reactions" and is the only way to plan something going wrong. We might be discovered by accident, or ambushed because of a leak in field security.

For every stage of a plan as complex as Spring of Youth, between ten and twenty possibilities for accident, error, or unexpected interference need to be taken into account. All are brainstormed and listed, and theoretical responses planned. About half a dozen of the most critical are tested and practiced in real time, with enemy role-playing practiced over and over again.

We did not know when or where we might be attacked—on the way to the target, back down the stairs, in the building, in the street, in the car, on the beach. But we prepared for it each step of the way.

As usual, Dado and Mano watched our practice that last night. On one drill they watched from inside the apartment. As we began the retreat, Dado suddenly shouted, "Contact from the rear. You have one man wounded!" A classic "case and reaction" ploy; he pointed at Zvika Livneh. We picked him up and ran down six flights of stairs with him. A few minutes later, Dado came out of the building and called our retreat weak. Mano told us to do it again.

"What should we do about this?" I whispered to Yonni under my breath. He knew exactly what I meant. Every once in a while a senior officer needs to show off "leadership" to an officer even more senior. The drill had gone fine, and we knew it.

"One more remark out of him," Yonni hissed back under his breath, "and I'll tear-gas him."

"You have any?" I asked.

He smiled and patted a pocket as Mano and Dado disappeared inside the building.

With me in the lead and Lonny, Zvika, and Yonni in the rear, we ran back up the stairs for the tenth time that night. We paused outside the front door to the apartment, waiting for Ehud's signal—five clicks on the Motorola transmitter clipped to the inside of my jacket—then waited another five seconds for the explosion on the door handle.

I burst into the main corridor of the apartment. Mano stood in the corner. I ran past him, leading the force into the flat. "Enemy contact!" Mano shouted as Yonni ran by.

Yonni swirled, pulled out the Mace canister, and let loose a spray that went right into Mano's eyes. Mano wanted a reaction. He got one. He started rubbing his eyes, which only makes the sting of the tear gas worse, and in his confusion he crashed into a pile of pre-fab window frames piled in a corner of the apartment living room, shattering the glass. (After the operation, the army reimbursed the contractor for the broken glass and frames, which the contractor thought vandals destroyed. But when he learned what we used his buildings for, he donated the money to the Soldiers' Welfare Association, Israel's equivalent of the USO.)

Pleased with our reactions, Dado said no more about the proficiency of our performance, or anything about Yonni's reaction. Neither did Mano. Mano never said a word about it. The Unit, after all, once kidnapped half a dozen unsuspecting senior officers from the general staff one day—including blindfolding, handcuffing, and ferrying them from one vehicle to another—when they asked us to prove a capability we had promised them.

Always protected by a halo of glamour—for good and for bad—special forces units are usually allowed certain liberties with respect to the formal hierarchy of the big army, and in the IDF, no unit was more special than Sayeret Matkal.

The next day we moved to Haifa to conduct drills in the seaborne aspects of the operation, and to hold a full dress rehearsal with all the elements of the mission. From missile boats into the rubber boats at sea, to a beach landing on the Haifa coastline, where Mossad cars and drivers waited to take us up the Carmel to a neighborhood similar to the target in Beirut, we covered everything except a break-in to an apartment.

In terrible wintry conditions at sea, learning to move back and forth from the deck of the missile boat to the Zodiacs looked like the most dangerous part of the mission. Two commandos from the Shayetet, the navy's *sayeret*, held me as I stood up in the rocking boat, reaching for a rope to pull myself aboard the missile boat. For a moment, the ship's roll appeared certain to crush us all. Just then, the rope snapped in front of me. I grabbed it, and the naval commandos heaved me upward to the deck.

On our way into Haifa, one of the sailors told me that during exercises the sea is always at its worst. "But when the real thing comes," he promised, "God will make it calm and peaceful." I hoped God knew what the sailor knew.

Dado and Eli Ze'ira, commander of Military Intelligence, came to see us off at the naval pier in Haifa on Monday, April ninth. They began with the usual speeches of encouragement and motivation, but suddenly Dado said, "We've got to kill those bastards."

I raised my hand. "Did you say kill?" Until then, we had planned the operation as a kidnapping, to take them back to Israel to stand trial. We did not regard prisoners from our encounters with the PLO as POWs but as criminals who had committed murder. None of us expected that any of the targets would simply raise their hands and surrender, but if they did, we practiced to take them prisoner, tying their hands and feet, and carrying them back home with us.

Dado looked at Ze'ira and then turned back to us. "Yes. Kill them," said the chief of staff.

* * *

It is traditional in Sayeret Matkal for the cooks to prepare something special before an operation—but the expectation of a seven-hour boat ride on the wintry seas like we had experienced the day before left none of us with an appetite. And just in case, we all took anti-nausea pills before leaving the base for the ride to Haifa. But, like the sailor said, God made the sea calm for us that night. Flat and smooth, it turned into a pleasant ride.

The missile boats stayed far off the coast, running lights dimmed. Beirut sparkled at night like the jewelry in its fancy shops. The missile boats slowed down until steady in the water, the Zodiac boats lowered. Each of us pulled on plastic sheeting to keep our civilian disguises dry for the trip, then we climbed down into the boats.

The naval commandos used outboard motors for most of the ride. But several hundred meters off shore, they turned off the motors and rowed the rest of the way in. Usually, we would have helped with the rowing and the swimming. But we sat in a pastoral quiet, under plastic sheets, watching Beirut come closer like tourists on a cruise ship arriving in port. Reaching the surf line, the frogmen steered the boats in like surfboards, and then the last few feet they slipped into the water and pushed and pulled until the boats beached. Even our feet did not get wet.

Three cars with Mossad drivers waited for us, just as planned. Lonny, Zvika Livneh, Yonni Netanyahu, Ehud, and I piled into the first Mossad car. Ehud slid in beside the driver, and I took the window seat beside him in the front seat. "Go!" snapped Ehud from under his brown wig.

But as the driver made the car slide slowly forward, he spoke softly, the tension unmistakable in his voice. "I just came from there for a last look," he said. "Three gendarmes, armed with submachine guns, are patrolling the street below the apartments." We knew about a Lebanese police station about two hundred meters away from the target buildings at the intersection in A-Sir.

Ehud bit his lower lip, remembering the kidnapping of the Syrian officers and how Dado had called off the mission because of the unexpected APC. I read his face as he wondered whether to report by radio back to the command-and-control field headquarters on board the mother ship and risk the entire mission being canceled.

"Go," Ehud repeated, making up his mind. We had practiced for just such an eventuality. The driver slowly drove from the darkened beach to the coastal road that leads into Beirut. On the way, all three forces in their cars tried out the radio frequencies we had selected for the operation.

Driving with traffic, the three cars moved within visual contact of one another, but not too close to be recognizable as a convoy. At the first set of traffic lights, we stopped for a red light. I glanced out the window to a car next to me. An elegant woman in the backseat, her driver in the front, looked over at me. Something soft in her face made me smile at her. She turned her head away. If she only knew what was going on, I thought.

On a mission like that, the paranoia begins with the conviction that everyone around you is completely aware of a foreign presence in their midst. As a security officer flying in and out of Israel in the early seventies, I knew those feelings. But the exchange of glances with the woman snapped me out of the paranoia that the whole city knew of Sayeret Matkal's arrival in town. The silence in the car started to grow comfortable as we settled into the seats of the Buick Skylarks that the Mossad agent rented in Beirut.

But the driver suddenly broke the quiet when we reached a second red light. "There are policemen in the area," he repeated, obviously worried. A fully trained Mossad agent, the driver recognized risk when he saw it.

I glanced at Ehud, thinking of the Syrian officers. If he broke the radio silence to update Mano Shaked on board the missile boat in the darkness far off the coast, Mano would contact Dado. He would discuss it with the chief of the Mossad. They might go to the defense minister, who would call the prime minister. By then, the mission would be scrubbed.

Everyone in the car waited for Ehud's answer. Everything was so delicately planned, we worried that the slightest bit of information that departed from the plan might spin the command post into panic. My body tensed waiting for Ehud's answer.

The light changed. "I heard you," Ehud finally said to the driver. "Go." The car lurched forward, and I relaxed into the soft upholstery of the big American car, watching the scenery of Beirut like a tourist on my way to A-Sir. I understood exactly what Ehud meant, and it made me glad. We would see for ourselves and then decide.

The ride into the hills passed quickly, and then we drove slowly into the target neighborhood, finding parking places off the Rue Verdun. Just as we had practiced, Ehud and I walked first.

Cars drove by on the street. A few people out for late-night strolls, not untypical in a Mediterranean city. I put my arm around Ehud's waist, like a lover. "It reminds me of Rome," I whispered into his ear as we moved along the sidewalk.

At first, we didn't see any of the policemen reported by the Mossad driver. But suddenly, two gendarmes came out of the shadows ahead, pausing on the sidewalk to light cigarettes. A street lamp made their brass buckles glisten in the night. Submachine guns hung from straps draped over their shoulders. They blocked the sidewalk. I felt Ehud tense.

"We're tourists," I reminded him, "civilians. They're the ones who should get off the sidewalk, out of our way."

So, Ehud and I continued our stroll, heading straight for them. But they ignored our approach. We hugged a little closer and narrowed our path to the edge of the sidewalk. Still the cops did not move. As we crossed their path, my shoulder brushed lightly against one of the gendarmes'. He didn't even turn to look at me.

Ahead of us, everything looked perfect. I knew the corner and the alley by heart. The glass doors to the lobby of my target's building shone brightly ahead.

We knew the guard sometimes napped. But no guards appeared in view as we moved closer to the building. "This is it," I said to Ehud, dropping my arm from his shoulder and leaving him in the street as I headed toward the glass doors.

Through the lit lobby behind the doors, I saw the staircase. Zvika, Lonny, and Yonni followed me. Ehud, Amiram, and Dov Ber, the liaison officer from the Shayetet assigned to the mission, stayed in the street.

Inside, I drew both Beretta and Uzi. We moved fast, in stages, taking each landing and then moving to the next in a fast half-run, half-walk, two or three steps at a time. Six flights up the stairs, we counted each landing, trying to keep our steps, even our breathing, quiet.

Finally, in front of the door, Zvika knelt to attach the explosive to the door handle. I stood behind him, covering his back. Lonny and Yonni took each side of the door.

I looked at Lonny watching Zvika prepare the plastique. Lonny's blond wig really made him look like a girl. He glanced at me. I grinned. He tried to smile back, but the tension made his smile forced and tense. I felt calm. I winked at him, and then nodded to Zvika to get ready. I clicked the radio mike three times, letting Ehud know we were ready.

The silence stretched on as we waited for Ehud's five clicks, signifying that each of the three forces had called in their readiness. Finally, the clicks began. I counted them off with my fingers—one, two, three, four, five. With the fifth click my open palm turned into a fist, and I pointed at Zvika. He activated the fuse and stood up. I leaned against the wall, Lonny to my right. Zvika took the other side of the door, Yonni to his left.

All three forces set their fuses to the same amount of time. The explosions were Ehud's signal to report back to the mother ship that the operation had begun, setting in motion the rest of the IDF forces in Beirut that night.

The seconds passed slowly waiting for the fuse. But just before the explosion, shooting broke out in the street below. Those last two seconds waiting for the fuse to work seemed endless as I listened to the fire in the street.

Finally, the explosion blew open the door in a blast of smoke. I burst in with Zvika, instinctively taking the left-hand turn into the main corridor of the apartment, running down the hall I knew so well from the drills.

Four strides and I reached my target's office. Half a dozen empty chairs faced the desk. Behind it, filing cabinets reminded me that Military Intelligence wanted any piece of paper we found. To my right, said the architectural plans I had memorized, was the master bedroom door. I swung in that direction just as the door flew open.

The face I knew from three weeks of carrying his picture in my shirt pocket looked at me as I raised my gun. He slammed the door. Bursts from my Uzi and Zvika's stitched the bedroom door. I rushed forward and kicked through the remains of the door. The man responsible for the Munich Massacre lay dead on the floor.

More shooting from the street made me turn away from the sight. The piles of paper on the desk and the filing cabinets behind it made me pause for an instant. But the shooting continued downstairs, and no matter what Military Intelligence wanted, the firefight below changed everything. "No time for documents!" I commanded, already running through the apartment corridor. "They need help downstairs."

Yonni and Lonny guarded the apartment entrance from the foyer. They followed me and Zvika out as I ran down the hall to the stairs, leaping from landing to landing, on our way to the street, where the firefight grew louder.

Out the front door, I ducked into the shadow of a tree, scanning the intersection just as a burning Lebanese police Land Rover rolled through the intersection. Straight ahead, Amiram Levine in a blond wig looked like a crazed dancer in the middle of the intersection, his tiny, powerful body swinging his Uzi back and forth from target to target.

To my right, Ehud stood in the middle of the intersection, doing the same. I added my own fire at the Land Rover, giving Amiram cover for him to run toward me. The Land Rover crashed to a halt against a building. But a second vehicle, a jeep full of reinforcements, came screeching into the box of fire we created at the intersection. Bursts of gunfire knocked the four passengers out of the vehicle as our fire strafed the jeep.

For a second, silence fell over the neighborhood. From the far distance I heard sirens. And explosions. Amnon Shahak's crew at work on the Habash headquarters, I figured.

"Muki!" Amiram called out. "The guard. He's in the Dauphin." He pointed to a squat little Renault parked across the street. "He started the firing," Amiram shouted. "I shot him—but I'm not sure he's dead." A bullet ringing against the asphalt a few feet from me confirmed Amiram's doubts.

"Let's get him," I said. Amiram and I ran diagonally across the street, flanking the Dauphin and firing into it as we moved. But as we charged into our final approach we saw Dov Ber, the liaison officer from the naval commandos, also attacking—from the opposite direction. Brave but wrong, he ran directly into our line of fire. Luckily, Amiram and I spotted him just before we fired, eliminating the driver.

The Mossad drivers pulled into the intersection, tires screeching as they braked to a halt beside Ehud. The teams of fighters from the other two targets suddenly came into view, hurling themselves into the first two cars.

We ran toward ours. The sirens came closer. A roar of flames burst from the spilled fuel tank of a jeep. But before I reached the car, a third jeep with reinforcements pulled into the intersection. I pulled a grenade from its clip under my jacket. The jeep braked hard and a gendarme jumped out. I fired at him with my Uzi, but missed. He ran inside and disappeared in the lobby. I threw the grenade at the jeep. It flew through the air in what seemed to be slow motion, bounced off the tarpaulin roof of the cabin, landed on the street beside the jeep, and exploded. Four gendarmes tumbled out of the jeep, either wounded or dead.

For a second time, sudden silence descended on the neighborhood like an envelope sealing it off from the rest of the world. The shooting halted. Barely two minutes had passed since we hit our targets. I ran toward our car. The door flew open. I threw myself head-first into the front seat beside Ehud. The car lurched forward.

"Hey!" we heard a shout from behind, "don't forget me!"

Zvika flung open the door, and Yonni jumped in, too.

"Go!" Ehud commanded, and the driver began speeding out of the intersection, down the hill, while Ehud used the radio to collect reports from the other two Mossad cars.

Amitai Nahmani's task force reported that all went well. But in the third car, a fighter named Aharon was wounded. When the shooting started, Kamal Nasser had hidden under his desk with a gun and managed to get off a single shot that wounded Aharon in the leg before the terrorist leader was killed by the team commander, Zvika.

Ehud cut off the radio contact and we rushed in a crazy race down the hills of Beirut. The Mossad drivers knew the city and they knew the big American cars well enough to make them slip and slide around the corners as we raced along. No whooping and shouting broke out inside the getaway car. Each man sat alone with his thoughts, alert for enemy forces taking chase.

As we passed a gas station, a uniformed attendant ran into the street, waving at our speeding car to slow down.

"Shoot him, Muki," Ehud said quietly beside me.

"He's a gas jockey, not a cop," I said just as quietly.

We passed the man. I did not shoot him.

A few blocks out of the neighborhood, the drivers slowed down to normal, quiet driving. Thus we made our way down to the shore road and started heading south on the highway to the landing spot. But half a kilometer before the gravel road that led down to the beach to our rendezvous with the Zodiacs, a routine patrol in a Lebanese Army armored personnel carrier rolled slowly along the road, scanning the shore with their klieg lights. We did not want any more shooting, especially so close to escape.

Tense with expectation that their lights might yet uncover the naval commandos waiting for us on the dark beach, we crawled behind them instead of passing, a civilian car respecting the army's right of way.

For a very long minute we crawled behind the APC, like frustrated commuters stuck behind a wide truck on a narrow road. The path down to the beach approached. The APC passed it. We slowed down even more, easily taking the turn.

On the beach, we tumbled out of the cars, running toward the naval commandos waiting for us. We left the cars behind, and the Mossad agents joined us on the rubber boats. But we remained silent until far past the surf line. Our plan said the whole thing would take twenty minutes. From the time we landed on the beach to the time we left was exactly half an hour.

Only when all the troops from the other forces operating in Beirut that night reached the missile boats did they learn what had really happened. Two main task forces went into Beirut that night, ours and Amnon Shahak's paratroopers, who hit Habash's headquarters.

Three top leaders of the PLO lay dead in our wake. And the six-story headquarters of George Habash's Popular Front for the Liberation of Palestine was demolished. But the attack on Habash's headquarters cost the lives of two of our boys. Amnon Shahak, who had won a first medal at Karameh, won another for valor, keeping his cool as he rescued wounded soldiers.

The question came up after Spring of Youth whether we hoped to catch Arafat that night in Beirut. I had missed him at Karameh because of bad planning. In Beirut, the planning was excellent. We did not go in expecting to get Arafat, but hoped for that kind of icing on the cake. Arafat regularly visited those three apartments, and usually worked late at night, the hour we chose for the mission. But Arafat also never stayed in the same place for very long, lest he turn into a sitting target.

The mission filled the newspapers the next day, of course. The raid against three of the most notorious terrorists in the world inspired gushing praise from many of the Western world's newspapers. In the Arab world the rumor went out that we escaped through the American embassy in Beirut. Nonsense, of course. But the Lebanese government collapsed.

None of our names—or the very name Sayeret Matkal—appeared in the papers. But I understood why the eyewitness reports in the Lebanese press described "two beautiful she-devils, a blonde and a brunette, who fought off the police and army like dervishes with machine guns."

Rules of Combat

Ehud Barak left the Unit in June 1973 for studies in the United States, choosing a very special person to replace him as commander of Sayeret Matkal—Giora Zorea. Strong-willed and principled, Giora came from Kibbutz Ma'agan Michael, rising from soldier through squad commander in Sayeret Matkal. He came from a tradition of iron-willed fighters—his father, Meir, had enlisted in the Jewish Brigade of the British Army to fight the Nazis in World War II, and eventually rose to become a general in the IDF. Giora made a name for himself as honest, an extraordinary soldier, and an independent thinker.

But Giora was only a reserve captain. So, to give him some experience, six months before the handover, Ehud sent Giora to Egoz to do my old job—commander of the reconnaissance company. A forty-day course for armored infantry company commanders would follow before he took the handover from Ehud. But after the stint with Egoz, Ehud signed him up for a three-month course. It didn't take long for Giora to decide that he could live without being commander of Sayeret Matkal if it meant more courses. Like me, he wanted targets and action, not theory and routines.

He packed his bags and went back to Ehud. "Thanks, but no thanks," Giora said. "I really don't need this, you know. I'm going back to the kibbutz."

145

"I still want you to replace me," Ehud insisted.

"I don't have the patience for another course," said Giora, a stubborn kibbutznik. Within a few weeks, Ehud convinced Dado that Giora was right for the job.

Promoted to major without any formal training as a company commander, Giora took over Sayeret Matkal. For his deputy he chose Amiram Levine, a career officer who would become a general in 1992, and in 1994 head of the Northern Command. Yonni went to the national staff college, an advanced-studies academy run by the army, Defense Ministry, and Foreign Ministry.

That left Amitai Nahmani and me as the two most veteran regulars on the officers' staff, the two senior captains in the Unit. And I began looking ahead to mustering out and going home to Nahalal.

Interested only in special operations, in "the little army," which I loved for its position at the very tip of the spear, eighteen months of service in Sayeret Matkal seemed to be enough for me. Back at home, Nurit had ailed ever since our return from Africa, and though our families helped, I wanted to be with her and Shaul.

But that spring, just before Giora took command, he came to me with the request that I stay in the job for a few more months. "You know the Unit better than anyone," he said. "Please stick around. At least as long as it takes for me to come to grips with the job," he said. I did not expect Giora's acclimatization to take very long. Instead of leaving the Unit in September 1973, to begin civilian life in Nahalal, I agreed to stay through October. Little did I know that once again, just as I readied to muster out of the army, war was going to change my life.

Spring of Youth hurt the PLO but did not stop terrorism. So my military career continued. Sometimes we planned and practiced for a specific operation, like Spring of Youth. Sometimes we took an assignment on a few hours' notice.

One Friday afternoon Giora ordered the staff to assemble a large force at the Ramat David air force base in the Jezreel Valley as soon as possible. "Take all operational gear for a hijacked plane—and make sure everyone wears a clean, pressed uniform," he added, without any other explanations. It didn't take long for us to get to Ramat David, across the valley from Nahalal, and learn the mystery. "We're going to intercept an Iraqi commercial airliner carrying George Habash," Giora told us at the air force base.

146

Amnon Shahak's attack on Habash's headquarters during Spring of Youth demolished the building and killed many terrorists, but it cost two Israeli lives and did not eliminate Habash. Best known for plotting airline hijackings, Habash broke away from the PLO, which he regarded as too moderate.

A medical doctor preaching extremist Marxism, his international connections with neo-leftist organizations like the Japanese Red Army and West Germany's Bader-Meinhof gang helped him mastermind his campaign of international terrorism against Israel—and the West. His operatives attacked targets throughout Europe, as well as Israel, and aided other international terror groups with their operations.

"He's on a routine shuttle flight from Beirut to Baghdad, probably traveling with bodyguards, as well as the ordinary passengers on the flight," said Giora. "Two combat pilots will pull up behind the Iraqi airliner, out of sight of the commercial plane. They'll get on the pilot's frequency and say that he should follow them back to Israel— or else we'll shoot him down."

It was a bluff, of course, but one that no Arab airline could dare call, especially after what had happened in Sinai a few months earlier, in February. Libya's Moammar Qaddafi had long offered a million dollars to the family of any pilot who flew a planeload of explosives into downtown Tel Aviv. When a commercial Libyan jet appeared on the Israeli Air Force's early-warning radar scopes coming out of Egypt into Sinai toward the center of Israel we took Qaddafi's threats seriously.

Fighter jets scrambled to meet the Libyan plane, trying to make radio contact with the pilot. But he ignored all their calls. The plane flew on. The decision rose all the way to Dado, at home. He made the fateful decision.

The black box found in the desert proved the pilot made the mistake. Lost in a sandstorm, his airplane carrying more than a hundred passengers, he ignored the calls to follow the fighters to an airport. They all died.

The tragedy shocked Israel and the world. The government offered compensation to the victims' families and eventually paid through a third party in Europe.

But the tragedy also made it possible to try capturing Habash. No commercial airline pilot would ever again ignore an Israeli Air Force (IAF) interception. As seriously as we took the Libyan threat, they would take ours. "Tell them there's been a technical malfunction and you're flying back to Beirut," the IAF pilots would instruct the Arab pilot if anyone on board noticed he was changing course.

The passenger jet took off from Beirut at eight that night, giving us about an hour to prepare its reception at Ramat David. We knew what to do. We had drilled it hundreds of times. An hour gave us plenty of time to prepare.

Waiting near the end of the runway, hidden in tall grass beside the tarmac, we would follow on foot as the plane rolled past, breaking up into separate crews for each of the openings to the plane: the emergency exits above the wing and in the rear, a hatch underneath the cargo area where an interior door leads to the passenger cabin, and of course, the main door behind the cockpit.

My El Al experience made it clear to me where I wanted to be: the main passenger door at the front, on the left-hand side of the plane. While my comrades dealt with getting in through closed doors, the airline stewardess would open the door for us, thinking they had landed in friendly territory. Giora wanted us in clean, pressed uniforms, our paratroops wings shining, the red berets on our heads, and pistols, not Uzis, drawn. "I want him to see the dignity of the IDF compared to his terrorists," Giora said. And I wanted to be that first Israeli soldier Habash saw.

We deployed a few minutes later, when word came through Intelligence that the plane had taken off. Half an hour went by, then twenty minutes, ten, five. Finally, the plane lights appeared on the horizon, two fighter planes escorting it from behind. The plane touched down and then raced down the tarmac toward us, while the two fighters swept up overhead and then looped back down for their own landing on another runway.

We had prepared for a Boeing with Iraqi markings. A Caravelle, with Lebanese airline markings, raced past us in the dark. With no time for questions, we sprinted onto the tarmac in two columns. The columns broke up into teams running with ladders to their break-ins.

The crew slapped the ladders against the wall of the plane and I ran up it first. Just as I expected, a stewardess opened the door. Confusion froze her face. I rushed past her silently, and while the other three members of my break-in team took the cockpit, I burst into the passenger cabin corridor, scanning passengers' faces just the way I did for eighteen months with El Al security. But instead of moving slowly down the aisle in civilian camouflage, my weapon hidden beneath a sport jacket, I wore pressed IDF fatigues, with dress-metal bars instead of cloth epaulets, and carried my pistol cocked and drawn, ready to fire at any opposition from Habash or his guards.

I shouted the English phrase "Hands up!" and in an instant they all understood, throwing their hands in the air. I strode the length of the cabin, looking right and left, pistol ready, looking for Habash. But he was not on board. Just then, Amitai Nahmani broke through the back door, the second squad into the plane.

"You can relax," I said, disappointed. "He's not here."

"What do you mean he's not here?" Amitai asked. "How do you know?"

"I've already looked. You can search, but he's not here." Amitai headed down the aisle toward the front of the plane, where some of my soldiers already stood guard, and I began to follow. As I reached the middle of the plane, I noticed fighters on the wing struggling with the emergency door from the outside.

Locked from the inside, the door implodes inward when released from the outside. In the passenger seats in front of it, a woman and two children sat petrified with fear. The door was going to cave in on them. Pushing against it, I tried shouting to the soldiers outside to stop. "Habash isn't here" I shouted. But stopping a Unit force in mid-action is impossible, especially if they think they are about to get their hands on George Habash.

While I pushed against the door with my shoulder, I yanked the woman to her feet and hustled her kids out of the way. With the civilians finally clear, I stood back from the emergency door. It blew inward, soldiers tumbling in after it. By then, officers and soldiers swarmed through the plane, pistols drawn, the realization dawning on them that Habash had never gotten on the plane.

The plane sat at the end of the runway, lit up by klieg lights; rows of chairs and desks sat beside it, where interrogators sat questioning all the passengers. Base commander Zorik Lev, who would be killed a few months later in the Yom Kippur War, arranged for food and drink—sandwiches and fruit juice—for the frightened passengers. Gradually, they calmed down when they realized we were looking for Habash, not them. The interrogators uncovered three suspected terrorists on board the plane—small-fry, not the arch-terrorist we hoped to find. A couple of hours after the plane landed, it took off, with the passengers on board, including a Libyan ambassador and a Lebanese minister.

It turned out that at the last minute, the Iraqi Boeing developed a technical problem, so the airline rented the Caravelle. But Habash, concerned for his security, postponed his flight when he heard the routine flight schedule had changed. His office said that Habash was sick that day. To this day he is said to be ill, but that has not stopped him from killing many people.

From the moment Giora explained the operation, I had my doubts. Trying to capture the man who practically invented airline hijacking as a form of terrorism, we hijacked an airplane to do it.

Nonetheless, while I felt the attempt to capture Habash by intercepting a civilian plane undermined our own moral policy against terrorism, I regarded the international diplomatic reaction as hypocritical. Instead of joining forces against airline hijackings, they did not care if Arabs and Jews killed each other as long as we left air traffic alone.

CONQUERING SORROW

In the early 1950s, David Ben-Gurion, Israel's first prime minister, visited Nahalal. He called on the second generation of farmers in the established farming settlements to give up a year on their own farms to help new immigrants flooding the country to establish new farming settlements in other parts of the country.

My uncle Koba and my father's uncle Gami took up the challenge. As so often happened in Nahalal, they relied on relatives to take care of their farms. My father took Gami's livestock to our new farm in Moshav Bet Shea'rim, across the fields from Nahalal. At the end of the year he would return it all—but we could keep any offspring from the livestock.

Overnight, the barn and coop filled with cows and chickens. But to my eight-year-old eyes, the greatest wonder was the horse. We could not afford tractors yet, nor did we have a car or jeep. The horse, and its wagon, became our sole means of transport. I quickly learned to ride it bareback, and spent hours on it, riding the Jezreel Valley.

A year later, when the time came to return the livestock, my father decided to get our own horse. My father heard of a shipload of horses brought by the Zionist movement from Bulgaria to Israel to sell to farmers at cost. My brother Udi, at eleven, three years older then me, went with my father to get one of the horses from Kibbutz Hahotrim, on the other side of Mount Carmel from our moshav in the Jezreel Valley. All day long I waited anxiously for their return with our new horse. At dusk, my father walked in the front door. He had taken the bus home. Udi rode down the mountain and across the fields to our farm.

With night falling fast, my mother worried. But my father, as usual, said little, except that Udi would show up safe and sound. I waited up far past bedtime for the clip-clopping of the horse carrying my brother into the yard, bringing the horse to the new corral my father had built for it.

Finally, it arrived. I heard it first and ran out ahead of my mother and father to greet our new horse. We named her Sofia, after the capital of Bulgaria, her birthplace. Delighted to discover she was pregnant, I looked forward to the foal's birth with increasing excitement as the months passed. In the final weeks, the first thing every morning I ran to the barn to see if Sofia finally gave birth during the night.

One morning in early spring I went out to the barn to discover a beautiful brown foal born during the night. But its very first day of life, it somehow damaged its knee. It could not even stand. The veterinarian said the best thing to do would be to put down the foal.

"No!" I cried out, promising to take personal care of it, nursing it back to health. The doctor was skeptical. My father believed in me. Thus, for days afterward, I began my day before school by treating the foal with the medicines left by the doctor. I stroked it and petted it and whispered into its ear as I rubbed the vet's ointment into the infection. "You'll be fine, and one day I'll take you riding in the valley," I promised the little horse, deciding to call him Foal until he could stand by himself. Even the vet admitted after a few days that he thought my treatment helped my beloved foal, though he still needed my help to stand. And as soon as I returned from school, I ran to visit my little foal.

But one day I came home from school and found the barn empty. Maybe he finally healed, I thought, hoping to find the foal with the mare in the field. Instead I found Sofia with my father. "The foal died," he told me bluntly.

"Where is he?" I demanded.

"I took it to the wadi at the end of the field," my father told me.

Heartbroken, I jumped on Sofia and raced across the field to the distant wadi. As we approached the bulrushes lining the narrow creek, Sofia neighed shrilly. My father had hitched her to the wagon to carry the foal's body to the wadi. She knew the foal lay not far off. I did not want her to see her dead baby. I jumped off the mare, tied her to a tree, and ran to see the foal.

Nobody ever cried in our family. When I realized tears flowed down my cheeks, I ran back to Sofia and galloped away from that place, away from the death of my closest friend.

Finally, far from the dump and the moshav, I slowed down and slipped off Sofia in a eucalyptus stand beside a field, to mourn alone the loss of the young horse I loved so much. I sat that way for a long hour, letting the sadness and sorrow overwhelm me.

Only when the sun began its descent toward dusk did I get back on Sofia for the sad ride home. As we passed the wadi, Sofia neighed again, trying to call out to her foal, heading for the wadi. I, too, wanted to see the foal again—but alive, on its feet, growing up. But I knew that was impossible.

"No!" I ordered, reining her back forcefully to the route home. "It's time to look ahead," I whispered into her ear, leaning over her mane to her ear. "*Abba* will take you to a stud farm, and there will be another foal."

I heeled her into a gallop past the wadi. And as we rode past, I turned a switch in my mind, not forgetting the young foal, but looking ahead to Sofia's next pregnancy, already planning how to keep the next foal safe and sound. She neighed one last time, and we raced on. My tears dried in the wind. And just as I promised her and myself, Sofia gave birth to a healthy foal a year later.

YOM KIPPUR

"Intelligence says a large concentration of Syrian Army forces is lined up against the Golan Heights, and an even larger concentration of Egyptian forces along the Suez Canal," said Giora.

We were gathered in his office for our Friday afternoon staff meeting and the next day was Yom Kippur, the most solemn day in the Jewish calendar. On Yom Kippur a remarkable quiet falls over the entire country. No cars move on the roads. Many, if not most, are fasting and in synagogue. In 1973, the holiday fell on a Saturday. Most of us planned on spending a quiet day at home. A Sayeret Matkal crew to handle emergencies would stay on duty, of course, at the base.

"Intelligence estimates are calling it an exercise," Giora reassured us about the Arab maneuvers. "But it involves virtually all their armies—infantry, armored personnel carriers, tanks, surface-to-air missile batteries, engineering forces and artillery. Just in case, we're going to alert-level three."

The IDF's emergency reserve call-up system kicks in at the next level on the scale. Ordinarily, a soldier away from the Unit leaves a detailed report of how to locate him in case of emergencies, whether it is his parents' phone number or his girlfriend's. He also must check in every few hours to find out if the Unit called. And, like all combat units in the army, we have pre-established pickup points around the country, where transport vehicles gather to collect unit members.

154

The same system is used by the entire emergency reserve call-up system in the country, but we used it more often than other units and practiced it regularly, to make sure our call-ups could speedily return every Sayeret Matkal member—whether enlisted man on weekend leave or reservist at work—to base. In the Galilee we kept three pickup stations in centrally located towns, including one in the Jezreel Valley.

Listening to Giora's briefing, two things came to mind. In May that year, Egypt and Syria—the two largest and most dangerous Arab armies lined up against us—had gone into a week of massive troop maneuvering exercises along the Suez Canal and opposite our lines on the Golan. For a week the IDF stayed on alert, quietly calling up reserves throughout the army until the enemy exercises ended. So, as I listened to Giora explain that Military Intelligence regarded the Egyptian and Syrian maneuvers as an exercise, I decided that if they held two full drills in less than six months, they must be serious. War might not be imminent, but close.

The second thought echoed just as strongly. It was the memory of a prediction made by Moshe Dayan earlier that year. He believed that "an electronic summer"—high-tech air battles between our planes and theirs during the summer—would be a portent of war. In September, Israeli Mirages and Phantoms shot down thirteen Syrian MiGs in a dogfight over the Lebanese coast, a perfect example of the "electronic summer" Dayan predicted.

Dayan believed the Arabs knew they would never reach Tel Aviv or Haifa. But if they grabbed a piece of the Sinai or a chunk of the Golan, even for only a few hours, the diplomatic wheels would start moving. International pressure on Israel would do the rest. In those days, only Washington supported Israel. The Western Europeans, worried about their oil supplies from the Middle East, weak in the face of Arab terrorism, and anxious about the Soviet Union to their east, kept at arm's length from us.

So, driving home to Nahalal that Friday afternoon, I played war games in my mind, imagining the calculations the Egyptian and Syrian commanders must be making. Assuming Dayan was right, I thought, the Egyptians planned a canal crossing with the aim of taking a piece of Sinai. I wondered where they would try it. In the north of the Little Bitter Lake? Or south of the Great Bitter Lake?

Maybe at Port Said or Ras al-Ash, where I saw the War of Attrition begin. A Syrian attempt to break through into a pocket of the Golan Heights suddenly became easy to imagine.

Nonetheless, driving into Nahalal, I decided that whatever happened, the air force—with help from the armored corps—could take care of it in a pre-emptive strike. Full-scale war still seemed improbable, if not impossible. And if the Arabs attacked, I believed, the air force and armored corps would quickly turn the enemy back.

Falling ten days after the prayers for the New Year, Yom Kippur is a day for soul-searching about the sins of the past year, asking forgiveness, and wiping the slate clean for the coming year. At Nahalal, my grandparents and their comrades gave up the traditional religion of their own grandparents. Yom Kippur in Nahalal meant a quiet day with family and friends.

That night, while I was visiting some friends in the village, the wife of a pilot friend took me aside to ask a surprising question. "You're not at the base?" she asked.

"No," I said, "why do you ask?"

"They canceled all leave for the pilots," she said in a matter-of-fact tone, but with a slight tone of superiority, as if to emphasize the importance of pilots. But her comment reassured me. On alert, the air force had obviously studied the intelligence on the enemy maneuvers that summer, and drew up plans to combat those formations. Our pilots easily outmaneuvered their Syrian and Egyptian counterparts during the "electronic summer." We knew the Soviet-made surface-to-air missiles (SAMs) that Moscow supplied to both Syria and Egypt created problems, but I trusted our air force to overcome them. It had won the war in 1967, and proved its superiority in the air ever since. I decided not to worry.

Saturdays are for sleeping late. At ten in the morning, I sipped my first coffee of the day, sitting in the garden in front of our little three-room house, watching six-year-old Shaul show off on his bicycle in the quiet street in front of the house. The phone rang inside. A moment later, Nurit called out, "Muki, the Unit's on the phone."

"Muki," the secretary began. I heard something strained in her tone of voice. "You have to get back. Right away. They raised the alert." She did not need to add a word.

I grabbed a uniform and checked my *chimidan*—the duffel bag that I always kept handy. It held my Klatch, the AK-47 Kalashnikov I carried since Shaked after the Six-Day War, booty from Egyptian and Syrian armies. I always made sure to keep at least half a dozen spare ammunition magazines, loaded and taped into crosses for quick loading. A thick jackknife, full of tools, sat in a pocket just over my heart.

Nurit watched me check my equipment. "So, that's it," she said. She knew about the alert. "It's serious."

I nodded. "But don't worry," I promised. "Everything will be fine." An artist, after the Six-Day War she painted all the bomb shelters of the moshav, covering the gray concrete entrances to the underground rooms with bright splashes of color. Like so many of us, she believed we never again would need the bunkers. Now it looked like they would be used again. We kissed goodbye, and I gave Shaul a hug before climbing into my army-issued four-wheel-drive Dodge 200, a high-chassis jeep that can carry six fully equipped soldiers and a bank of radios.

Usually, nobody in Israel drives on Yom Kippur. Religious zealots are known to stone cars driving on the holy day; uncultured kids copy them for the fun. No radio or television broadcasts disturb the solemnity of the day.

I started the car and drove slowly out of the calm and peaceful moshav, a perfect blue sky above. Aware of neighbors' eyes on me as the car rolled through the village, I drove slowly, to prevent panic. But as soon as I reached the main road, I gunned the engine, racing on squealing tires through the curves of the Jezreel Valley road to Afula, without a single other car on the road.

Before I had left the base on Friday, Digmi, the reserve pickup driver, told me that I could find him either at home or at his neighborhood synagogue. Now, his wife sent me to the prayer house. I strode into the hall in uniform, my Klatch over my shoulder. Digmi put down his prayer book and hustled out after me, still wrapped in his *tallit* (the Jewish prayer shawl).

While Digmi ran home to get his truck, I raced on to the pickup point, finding a dozen Sayeret Matkal fighters waiting for him. I picked half a dozen to take in my jeep, and when Digmi showed up five minutes later, I put an officer in charge with instructions to wait another half hour for stragglers before following us south.

At first we were the only car on the road. But gradually, other speeding military vehicles appeared on the roads. I cut 30 percent off the normal amount of time needed to drive from the Jezreel Valley to the Unit's base.

I walked into Giora's office just as he announced to the already assembled officers: "Intelligence has adjusted its estimate. War is now probable. It will break out at eighteen hundred hours. We have to start preparing. And fast."

But we faced a major problem. For what, exactly, should we prepare? Sayeret Matkal, as Avraham Arnan conceived it, conducted special operations between wars. We planned in advance, on two or three targets that we defined or Intelligence gave us as an assignment from the general staff. No standing orders existed for Sayeret Matkal in case of war—and especially not a surprise attack on two fronts.

The realization sank in that we knew how to fight—but not where. Most horribly, I saw, we might even get an order to sit out the war. I did not want to let that thought even cross my mind. Neither did Giora. But other officers in the Unit, believing in Arnan's doctrine regarding Sayeret Matkal's value and purpose, raised the issue, indeed fought for us to stay at the base.

"We can come up with ideas for targets and suggest them to the general staff," Giora mused. But we all knew that whatever we suggested would need logistical coordination and distract the senior command from more pressing needs.

Meanwhile, soldiers and officers poured onto the base. By noon, dozens of fighters and administrative staff—regulars, enlisted, and reservist—were milling about in the parade grounds, gearing up with supplies provided by our quartermasters.

Commanders called together officers and then the soldiers, to brief them on what Giora had told us. But we knew little except that the latest word from "the Pit," the underground command-and-control center for the entire IDF, deep under Defense Ministry headquarters in downtown Tel Aviv, was still calling the likelihood of war "probable."

Around twelve-thirty, Giora called in the senior officers. We crowded around the table in his office, some sitting, others standing. Cigarette smoke filled the air. "Gentlemen," he began with a glance at his watch. "We have less than six hours to prepare. Intelligence says the Arab attack will definitely begin at eighteen hundred hours."

"What about the air force?" someone asked. "A pre-emptive strike?"

He shook his head. "The government decided against one. They want it clear to the world that the Arabs attacked, not us."

He sent Amnon Biran, Sayeret Matkal's senior intelligence officer at the time, over to Military Intelligence at the Defense Ministry compound in Tel Aviv. Giora hoped Amnon would rustle up an assignment for us.

I doubted it. Sayeret Matkal only handled operations it had planned for. Tradition would keep us on the base for the war, I feared. But we belonged on the front or behind enemy lines. We were Israel's crack commandos, and could not sit by idly while the IDF went to war. I raised my hand. Giora gave me the floor.

"We absolutely do not wait until they call us," I said, letting my instincts speak for me. "Our job as fighters is to protect the State of Israel and its people," I said. "We can't wait for an assignment we know we won't get, while war rages. We need to construct a framework to get us to the front as quickly as possible."

"For example?" Giora asked.

"We send half the unit to the south and the other half north. We leave a small task force here, in case of emergency—or in case the general staff does come up with an assignment. Once we check in with the regional commands, they'll know what to do with us."

The speech seemed to impress Giora, but others stuck to tradition, saying our value as special forces made it wrong to send us into the chaos of battle without a well-planned mission.

The argument went on for a few minutes. Finally, Giora made a decision. Two forces go north to the Golan—one for the southern Golan and the other for the northern part of the Heights. A third force goes south to the Egyptian front. A fourth stays on the base, in case of an emergency.

But less than an hour later, everything changed again. At exactly 1400 hours Egyptian and Syrian aircraft, artillery, and infantry began a concerted attack along the entire length of both fronts, across the Canal and into the Golan. Giora called us into his office for a third time, to break the news.

"Let's drop everything," I argued. "All of us, to the north. Whatever happens along the Canal, the Sinai's size can protect the Negev. But the Golan's tiny, with settlements on the plateau and below in the Galilee." I made it a demand, doing something extremely unusual: I raised my voice. "We go north!"

I rarely shout. They listened.

Giora assigned Yonni, who had rushed in from the national staff college, to command a combined force of my regulars plus reservists under Yuri, a reserve major. Giora took command of Amitai Nahmani's regulars, also reinforced by a reservist group. A third force remained at the base.

Within the hour, our fighters were crammed into buses with all their equipment. Just before nightfall the buses pulled into a woods on the slopes of Mount Cana'an near Safed, where we established a field headquarters. Giora took Amiram Levine, Amnon Biran, me, and a communications officer over to Northern Command headquarters in Nazareth, to rustle up an assignment.

It did not take long to realize that the Northern Command could not help us. No orderly intelligence flowed from the Golan, only radioed observations from front lines, where positions were falling up and down the Golan. The Syrian onslaught caused heavy casualties, and pressed toward the center of the Heights on its way to the edge, with an open road to Galilee.

By Sunday morning, it became clear that looking for an assignment at the Northern Command, so close to the front, was worse than being back near Tel Aviv, so far away. At times, we heard the muffled artillery thumps carried south on the wind and saw bomb-laden Phantoms lumbering through the sky on their way up to the Heights trying to get through the Syrian SAM umbrella.

"Let's get hold of some APCs, half-tracks, anything to get us up to the Heights," I suggested. "We'll find Raful. He'll know what to do with us." By then, my former paratroops brigade commander had become a divisional commander on the Golan.

Giora and I started asking around for transport and quickly ran into another problem. The transport officers at the Northern Command threw us out of their offices with shouts that they had already sent everything up to the front. "I saw APCs in a lot at the end of the base," I pointed out.

"They're already assigned," a transport officer told us.

Dejected, Giora and I headed back to the camp near Safed. Overhead, Phantom jets raced low to the Golan, carrying bombs. Roads that ordinarily slowed down for tractors pulling trailers of hay were suddenly gridlocked with tank trailers. "We've got no choice," I decided as we pulled into the woods where our soldiers waited. "We have to steal some transport. Otherwise we'll be stuck here until the end of the war."

I put the most cunning soldiers in the Unit on the job. "Get out on the roads. Look for APCs. Do whatever it takes to get them back here. Beg, borrow, steal. Whatever it takes.

"And, Giora, give me the keys to your car," I decided. He drove a white Carmel, a boxy fiberglass car an Israeli firm once made, which came with the major's rank. He tossed me his keys.

"I'm going to head over to the emergency warehouses in Safed," I told him. "I'll talk someone up there into letting me have something. Half-tracks, APCs, something."

I started driving toward Safed along the winding, hilly roads of the Galilee. Only a couple of minutes after leaving the woods, I came around a bend in the road. Down the hill to my right a convoy of APCs made its way toward me. I started counting. Five, ten, twenty, more than thirty armored personnel carriers. Just what we needed. I pulled out my binoculars and took a good look at the brand-new open APCs heading straight for me, their caterpillar treads tearing the asphalt. From the top of the hill, I looked down into the transport bays of the APCs. Unmanned, except for drivers, they were just what we needed. A white Carmel, just like Giora's, led the convoy.

I sped toward them, stopping in the middle of the road and flagging down the Carmel. A transport major sat behind the driver's wheel, his secretary beside him.

"Where the hell have you been?" I started shouting before he even came to a halt. "There's a war going on! We've been waiting two hours for you!"

"I know, I know," the major answered through the open window. "Don't ask. It's crazy. Some officer tried to steal the APCs away from me . . . "

"I don't have time for history or excuses," I commanded him angrily, though captain's bars, not major's leaves, decorated my epaulettes. "Follow me," I snapped, "I've got fighters waiting for these APCs."

I turned Giora's car around and kept an eye on the convoy through the rearview mirror. Coming around a corner on the winding mountain road, I saw the woods where the force waited.

And coming around the corner, right at me, was a Military Police jeep. It flagged me down.

I held my breath as I rolled down the window to listen to the MP's request. It was one of those rare moments I remember from my army years when an MP proved to be useful. He asked if I needed any help.

"Sure," I said. "Make sure they follow me." I pointed over my shoulder at the convoy of APCs.

"No problem," said the MP sergeant, turning around in the narrow road in front of the APCs, then waiting until they all passed, taking up the rear of the convoy.

Less than fifteen minutes after I left Giora in the shade of the pine trees in the woods wondering where to get half-tracks, I returned with a convoy of thirty-three behind me, to the cheers of the eager Sayeret Matkal fighters, who ran, without any need for orders, to take over the APCs from their drivers.

The transport major climbed out of his car and pulled out a clipboard. "Sign here," he said. Giora looked at me. I looked at Giora. I shrugged.

Only then did the major realize what had happened. He raved and ranted, trying to get through to Northern Command headquarters and find someone with authority over the Unit. But nobody had time for an angry transport officer that day.

"Give me back the APCs," he shouted at Giora. "And you!" He turned to me. "You're going up on charges."

I was lucky the MP waved goodbye to us as the last APC rolled into the woods. Behind me, our fighters were churning up the ground turning the APCs into a convoy ready to leave for the war.

"What's your name?" the transport major demanded.

"Betser. Muki Betser."

He scribbled my name down on a page on his clipboard.

Giora took me aside. A gentleman of the kibbutz, he never would have stolen the APCs the way I did. "What are we going to do?" he asked me.

Missing the war worried me more than a court-martial after it. "What do you care?" I asked Giora. "So maybe they'll put me on trial after the war. I'll worry about it then. Right now we have the APCs. Let's get going."

He looked at the last of the fighters climbing onto the vehicles. Right then, nobody could have ordered battle-hungry Sayeret Matkal fighters to get down from the APCs. Giora told the transport major to file whatever report he wanted. Meanwhile, we had a war to fight.

The Special Gentlemen Are
Here

For all the sense of urgency and emergency, and even with planes constantly overhead rushing up to the battle, the war seemed like a distant thunderstorm as we rode the winding roads from Safed across the Galilee to the Golan.

But up on the plateau, inside the front, the thunder turned into war. Brushfires created by fallen shells in the farmers' fields and the wild ranges of the Heights blazed in the darkness around us. The thump, whistle, and rumble of artillery and cannon fire beat like drums beneath the constant roaring of warplanes above. The smell of smoke permeated everything.

As soon as we reached the plateau, Giora and his forces split off heading south to Hushniyeh, where the Syrian onslaught threatened the southern end of the Sea of Galilee.

We meanwhile raced due east toward Raful's headquarters at Nafah, radioing ahead to let them know we were coming, shocked to learn he had moved into the field out of the huge army camp when it came under heavy attack in the opening hours of the war. The mere fact he had needed to move his headquarters to an APC in the field proved the severity of the situation.

Favored visitors to the Golan, just a week before the war he had served us food straight from his personal refrigerator when we visited him in his Nafah office. Now, a few miles northwest of the fort, we found him in the center of a huddle of APCs, half-tracks, and jeeps, hunkered in the darkness of a rocky field for a quick consultation.

Yonni and I approached the open back door to Raful's APC. The dim lights of the interior revealed him in his trademark Australian bush hat, surrounded by officers. He pointed with a bandaged hand at a map in front of him. Later, I learned the injury happened in his carpentry shop back home, but then, it made a deep impression on me.

"Shalom, Raful," I said, standing in the open back doorway to his mobile headquarters.

He looked up from the map. Unshaven, his dust-covered face looked like war itself. But then he smiled, recognizing us. "Great to see you," he said. "How'd you get here?" he asked, making me wonder if he had already heard that Sayeret Matkal stole the APCs to get to the front. But as far as I was concerned, that was already ancient history.

"We've got two task forces in fifteen APCs, all the equipment and weapons we need, RPGs for tank-hunting. Whatever you want us to do," I spoke up. "We're ready."

"Great," he said. "Let me finish up here and then I'll take care of you, okay?"

Yonni and I waited in the field, watching the sky, listening to the tense discussions inside Raful's APC between the distant thumps of artillery and cannon fire. Raful's calm voice led radio conferences among him and Northern Command, Intelligence, and brigade commanders. But mostly he spoke with individual tank commanders left alone in the battle after the Syrians had destroyed the rest of their battalion. He encouraged them and comforted them, made wise suggestions, and never sounded under pressure.

Finally, he climbed down out of the APC to talk with us. "Okay," he began. "What do you guys want to do?"

Tank-hunting, we had decided while we waited for him. "We know the Heights," I pointed out, "can work at night, and have plenty of anti-tank rockets, and plenty of ammo. Send us out tank-hunting."

Raful loved the idea. He grinned and called for a handset to contact Zvi Barazani, left behind at Nafah to hold the base. "Barazani, the special gentlemen are here. I want them to start hunting."

While Raful took his staff to the field to run the division's counteroffensive, Barazani stayed in Nafah to hold the camp against an inevitable second Syrian attempt to capture the base at a major crossroads in the central Golan.

Over the radio, I could tell Barazani was not exactly delighted with the idea. He had only taken the brigade command the day before Yom Kippur, before anyone knew of the impending war. Maybe he thought it meant putting infantry forces at unnecessary risk; maybe he thought the air force could do the job better. Whatever the reason, he did not seem pleased with Raful's request. Nonetheless, Raful got off the radio and sent us to Nafah. "Work up some plans with Barazani for a night offensive, then get back to me," he said, sending us on our way.

I knew Nafah as one of the Golan's largest army bases, an armored corps regional command, full of tanks, APCs, half-tracks, jeeps, and trucks neatly parked in their proper place, every footpath lined by rocks painted white, epitomizing the armored corps' obsession with tidiness.

Now, wisps of smoke hung in the windless air like witnesses to horror. Cars, jeeps, and APCs still burned with final weak flames. Smashed and broken, the destroyed vehicles lay about like corpses.

We drove slowly into camp, astonished by the sights around us. Soldiers started coming out of buildings darkened by the blackout. Dark smudges of soot and the even deeper darkness of sleepless worry shaded the fear in their eyes. For the young, the Syrian onslaught became their first encounter with the death of friends and the feeling of survival after a battle. Looking at them made me think of myself at Karameh, walking off the battlefield, feeling let down by the generals and the politicians.

At one point in the fighting, said the soldiers, Raful and his staff shot their way out of a bunker, reduced only to their Kalashnikovs, a few bazookas, and RPGs. Shooting at the advancing Syrian armor, they made it to the APC that became his mobile field command. Just when it seemed that all the fighters in the fort needed to withdraw, the enemy advance stopped as suddenly as it had begun.

Tanks led the Syrian push into Nafah. The soldiers halted the advance, but it cost a great many casualties on both sides. Syrian tanks reached into the camp, gun barrels pointing over the fences — and through them.

It reminded me of something that had happened during the War of Independence at Degania, the kibbutz settlement started by my grandparents at Umm Juni. A Syrian tank reached the main gate of the kibbutz, halted only by the willpower of kibbutzniks using handguns, rifles, and homemade grenades and Molotov cocktails. To this day, an old Syrian tank sits in the yard of Degania, a monument to Israel's survival of the War of Independence.

We found Barazani in the operations room.

"Listen," said Barazani as soon as he saw us come into the operations room. "There's no intelligence that pinpoints tanks, so I'm not recommending you look for them on foot."

"Why not?" I wanted to know. "Show us on a map where there's a concentration of tanks, and we can take them out."

He shook his head. "No intelligence," he repeated, reiterating the severity of the situation. "All I have are reports from individual positions along the lines. They're under fire. They have casualties. Aircraft is hitting them. Cannon is hitting them. But no intelligence. The air force faces serious problems with the SAMs. And if they can't get through the SAMs, we can't get good aerial photos. No intelligence on their positions."

"Look, Zvi," I said. "We were here last week. We know the area. We know the field. We can go out as a recon unit and get the intelligence."

He knew me from the paratroops, and he knew the Unit. But despite all my efforts, he did not want to take responsibility for sending us out on such a dangerous mission. To get an operation going without intelligence is nearly impossible; and as a new commander in the area, unfamiliar with the nuances and details of the terrain, he did not want to make a mistake.

"Zvi," I tried again, repeating the argument that had won over Raful. "Nobody can beat us at night. We can get right up to the tanks at night without being spotted, we can go out and find them, watch them, observe, identify, and hit. Nothing is going to happen to us. So what are you afraid of?"

Awake since the first signs of an impending Syrian assault on Friday, Barazani scratched the dark stubble on his chin. "Let's wait until morning," he finally said. "We'll get through the night and maybe by tomorrow we'll have better intelligence." He read the impatience in my face. "Listen," he added forcefully. "There's no choice tonight. You boys want to do something? Secure the camp perimeters. I'm sure there's going to be another attempt to take the base."

"And tomorrow we'll get going on a tank-hunting operation," I added. I still felt we should go after enemy tank concentrations. We could either take them on our own or radio their coordinates back as targets for the air force or artillery to strike.

But Barazani did not want to take the chance that Sayeret Matkal might be seriously damaged under his orders. Avraham Arnan, though officially no longer responsible for the Unit, still wielded a moral authority in certain circles of the army. Though still in uniform, he held no formal position of authority over the Unit. But he also never forgave anyone who endangered his baby.

I took a junior officer and we made a quick tour of the perimeters of the camp, finding high-ground points of observation in the direction we expected the Syrians to use when they resumed their attack on the fort.

While we toured the camp looking for good positions, the Syrian shelling resumed. Mostly cannon fire, it included occasional mortars, which meant the enemy was only a couple of thousand meters away.

Inaccurate but annoying, it slowed down my steady progress from one position to the next. But we found several good points to deploy crews for a perimeter defense of the camp in the east and the south. As I was instructing one of the crews, a shell fell in the direction where I had just deployed another squad. It looked like a direct hit.

I grabbed the radio microphone, but before I asked, the officer in charge at the position, Shai Avital, came on the air. "Nothing to worry about," he said, cheerful as usual. But I worried. I jumped into the jeep and raced to the position. "Some guys flew a little, that's all," Shai said, smiling when I came to a halt beside him. "We've got bruises, not wounded," he said.

"Okay," I told him, relieved. "Stick to your positions."

The shelling continued, but not intensely enough to drive me to cover, indeed ever more sporadic, like a heavy storm turning into a drizzle. I scouted the eastern fence of the fort that faced the Syrian forces. A blackened Syrian tank, still smoking from the fire that engulfed it the day before, nuzzled the fence with its gun barrel. I touched it. When I had noticed the Syrian tanks before, thinking of Degania, I considered the tanks against the fences as an abstract thought, a curious, almost surrealistic idea. But now, up close, the idea that Israel was on the defensive blackened my mood as much as the soot darkened my fingertips. I decided to press Barazani once again for a tank-hunting mission, and went back to his operations room.

"Avraham Arnan called me," Zvi said as I came in. "He's against you guys being here. He wants you to go back to your base."

I just shook my head in dismay, unable to understand the idea that the best fighters in the country should not be helping. But I knew Arnan's call scotched any chance of Barazani giving us the okay for tank-hunting.

I wandered around the camp, thinking about Karameh, where I first saw the fallibility of the Israel Defense Forces, and about Degania, where my grandparents helped lay the groundwork for the active defense of the Jewish people in their land.

Crossing one of the craters made by a Syrian shell, I looked up and saw the entrance to Raful's headquarters. I entered the two-story blacked-out building. Used to seeing it full of staff officers and secretaries, now its empty offices symbolized the IDF's failure. I moved down the dark corridors to Raful's office, realizing that I wanted to eat something other than the hardtack of our field rations.

There it was, just like last week—his refrigerator. I pulled open the door. The light went on. As if nothing had changed since last week, the best of Israel's farms filled the fridge: cheeses and cold cuts, fruits and vegetables.

"As if nothing has changed," I said aloud, repeating the thought, realizing at that moment that whatever the outcome of the war—and I had no doubt we would eventually prevail—nothing would ever be the same again.

I dug out some bread, sausage, and cheese and found a jug of orange juice, then sat down at Raful's desk to make a sandwich. A black civilian telephone sat on the desk. If there's food here, I thought, and the refrigerator light went on, maybe . . . ? I reached for the phone. The banality of the working dial tone surprised me. Amazed, I called home.

It elated Nurit to hear from me. After I left Nahalal on Saturday morning, she helped organize the bomb shelters in the village. "And good we did," she said. Syrian missiles had fallen in the Jezreel Valley. One hit a building at Migdal Haemek, a nearby town. Another damaged an empty school building at Kibbutz Gvat. The electricity at Nahalal went out on the first night of the war, because a missile hit power lines down the valley. She knew never to ask about any details of my work. She did not even ask from where I was calling.

"Don't worry," I told her again. "We'll hit them back twice as hard." As we talked, Raful's deputy walked in.

"Muki, what are you doing here?" he asked, so astonished to see me behind Raful's desk that he did not notice the phone in my hand.

"I wanted to call home." I smiled, showing him the phone in my hand.

"My God, the phone lines work!" he shouted. "Give me, give me, I want to call home. Let them know I'm okay."

"Okay, okay, relax, hold on," I said, "I'll finish my call and then you can make all the calls you want."

I said goodbye to my wife, then handed over the phone. But almost as soon as he started talking, a massive Syrian artillery barrage began, much more concentrated than the one an hour earlier. He shouted down the line to his wife that he was okay and then we both ran back to Operations to find out what they knew.

Tank battles raged all over the Golan. The Syrian tanks outnumbered us ten to one. The 188th Armored Brigade began with fifty-seven tanks and held off six hundred enemy tanks, at a cost of 90 percent casualties. The Seventh Armored Brigade began with seventy tanks and was decimated.

More news came in. Reservists arriving on the front reported that chaos in the rear had slowed their arrival. General headquarters back in Tel Aviv sent word for everyone to hold on until reinforcements arrived. But nobody could say how long it would take. Meanwhile, a handful of tanks held back endless waves of enemy armor trying to get across the plateau.

But Barazani had some good news for me. Raful had made a decision. He wanted Sayeret Matkal squads to go tank-hunting in the morning. I could finally get some rest, knowing that the next day we had a mission.

COMMANDO VS. COMMANDO

There's no sleep during a war. Not a real sleep. Not a deep sleep in a bed. I catnapped here and there, and on a few rare and lucky occasions, I grabbed an hour or two. In Nafah that first night, I went into an empty office, pulled up a chair, put my feet on the desk, and leaned back, making sure to face a window so that daybreak would wake me even before the sun came out.

When it did, I ran cold water over my face and went out to check the troops deployed in their positions around the camp. Morning mists veiled the scene, but as daylight rose, the scene became vividly clear. Our American-made Pattons, and British-made Centurions, their Soviet T-52s and T-54s, the tanks and jeeps and APCs and half-tracks that went into the battle of the first two days of war, lay about the camp like so many broken toys.

While I was inspecting a post hit during the night by a Syrian shell, a radio call suddenly came in from an officer at the northern edges of the camp. "Helicopters," he reported. "Coming in from the northeast." I looked up in that direction.

Three enemy helicopters crossed the horizon from east to west. I expected them to break south along the Tapline Road, which runs north-south across the Heights and used to carry oil from Iraq to the port of Haifa when the British ruled the Middle East.

Now, just off the Tapline Road, the choppers began descending into a field about two kilometers north of Nafah.

"Yonni!" I called on the radio. "Choppers landing about a kilometer and a half north of us." We both knew that we needed to get to the choppers before the enemy soldiers they carried managed to deploy, obviously heading toward Nafah. Sayeret Matkal always prefers attack over defense.

As soon as Yonni confirmed, I put out another message to all the team commanders to get the fighters onto the APCs on the double. We converged at the APC parking lot and together we raced out of camp heading north on the Tapline Road.

The whole terrain in that part of the Golan is undulating hills, wild fields of rocks and boulders and dry, thorny brush. From the road, we saw the choppers disappear behind one of the hills and then, a few moments later, rise into the sky and start heading east toward the Syrian border.

Yonni led the force in the front APC, my company behind him, followed by Yuri's unit. A dozen APCs stormed up the Tapline Road toward the landing point of the three choppers, which I figured could carry about fifty soldiers. We had almost twice as many fighters.

Yonni ordered a halt on the road about three hundred meters from the hill where the Syrian forces had landed. We leapt down from the vehicles, moving in a classic assault-force deployment. Everyone knew what to do.

We raced forward, producing as much firepower as possible, using it as cover while we advanced from boulder to boulder. Assault is the essence of the IDF combat doctrine, and we needed constant fire and movement forward to avoid being pinned down.

Just as we reached the halfway point up the hill, about twenty meters from the top, their fire began hitting us. We shot back, continuing our attack, running and shooting, running and shooting, without stopping for any cover, all of us knowing exactly what to do. Hand grenades began flying through the air.

"Grenade!" I heard someone shout. Three hand grenades tumbled through the air over my head. I threw myself to the ground to take cover. Back on my feet before the dirt finished hitting the ground, I continued my advance, pausing only to reload my Kalashnikov.

Nearly at the top, we began throwing our grenades. More than a dozen flew into the air at the Syrians. The explosions clapped thunderously, putting an end to all the shooting, leaving us in control of the hill. Around us, twenty-five Syrian commandos in brand-new camouflage uniforms lay dead. We grabbed vantage points all around the hill, scanning the area for more Syrian commandos.

My force lay to the east of Yonni's on the hill. We communicated by radio, yet we were close enough to hear each other's shouts. We knew we had conquered the hill, but the morning mist and the ragged terrain of the brush—boulders, natural ditches, and old tank trenches below us—were perfect camouflage for the enemy in hiding. Every once in a while, one of our boys shot at something moving suspiciously in front of us.

The mists evaporated in the morning sun. Looking east, I saw a helmeted head rise and then quickly duck out of sight about thirty meters ahead of me. I recognized the depression in the terrain as an old tank trench. "Yonni! Enemy in the tank trench! Cover me! I'm attacking!" I shouted, and at the same time signaled my force to follow my assault. But as we rose to attack, I saw Yonni, followed by about ten fighters, already heading toward the enemy position, firing as they moved.

I quickly ordered my force to change tactics and provide covering fire to keep the Syrians' heads down while Yonni and his soldiers ran toward the trench. We improved our positions as we continued firing, heading toward the tank trench.

A sharp cry burst out of Gidon Avidov, a young officer from Nahalal, a few meters away from me. He looked down at his belly and collapsed.

"Medic," I called out. Two soldiers grabbed Gidon and pulled him to cover. Yonni and his forces reached the trench, shooting down into it. I ran the last ten meters, followed by a dozen of my men, adding our gunfire to the trench.

Enemy soldiers, all dead, lay piled together where our fire drove them into a corner of the tank trench. But did we get them all? Yonni and I wondered. We took cover amidst the boulders and brush, surveying the scene ahead. Again we lay on the ground in the silence that followed so much noise, listening for the presence of any survivors trying to move across the terrain. Occasionally, the crack of a rifle fired by a soldier thinking he spotted something moving ahead broke the silence.

Finally, a Syrian wearing officers' insignia rose from behind a boulder ahead of us, hands over his head. "Don't shoot!" he shouted in English, and then limped forward, his camouflage fatigues dripping blood from a wound in his leg.

"Don't move," someone shouted in Arabic at him.

The Syrian stopped. "You've killed them all," he said sorrowfully as we approached carefully, making sure he was alone.

"How many?" Yonni asked.

"We came with forty-two soldiers," the Syrian admitted.

Yonni and I had our men count the bodies. When we added the prisoner, their commanding officer, it came to forty-two.

Gidon Avidov later died in the hospital. Baruch Tsur, a reservist from Moshav Hatzeva, died in the field, despite the medic's efforts. A few other soldiers suffered light wounds.

Well equipped, the dead Syrian commandos carried new AK-47s, East German binoculars, commando knives, and food. The Syrian major told us we had taken out the most elite commando force in the Syrian Army. Determined, aggressive, and motivated for battle, we could not allow ourselves anything less than our best performance. But we didn't give them any time to appreciate the professional reception we gave them.

THE HILL BEYOND THE VALLEY
OF TEARS

I still wanted a proper assignment from Raful to take the Unit across the lines to go tank-hunting. But Raful had other problems on his mind that Monday, forty-eight hours into the war.

Fifteen hundred Syrian tanks had attacked on Saturday afternoon. By Monday morning, Avigdor "Yanosh" Ben-Gal, commander of more than seventy tanks in the Seventh Armored Brigade when the war started, was down to his last seven. The 188th Armored Brigade was almost gone. Its commander, Itzik Ben-Shoham, and his deputy died trying to hold the Tapline Road running north to south on the Heights.

I tried to be patient waiting back at Nafah for a connection through to Raful. At midday, in the Operations office, Barazani answered a phone, listened for a minute or two, and then said, "He's right here." I was certain Raful was on the other end of the line with the tank-hunting assignment when Barazani handed me the phone.

But Avraham Arnan's clipped voice spoke to me from the other end of the line. "What you doing there?" he began. "I'm coming to . . ."

I interrupted him with my answer to his first question. "We're chasing the war, Avraham," I said. "We fought a Syrian commando unit. Baruch Tsur and Gidon Avidov are dead." Silence fell on the line. Baruch Tsur had served under Avraham in the early days of Sayeret Matkal, when Arnan still commanded the Unit.

175

But then his crisp voice repeated his first question. "What are you doing there? Get back to camp. Our soldiers are too valuable to be killed in battle."

"Avraham, what's wrong with you?" I asked him. "The country's at war . . ."

"Stay where you are," he interrupted me. "I'm on my way."

He pulled up in a jeep half an hour later and came into the operations room, calling me outdoors for a private conversation.

"Listen," he began, without any formalities. "You must return those soldiers to the base. They are special. Very special. You know that. They are for missions between wars, not during them. Let the armored corps take care of it."

Because he was the Unit's founder, our relationship with Arnan was special, especially because of his private fight with cancer, to which he refused to surrender until the very end. But I disagreed strongly, and spoke my mind.

"This is the people of Israel's war," I told him, "not a private war between the armored corps and some enemy. No soldier has blue blood. The Unit is in this war and we will fight it, the best way we know how."

He thought for a moment, and then came up with an idea. "If you want to do something, there's a mission for you. Capture a SAM-6 for intelligence."

The newest Soviet SAMs made an umbrella protecting most of the enemy's side of the battlefield, foiling the air force's attempts to hit the advancing Syrians, or even collect aerial intelligence on their positions. We both knew stealing a SAM-6 was something Sayeret Matkal should have prepared for before the war, not during it. But I did not want to argue missions with him.

"Fine," I said. "We'll try to do that, too," I promised. "But you cannot expect me to sit by idly while the country fights for its life," I added.

"I want to speak with Yonni," he insisted.

I shrugged. "Do what you want," I told him. Nonetheless, as he crossed the field where we stood outside the operations bunker in Nafah, I thought about what he had said.

True, our vocation was for the little wars between the big wars, for special operations. We had practiced ways of taking out

SAMs of all sorts, using models of every known surface-to-air-missile system.

During the War of Attrition, an IDF operation literally plucked a Soviet radar station out of its position in Egypt, a coup for our intelligence. And we knew how to neutralize a SAM-6 by striking at the radar guidance systems, not tediously trying to destroy the missiles themselves.

We could go in and stealthily take a SAM-6. But a job like that required planning, logistics, intelligence. Just as we needed some intelligence to show us where to find tanks, we needed intelligence to show us where to find the mobile missile batteries, which the Syrians constantly moved, precisely to stymie our efforts to locate them.

Caught in the vicious circle of not having aerial photographs of the SAMs, because the air force could not get over the mobile batteries, I felt frustrated, yet also inspired with an idea. As soon as the war ended, I decided, we would begin preparing dossiers for action in case of the next war, and not just special operations between the wars. Meanwhile, we had a war to fight.

I did not wait to hear about Arnan's conversation with Yonni. If Yonni would have told me that he agreed with Arnan, I would have said no, just as I told Avraham.

But the conversation with Arnan made me impatient for work. I decided to go see Raful. I drove out of camp alone in a jeep to Raful's mobile division headquarters, still run out of an APC in the wild fields of the central Golan, a couple of kilometers away from where we beat the Syrian commandos.

"Yesterday we talked about tank-hunting," I said when he became free for a moment from the radios and the maps. I said nothing about our success against the Syrian commandos. "We await your orders."

He stared at me for a long second through tired eyes. "Come," he finally said, jumping down from the back of the APC. "Let's go see Yanosh."

I followed him to a jeep. He drove in silence past destroyed tanks from both armies, heading east. Suddenly, he began mourning aloud lost soldiers of the 188th and the Seventh brigades by naming them. He used words we rarely let cross our lips, like *bravery, dedication,* and *heroism.*

"The best two armored brigades in the IDF," he grieved. "Nobody ever did such good, serious work." It was the highest praise of all from a son of the Jezreel Valley.

He praised their officers, like Itzik Ben-Shoham, the 188th Brigade commander, who fell trying to hold the Tapline Road, and Yanosh Ben-Gal, who pulled together the remains of the Seventh and 188th, to hold the line against the Syrians. He referred to Itzik in the present tense. But we both knew that Itzik had died on Sunday morning, holding the Tapline Road.

We joined Yanosh on a hilltop overlooking a valley that would become known as the Valley of Tears for all the killing that went on there in the first days of the war. Together, we counted killed Syrian tanks, most facing east as if they had tried to escape back across their lines. We lost count at 120.

Many of the enemy tanks looked unscathed, abandoned before they even fought. And through binoculars, we saw Syrian tank crews walking away from the battle, toward home. For a moment, it reminded me of the Sinai in the Six-Day War. But I shook the comparison out of my head, knowing too well what had happened in the first sixty hours of the war. In 1967, the Arabs ran. They fought in 1973.

Raful broke the silence. "Here's what I suggest," he said to Yanosh. "Muki and his guys can hit the tank crews refusing to surrender and can bring back the usable tanks." Not a bad idea, I thought, though I preferred hunting tanks still on the attack.

But Yanosh had a better idea. "This battle is over," he said. "I think it's time to begin preparing a counterattack." He pointed east into the valley, over the dozens of broken and abandoned tanks. "They're done here. We should use the Unit to go on the offensive."

In our army, a subordinate officer can disagree with his commander and not be afraid to say so if he thinks he has a better idea. I agreed with Yanosh. He looked ahead, a critical skill for a leader. We both waited silently for Raful's answer. I thought about the considerations going through his mind.

Battles still raged on the Golan. The Syrians took the strategic reconnaissance post we won from them in 1967 on the snow-topped peaks of Mount Hermon to the north. We had used that position to look down on vast swaths of Lebanon, Syria, and Jordan, filling it with the best electronic surveillance system available to us. Now, the Syrians could use it to watch the entire northern half of our country.

Tough tank battles continued in Hushniyeh, south of us on the Golan, where Giora Zorea took the other half of the Unit when we first reached the Heights on Sunday in our APC convoy. And much further south, Egyptian forces continued pouring across the Suez Canal into Sinai.

I agreed with Arnan about one thing: the armored corps bore the brunt of the war, not the infantry. The war began with the largest tank battle in history, fought with incredible courage, in one-against-many tank battles. Looking out over the Valley of Tears I felt a tremendous appreciation for the hundreds of tankers who died halting the enemy attack.

But I also saw a lack of sophistication in the battle. Force against force, like in World War One, the battle lacked all the technological and tactical skills that I believed gave Israel the advantage on the battlefield. We were the best night fighters in the Middle East, but the generals did not use us at night. We surely could have done a lot more: reconnaissance missions to locate targets; hitting enemy supply convoys and Syrian tank parks; sabotaging operations behind enemy lines.

In those first few days, the war's course was set at the level of individual soldiers, by people like Avigdor Kahalani. All of Yanosh's battalion commanders received medals for valor after the war. Kahalani won the medal for courage, the highest decoration of all. His battalion decimated, he fought back from his lone tank an endless wave of Syrian tanks trying to pass through the Valley of Tears east of Kuneitra, an abandoned Syrian town we took in the war in 1967.

I had listened to Raful on the radio network talking with Avigdor, whom I knew as a shy, smart fellow who survived massive burns in the Six-Day War as a young armored platoon commander and stayed in the army over the years, rising to command a battalion. After he finally retired from the army, he went into politics.

Raful did not command or give orders. He coached and encouraged Avigdor until finally, out of fuel and down to his last shells, Avigdor pleaded that all was lost. "Hold on," Raful asked. "Just five more minutes."

A request, not an order, it comforted us all with its calm, human understanding of how to overcome fear by looking beyond it. "You think it's tough for you? It's tough for them, too," Raful went on, with the certainty of an experienced combat soldier, and an almost jocular tone that conveyed confidence. "Give it five more minutes," he repeated. Those five minutes seemed endless, but just as Raful's instincts predicted, the Syrian assault halted.

Now, on the hill overlooking the Valley of Tears, waiting for Raful's decision concerning our mission, I agreed with Yanosh. Chasing after fleeing Syrian soldiers was a waste of the Unit's talents. We belonged at the tip of the spear, as an integral part of our counterattack to push the Syrians back over the lines they crossed when they opened fire on Yom Kippur.

Raful finally spoke. "All right," he said, turning to me. "Take your boys and join Yanosh's brigade. Start pushing them back."

Yanosh grinned, and decided on the spot to attach us to Yossi Ben-Hanan, a brilliant, brave armored corps officer who had arrived on the Golan that morning straight from the Himalayas, where he was honeymooning when the war broke out. Now, we began to push the Syrians back to the Purple Line drawn at the end of the Six-Day War, when we took the Heights to stop Syrian shelling of the Galilee.

Unlike during the Six-Day War, when as a reconnaissance force for a brigade we moved ahead of the armor, Yossi Ben-Hanan's tanks now moved ahead of us and we followed in APCs and half-tracks. In short, aggressive battles, we forced the enemy back. While the tanks shot it out, we flanked the combat zone on foot and took out enemy tanks with RPGs and bazookas. We eliminated stubborn enemy infantry posts encountered on the way, and when the daytime battles slowed down, we guarded the sleeping soldiers and the parked tanks of the little five-tank battalion.

By the end of the fifth full day of battle, on Wednesday, we reached the Purple Line in our sector. The road from Kuneitra to Damascus lay in front of us. Chief of staff Dado Elazar wanted the government to give the order for us to push forward, to threaten the Syrian capital. On Thursday morning, the order came down to cross the Purple Line. By Friday morning, exhausted after non-stop fighting, we reached Hales, able to rest in an abandoned Syrian fort while the generals planned the next move, across the Leja, a bleak black stretch of volcanic rock between us and Damascus.

Notoriously impassable, especially for half-tracks with their rubber tires on the front axle, the Leja's pumice was like a grater on cheese to the rubber soles of our paratrooper boots and the front tires of a half-track. Even an APC's metal treads would be vulnerable to the hard, brittle rock when crawling across the Leja. But we needed to cross it, to bring our long-range artillery within range of the western outskirts of Damascus.

Now, stretched out on the metal bench of an APC, I waited along with the rest of the command for Raful's orchestration of the assault. But as I listened, half-awake, to the radio traffic, I realized that Yanosh had continued sending forces ahead, including Yossi Ben-Hanan, leading his tanks onto the jagged rocks of the Leja, heading to Tel Shams, a Syrian fort halfway across the volcanic field.

Right after Yossi got the order for his five tanks to move forward, Raful sent down an order. "Stop all forces," I heard him say, "until the start of the next move."

"Yossi, stop your advance," Yanosh relayed to Ben-Hanan.

The radio crackled with static. "We can't turn back now," Yossi finally said. "We're in the middle of the Leja, about to attack. Let me continue with my assault."

A long pause followed. Then Yanosh said, "Okay, proceed."

That's strange, I thought. Raful didn't notice that Yanosh agreed to Yossi's move. Yanosh said nothing to Raful about Yossi going ahead on his own.

I heard Yossi shouting at his soldiers over the radio. "Keep advancing, follow me, keep moving." His voice trembled with excitement as he gave his orders, and they advanced on the Syrian position.

But suddenly a roar of Phantom jets drowned out all the sounds. I looked up. Two of our Phantoms, pursued by four Syrian MiGs, raced overhead.

The MiGs seemed very agile compared to the heavy Phantoms. But suddenly both Phantoms, the MiGs on their heels, rolled up and over so that they came out behind the MiGs, firing at the Syrian planes.

I tried waking Yonni to watch the dogfight but, exhausted, he only opened his eyes and then closed them, missing one of the MiGs trying to avoid the missiles by heading straight up. It turned into a tiny speck high in the air. Suddenly, a parachute opened high in the air and the MiG began tumbling and spinning out of control, until it crashed in a fiery ball of flame that quickly turned into a tall plume of black smoke on the horizon.

The dogfight over, I turned my concentration back to the radios, just in time to hear Yossi say that his force had reached the edges of Tel Shams. "We're coming at them from an unexpected place and we'll be able to surprise them," he said, adding, "I'm going to make them pay for my ear." A Syrian rocket exploding nearby on his first day in the war had damaged Yossi's eardrum.

I did not hear Yanosh's response, but after a long pause, I heard Yossi's command: "Forward! Attack! God is with you." I never found it appropriate to call on God going into battle.

The shooting at Tel Shams could be heard clearly over the radio. First one tank, then a second reported successful hits—and then being hit. Suddenly, only a crackling static came over the network, and then the radio fell completely silent.

Yanosh's voice broke the eerie silence, calling out Yossi's name. Nothing.

I started waking Yonni, to tell him we had work—rescuing Yossi and his force—when Raful came onto the radio network, talking to Yanosh.

"Okay, how many tanks do you have?"

The tension in Yanosh's voice revealed his feelings as he told Raful about Yossi's move. "I don't know what happened to him," Yanosh admitted.

But before Raful answered, Yossi's voice came over another radio, a small infantry set tuned to our frequency that we gave him while assigned to his battalion. Compared to the excitement and energy of a few minutes before, he sounded calm but very tired. "Yanosh," he said. "We're hit. All the tanks. Casualties. My leg is gone."

"Where are you?" Yanosh asked, worry in his voice. "Where are you talking from?"

"Outside my tank," said Yossi in a very weak voice. "My tank . . . is gone."

Silence replaced the voices, and with each passing second, the tension grew. Then Yossi's tired voice repeated, "Yanosh. My leg is gone."

I knew they were close friends. "Don't move," Yanosh pleaded. "Drink some water," he suggested. "Close your eyes," he tried, then realized the mistake. "No, don't close your eyes." Until then, his voice had calmed and reassured all who heard him. For the first time, I heard anxiety in his voice.

Now totally focused on the drama, I shook off my exhaustion and insisted that Yonni wake up. I briefed him on the situation and we called together about a dozen fighters, taking six apiece on two APCs, and started speeding toward Yanosh at his command post about half a kilometer east. The radio drama continued with Raful's nasal drawl, easily recognizable over the static-rife radios.

"Your forces?" Raful asked Yanosh. "How many do you have?"

Yanosh's voice trembled, very unlike him. "Five of my tanks were hit in an attack on Tel Shams. Yossi is hurt, his leg is gone." He said it in a rush of words, getting it off his chest.

I waited for Raful's reprimand. Instead, he calmly asked, "Why did you move without an order?" But he did not wait for an answer. "Okay, where's the force now?"

It amazed me that Raful did not admonish Yanosh. Every tank was crucial to us. Yossi's five tanks constituted nearly half the battalion at the time. And he lost them in an unauthorized assault deep into enemy territory, after Raful specifically asked for a postponement until he coordinated the maneuver.

But Raful listened without questions to Yanosh's explanation. Just as we pulled up to Yanosh's front command, Raful's voice came back on the air. "Okay. We'll take care of it." That's Raful, I thought. Never losing his cool. It took him a second to understand what had happened, and, that the problem needed a solution, not recriminations.

Nobody yet had mentioned us as the solution. But as the only unit in the area capable of such a mission, I knew it was ours to solve. I jumped down from the APC and walked into the circle of worried officers, hoping my smile would help reduce the obvious tension. Yanosh and I are the same height, a head taller than the other officers under the camouflage net. "Yanosh," I called to him over his staff. "We'll get your men out."

His deep-set eyes burned red with worry. "Bring me Yossi," he said. "You've got to get Yossi out of there."

"Why only Yossi?" I asked with a grin. "We'll get them all."

As the daylight began to wane, Yonni and I took six fighters apiece in two APCs across the lines, to race across the Leja, following the trail of broken rock left behind by Yossi's tanks.

About eight hundred meters from where Yossi began his assault on Tel Shams, the Kuneitra-Damascus road cut through the rocky plain, separating us from the fortified mound in the distance. We pulled to a stop in the vehicles. From then on, we went by foot.

Crossing the road, we encountered soldiers from Yossi's force. They had abandoned their wounded tanks and had begun the crawl back to our lines. They walked hunched and apathetic, dejected and defeated. Some carried pistols, others Uzis. Several left behind their personal weapons. Their defeated manner perturbed me. But with Yossi still in the field by his tanks, I had no time to discuss the proper behavior of an IDF combat soldier.

"What happened?" I asked an officer among them, a fellow I knew from the Jezreel Valley. He later died elsewhere on the Golan during the war.

"They hit us bad," he said. "Very bad. We were completely screwed. We managed to escape," he said, indicating the soldiers coming across the road to us. "The rest . . ." he pointed to the burning tank in the distance. "I don't know . . ."

"Where's Yossi?"

"The burning tank," said the officer. "Right in the middle."

He seemed apathetic about leaving his commanding officer behind. It seemed strange they did not try to rescue Yossi. "What happened back there?" I asked again.

"Yossi pulled out his gun and threatened to shoot anyone who refused to follow him into the action. But it was crazy. Five tanks in broad daylight against the whole fort. It was crazy."

His charge could be investigated later, I figured. Meanwhile, if anyone had survived, they awaited rescue before the Syrians from the Tel Shams fort went down to investigate and take prisoners. Ever since Yossi said he lost his leg, I envisioned him lying in the field bleeding away the last of his life. I called my men forward and we raced on, heading for the fort on foot as night's darkness enveloped the plateau.

The night covered us in our final approach to Yossi's tank, still glowing with a flickering fire from its open turret. I raced ahead to find Yossi, lying semi-conscious beside the tank. His leg was not gone, but, twisted into an impossible position, it was badly broken.

Crouching beside him, I smiled. Yossi drifted between consciousness and sleep. "I've been through it," I said, remembering Karameh. "Your leg will be fine. You'll be fine."

A minute later, Yonni came with a medic, who began splinting Yossi's leg for the stretcher ride back across the Leja. "I'm going to check the other tanks for survivors," I told Yonni.

We moved quickly from tank to tank in the dark, knocking on the steel hulls, calling out for survivors. But after checking all five tanks, the only other fighter from Yossi's force we found left behind at Tel Shams was a radio operator named Zvika.

The hike back to the APCs went slowly. We carried Yossi on a stretcher, while the volcanic pumice tore the soles of our boots to shreds. Once back on the APCs, we began to move, but the going was too slow. We decided to call in a chopper for Yossi and Zvika.

We found a narrow stretch of flatland where the jagged rocks thinned out, and the pilot negotiated his way in, trusting that we knew how to bring in a helicopter in an apparently impossible spot.

Quickly, we loaded Yossi and Zvika aboard and then watched the helicopter take off, heading toward a hospital inside Israel. For them, the Yom Kippur War ended that night. For us, it was barely half over.

GOING SOUTH

Exactly one week after the war began, the paratroops brigade took Tel Shams with only four lightly wounded casualties. New lines stabilized inside Syrian territory on the central front where we operated. We fell into a routine—if war can be called routine. I did not think the generals made the best use of our skills, but we kept busy through good old-fashioned behind-the-lines commando missions.

Our tasks ranged from crossing the lines deeper into Syria at night to reconning enemy positions and sabotaging enemy supply routes to hunting down tanks and foiling Syrian efforts to hunt our tanks.

Yonni and I divided the force in half, rotating assignments and missions. One night he went over to sabotage a Syrian supply convoy, the next night my force went over to take out a tank.

One night I crossed into enemy territory with a team of sixteen fighters to gather intelligence on Sasa, a Syrian position about three kilometers northeast of Tel Shams. We moved under the light of a half-moon, coming right up to the edges of the Syrian fort at midnight. We saw parked armor but no movement in the trenches.

We took positions, watching the quiet fort. There was only one way to test their strength—I gave the order to fire a short burst of fire. I have to admit that to the Syrians' credit, they shot back. We waited until they stopped and then fired again into the fort, just to make sure. Answering fire came back immediately, inaccurate but intense. I reported back to headquarters that the Syrian position was well manned.

By the end of the first week of battle, Jerusalem wanted to send a clear message to the Syrians that if they did not let up their pressure, we could strike even deeper into their territory. But for our 175 mm cannons to hit Damascus, we needed to be at least three kilometers closer than our lines. Yonni took the assignment to get the cannons close enough to shell the outskirts of Damascus and then get them back to our lines before the Syrians responded.

The Golan stabilized, I knew the land still burned in the Sinai, where the Egyptians kept up their attacks, still pouring soldiers over the Canal at various points. I decided to go south, taking my regulars with me, and went to see Yonni with the proposal.

A few days after Avraham Arnan's visit to the front, Yonni confessed to me that he agreed with Sayeret Matkal's founder's insistence that the Unit go back to base. "Arnan convinced me," Yonni admitted. "So I went to Raful and told him I thought the Unit should go back to base."

"What did he say?" I asked.

"He shamed me," Yonni said, smiling weakly with embarrassment. "Raful said, 'We did without you before you came, we can do without you now.'"

When I told Yonni I wanted to go south with my soldiers, he decided to stay on the Golan with Yuri's reservists. The decision heartened me. The casualty rate among Yuri's soldiers undermined the reserve officer's confidence. I worried for him and his soldiers, and often during the days on the Golan I suggested to Yonni that he stick with Yuri's force. But he preferred us. In any case, now, as I prepared to leave the Golan, Yonni finally moved to Yuri's command car, and together they eventually ended up in the northern Golan helping to recapture the peaks of Mount Hermon from the Syrians.

I gathered my fighters, recapped the war as I understood it, and praised them for their good work.

By then, we all knew that the other force from Sayeret Matkal on the Golan, under Giora Zorea's command, went south to Hushniyeh but did not find any work so they headed back to base after a few days. Meanwhile, Amiram Levine had taken another force south to try to find work on the Egyptian front.

I told my soldiers to get ready for the trip back to the base, where we would gather assignments for a second phase of fighting. Although they knew me well, my soldiers decided I meant that we had finished our job in the war. Bearded, filthy, and hungry for a real meal after ten days of field rations, back home the soldiers went straight to the showers and then gathered in the mess hall for a proper meal, while I went to see Giora.

He had already lost his older brother, who fell as a combat pilot shot down over the Golan in the Six-Day War. Now, a second Zorea brother had died in battle. Yohanan had served in Sayeret Matkal for a while, and then transferred to the armored corps, planning on an army career. An Operations officer on the Golan at the outbreak of the Yom Kippur War, he fell in the first hours of the Syrian onslaught. From the very highest levels of the army, a decision came down forbidding Giora to cross the border ever again. With two of six brothers dead in war, the generals decided the Zorea family had sacrificed enough.

"I'm going down south," I told Giora.

"Amiram Levine and Amitai Nahmani are already down there," he said. "After we didn't find work on the Golan, they decided to go south."

Like me, Amitai was a captain, a senior staff officer in Sayeret Matkal. As deputy commander of the Unit under Giora, Amiram took command of both Amitai's force and a group of reservists attached to it.

"I'll meet up with them," I said.

"Listen, Muki, they've been down there ten days, looking for action. They have not seen a single bullet or Egyptian. You fought every day for almost a week and a half. Why don't you wait here for a day or two, rest a bit?"

I took a sip of hot black tea before answering. "Giora, I'm going down," I insisted.

"We might need you here," he tried.

"You've got enough fighters here," I shot back. "I'm sure that if we go down, we'll join the battle. At the very least, I want to know that we tried. Just like in the Golan. Whatever we can do, we'll do." He gave up the argument, knowing I had already turned down Avraham Arnan's pleas for me to return the Unit to base.

I told the staff to prepare what I needed: all the maps and aerial photographs from the south, as well as the Southern Command's radio codes, and replenished equipment. I arranged for an air force flight down to Refidim, the huge air force base in the Sinai, then I called together the crew commanders and then afterwards the entire force.

"We're flying south to Refidim tonight, to meet up with Amiram Levine's force," I began. I saw the shock in their eyes, but plunged on, not giving them time to protest. "We'll continue our involvement in this campaign, just like we did on the Golan Heights. It's another front, and another enemy—Egypt. But it's the same war and we're the same fighters." To them, it sounded like they had just finished a 120–kilometer march and I told them to do another hundred. But none questioned the decision or complained.

While they went over their equipment, I took a briefing from an intelligence officer on the state of the war in the south. We had managed to stop the Egyptian advances, and Arik Sharon's division had crossed the Canal west into Egypt, north of the Great Bitter Lake. But the Egyptian Third Army held on to the east bank south of the Great Bitter Lake, and the Second Army, pushed back across the Canal, was pounding Sharon's forces to the south as well as keeping a full press on the IDF reoccupying the east bank.

At midnight, we flew into Refidim. Amiram Levine met us with APCs. We went to Umm Hashiba to meet Shai Tamari, chief of operations for the Southern Command, who brought along the command's intelligence officer. But going over the maps and latest reports, it became obvious they did not have an assignment for us.

So, we went to see Haim Bar-Lev, the former chief of staff now running the Southern Command. Disagreements between Gorodish, named Southern Command commander in July, and Arik Sharon, his predecessor, forced Dado and Dayan to name Bar-Lev as supreme commander for the southern front.

Bar-Lev's icy blue eyes considered us for a few minutes as we presented our argument in the crowded headquarters bustling with officers and messengers. Squawking radios and the distant thumping of artillery and tank fire punctuated the conversation.

"If you get to SAM-6's," Bar Lev finally said, in his slow, drawn-out drawl, "that could be helpful." Shades of Avraham Arnan all over again. The meeting turned into a long-drawn-out affair.

"We can take out missile batteries," I argued. "But it's precisely the kind of assignment we should have prepared for in advance in case of war. Now, logistical pressures make it absurd to think we can manage to get what we need to do it."

Bar-Lev listened carefully, but had nothing more to suggest. Toward the end of the meeting, he surprised me with a question. "Where's Omer?" he asked.

His son, Omer, served as a regular soldier under my command. A decade later he would become commander of Sayeret Matkal. I noticed the general did not ask how Omer was, just where.

"He's with me," I said. "He's fine. We finished on the Golan so now we're here. He's fine." Bar-Lev smiled, asking nothing more. But when our audience with him finally ended — without any decision — he asked me to pass on a message to his son.

"Tell him his sister Zohar got married yesterday, just as planned," said Bar-Lev, who would pass away twenty years later while serving as Israel's ambassador to Russia after the fall of the Soviet Union.

At the end of our inconclusive meeting, Arik Sharon walked in, a white bandage on his forehead. I heard he was hit by some slivers of shrapnel. He and Bar-Lev huddled in the corner for a few minutes, then went into the briefing tent for about fifteen minutes before leaving the front command headquarters.

I followed the burly general who founded the 101st, the first of the elite reconnaissance forces in the IDF, out of Bar-Lev's command trailer.

"Arik," I called out to him. He turned his heavy body and, recognizing me, grinned broadly. "We're here with several dozen fighters," I said, "with APCs. We want to join in."

"Come," he said, without hesitation. "These people here have no idea what's happening. We've been across the Canal for three days, but now I'm stuck in the orchards south of the Ismailiya-Cairo road. I have a force from Shaked, but I have plenty of work for you."

I jumped at the opportunity and called Amiram out of Bar-Lev's headquarters, telling him about Arik's invitation. We grabbed a chopper back to Refidim, planning to get the crews organized on the APCs. But Elazar "Cheetah" Cohen, an air force colonel famous as a chopper pilot, intercepted us at the landing pad, maps in hand.

"We've got forces past Fa'id," he said, referring to an Egyptian air force base on the western bank of the Great Bitter Lake, inside Egypt. "The Egyptians ran away, but we want to take the air base, turn it into an advance air field for transporting fighters and supplies."

"Now, that's a mission for us," I said to Amiram. Taking an air field out of enemy hands was right up our alley. With Arik's headquarters between Fa'id and Deversoir nearby, the air field mission gave us something specific to do, not a vague request.

Cheetah gave us some aerial photos, and Amiram and I started making plans. Cheetah promised us two Sikorskys, to carry a few dozen soldiers and four jeeps. We had pretty much finalized our plan when Amitai Nahmani came over to me, a determined look in his eye.

"Muki," he said in a tone of voice that worried me. "It's not fair."

"What?" I asked, but I already knew what he meant.

"You already fought up on the Golan. It's not fair that you take this mission and we have to stay behind again."

He was right; it would not be fair for my boys to get the assignment when his still had not see any action. I handed him my notes, and we shook hands. I watched Amiram join Amitai's company as they boarded the two choppers, unhappy to be waiting behind.

After an hour went by without word from them, I decided not to wait any longer and told my staff officers to ready the fighters for the APC trip over the Canal to Arik's command. But I also kept trying to get through to air force headquarters at Umm Hashiba to find an airlift. While I was working the radios, Amiram's code came on the air. "We're coming back," he said. "We have casualties. I'm wounded."

"Where's Amitai?" I asked.

"Amitai too. You're in command now, Muki."

"Okay, no problem. Where are you?"

"Landing in Refidim. Dropping off Cheetah. But we're not getting off. We're going back to Israel. To the hospital."

I took two officers and raced by jeep to the pilots' quarters at Refidim, asking for Cheetah. "He's in the showers," the desk man said at the entrance to the pilots' dormitories at the huge base.

I ran down the corridors to the showers and burst through the door. The humidity of the hot water heated by the solar panels on the roof of the building made a sharp contrast to the arid desert air. "Cheetah!" I called out.

"Muki?"

His soap-covered head came out of the shower stall.

"What happened?" I asked.

"God, we were stupid," he said. "We went into the field figuring they already ran away. Amitai drove the jeep. Amiram sat beside him. I sat in back with Moshe B. An RPG hit us. Direct hit. The jeep lit up like a flare."

He paused ominously, and then plunged on. "Amitai's dead," he said. "Amiram's legs are full of shrapnel. Moshe's face is burned bad. They should all be in the hospital by now. I'm okay. Just a torn eardrum." He scowled, and then ducked his head back under the water to rinse off the soap.

"Where's Amitai now?" I asked.

He paused before he answered, a tense moment for us both. "We left him there," he finally admitted. "At Fa'id. He's dead. By the jeep."

"The rest of the force?" I asked.

He looked down. "I don't know," he finally admitted.

I rushed out of the pilots' dorms back to the airfield, in no doubt about my course of action. I used the radio to raise contact with Amitai's force. Shlomo Baidatch, one of Amitai's junior officers, responded to my call.

"Where are you?" I asked him.

He named the twenty-first coordinate on the Barrel Road, a powdery-dust road that ran north-south parallel to the western bank of the Great Bitter Lake.

"Organize the force for an overnight stay," I ordered. "Stay there. We're on our way. We'll be there by morning," I promised.

We drove all night, through battlefields and around them, but we stopped for nothing. We drove across the pontoon bridge that Arik's engineers managed to erect at the end of the Canal, where it enters the Bitter Lake, and continued on, into Egypt, into Africa.

Just before dawn, we found Baidatch and the rest of the force, just where he had promised. "Amitai told us to wait behind while he went in with Amiram, Cheetah, and Moshe," Shlomo began mournfully. "They figured the Egyptians all ran away. We should have gone building by building." Although shaken up by what happened, he gave a clear and concise briefing. "They drove down the runway advancing on the field. That's when the enemy hit. Under fire, we got the wounded out. But we couldn't reach Amitai. He's still lying there."

I called together the force. "The first thing we're going to do is get Amitai out of there," I told them. I told Baidatch to organize a team for the mission.

This time, instead of driving in through the front gate, we flanked the air field's buildings, coming in through the fences around the base, working our way carefully toward the burnt-out jeep and Amitai's body.

In the dim light of dawn, the blackened burned body looked even more grisly than I had feared. I shivered in the desert chill at dawn and mourned silently for Amitai, another friend lost to war.

The Egyptians had gone, said crew reports from fighters dispersed throughout the base. But I did my own survey of the surroundings, wanting to figure out where the attack on the jeep had come from.

I found the answer in an underground MiG hangar with a view toward the runway. Beside an open, half-empty crate of RPGs, I found shell casings from Kalashnikovs. Most telling, I found a setting of food. Two half-empty bowls of corn porridge told what had happened.

The Egyptians fired from inside the hangar when the jeep came down the runway. But instead of holding out at the air field, they ran away while Baidatch and the company evacuated the wounded.

I reported to division that we held the field. They sent the Fiftieth Battalion to relieve us and hold the field. "Make sure they bring in a burial squad to come in and take care of a body," I added. The IDF's rabbinical corps handles burials for the army.

A little while later the Fiftieth showed up, led by my friend Yoram "YaYa" Ya'ir, who began the war as deputy battalion commander, taking command just before the war because his battalion commander broke his leg. We met in the middle of the runway.

"Amitai is dead," I told him. "But the field's in our control. Where's your burial crew?"

He jerked a thumb over his shoulder. A bearded soldier carrying a clipboard approached me. I pointed toward Amitai's body, lying on the runway. "His name is Amitai Nahmani," I began.

The bearded soldier held up his clipboard, as if it put him in charge. "What's the name of the dead man?" he asked.

"Captain Amitai Nahmani of Kibbutz Givat Haim," I said.

The student rabbi looked at the body and shook his head. "He's burnt. It is impossible to identify him. You absolutely sure it is him?"

"A hundred percent," I said, making no effort to hide my distaste for bureaucrats.

"And you are?"

"Betser, Moshe. Captain. Address: Nahalal."

He wrote very slowly and deliberately, and then handed me the form to sign. I had started to scrawl my name when I noticed he accidentally named me as the dead soldier and Amitai as the notifying officer.

"He's Nahmani," I said, handing the clipboard back to him with a smile. "I'm Betser. I think you got our identities mixed up."

It shocked him so that he began blessing me in Aramaic.

"It is okay," I said, embarrassed by his outburst. "You might be right, but I think it is a bit too soon, no?" But my joke left him speechless. "Relax," I chided him. "Nothing happened," I added, trying to ease his anxiety. "Mistakes happen."

But, trembling, he kept mumbling a blessing for long life over and over as he went through the process of filling out a new form.

DEATH IN THE MANGO GROVES

While the UN Security Council met in New York to discuss a Soviet demand for a cease-fire on behalf of Egypt, we met with Arik Sharon in a collection of mobile trailers and camouflage nets serving as a field command north of Fa'id in the flatland west of the Canal.

He pointed on the map to a five-hundred-meter-wide stretch of plantations to our northwest. "Beyond the groves is the Ismailiya-Cairo road. But the enemy's filled the groves with snipers and artillery spotters. It's difficult to get across and our progress is slow. But it's imperative that we be on the other side before a cease-fire," he emphasized.

"Okay," I said. "We'll look at it. Maybe we can handle it."

An uneasy quiet prevailed as I headed back to my half-track, a few hundred meters from Sharon's trailer. I looked back at Sharon's command center. Soldiers took down camouflage nets, readying for the move to the plantations. My uneasy feeling grew stronger, and I began running toward my vehicle.

Like a thunderbolt on a clear day, the incoming artillery burst down on us with angry thumping that shook the ground like earthquakes. Just as I reached my half-track, the battery of radios that I had collected to be able to listen in on as many frequencies as possible began squealing with shouts and cries. "Muki!" one radio squawked. "Muki, we're hit, we're hit. Wounded!"

195

I looked around. To my north, about seventy meters away, I saw a stricken half-track. I ran to it, where men lay scattered like broken chess pieces. Shmulik, Sayeret Matkal's doctor, worked on Yehuda Hever. I looked down at Hever. "He's dead," I said softly. Beyond Hever, Shlomo Baidatch lay badly wounded.

Shmulik looked up at me. Everyone loved Hever, a reservist. Shmulik nodded sadly, then scuttled over to Baidatch. I went from wounded soldier to wounded soldier, trying to calm them, smiling and reassuring them that the medics were on the way.

One of the toughest moments I ever faced was finding myself kneeling beside Shlomo Baidatch, a wonderful guy, a good friend, and a terrific officer, telling him he would survive. But it did not look good. Two of us picked him up, and with Shmulik at his side still trying to save him, we ran toward a medical tent. As we laid Shlomo down on a stretcher, Shmulik crouched, still at work.

A doctor came out of the field hospital, a blood-spattered white smock over his uniform. He took one look at Baidatch and then gently patted Shmulik on the back. "He's dead," the doctor said quietly. But Shmulik continued trying for a few more minutes, in vain.

Arik's command had already moved out of the area, heading toward the plantation he wanted to cross, while we dealt with our wounded. I radioed his command, reporting our delay and promising to catch up as soon as possible. Meanwhile, I wanted to make sure my two friends received proper handling at an evacuation point for the dead about a kilometer south.

I took Omer Bar-Lev and his crew. We put the two bodies on an APC and headed south. As the collection point came into view, I realized that it would be the most gruesome experience of my war.

Rows of bodies lay under the glaring sun. The young faces of regulars and the middle-aged faces of the reservists—they all wore the shock of their final moments, the unscathed innocence of sudden death. The flies swarmed over the blankets covering the bodies.

But the apathy of the soldiers on duty at the collection point disturbed me most. They sat beside the long rows of bodies, eating tinned corn.

"I have two dead men here," I said. "Where can I put them?"

One of the soldiers pointed over his shoulder. "Over there," he said, not even looking up, indicating the end of the row in the sand.

I looked around. I would not leave Shlomo Baidatch and Yehuda Hever on the ground. I went over to a truck parked beyond the bodies. A few bodies lay on stretchers inside. We made room on the truck for our two dead friends, then lifted the bodies onto the truck. We gave them one final salute and then went back to our APC. The entire time, the soldiers on duty at the collection point just watched, silently eating their tinned corn.

We caught up with Arik a little while later, finding him sitting in the open back door of his APC, reporting on the cease-fire announced at the UN, slating the fighting to end in twelve hours. Arik looked at me. I said, "We caught some direct artillery. I had a few casaulties. Two dead. One of them is Shlomo Baidatch."

"Uri's son?" he exclaimed. Uri Baidatch, a colonel in the paratroops, had served as Arik's deputy in the days when Sharon commanded the paratroops brigade.

Arik grabbed his head as if in pain, not caring if the dozen officers present saw him on the verge of tears. He held himself that way for a long minute. We remained silent.

But suddenly, he turned the switch that I knew from my childhood, from the day my young foal died, raising the wall in his mind that marked the point when he learned of Shlomo's death and yet enabled him to set it aside, to continue.

It is the survivor's wall, enabling us to remember and yet to continue, by preserving behind its apparently blank surface our memories—and the turmoil of our emotions. With each death, that wall both crumbles a little and strengthens a little. Learning to suppress the expression of our emotions became the way to stand up to the difficulties and tragedies of our lives. The wall's purpose is not to deny the emotion but to dam it, preserve it, protect it, and give us strength to continue.

Arik finally lifted his head. He looked at me. "The paratroopers have tried breaking through," he began, "and Shaked is doing a terrific job advancing. But I need your fighters to get through those groves." He pointed to the northwest.

About five hundred meters away, a wide green swath of plantations tended by the peasants of the area broke the flat scraggly plain of desert. I raised my binoculars. I saw orange trees, date palms, and a stretch of mango. The maps showed irrigation canals lacing the plantations, cutting through the red sand. To my farmer's eye, the groves looked very good, and well tended. Beyond them lay the strategic Ismailiya-Cairo road.

I took some soldiers and began walking toward the groves, hearing Arik on the radio talking to the armored crews. "Can you guys pinpoint the treetops, to get rid of spotters and snipers?"

A voice came back on the radio. "We've hit every tree. Believe me, whoever was in there is gone by now."

"It's a pleasure fighting with you," Arik said. But he knew as well as I did that we could not be sure the tank guns had hit all the spotters inside the groves, and that some had not remained behind to watch for us and radio our positions to their artillery.

I moved my forces forward onto the red soil, right up to the edges of the plantation, and then stopped to wait for Arik. A pair of Egyptian villagers on two donkeys loaded down with packages, rode slowly past, ignoring us, seemingly ignoring the war itself.

Arik caught up with us in an APC and we sat down on the sand behind it. "Here's the plan," he announced. "You go in with half-tracks, and Natan Ben-Ari will lead the tanks," said Arik, referring to the tank battalion commander with him. Natan and I exchanged glances and then we both looked to Arik, outlining his scheme. "You'll move ahead of us, creating a moving box of fire to your left, right, and forward, until you're on the other side in the open sand."

Natan rounded up a few tanks while I put together a dozen half-tracks. But neither of us liked the assignment. Without any intelligence about the whereabouts of the snipers, minefields, or any other defense the Egyptians had installed along the line, we might be walking into a death trap.

"What kind of assignment is this?" Natan complained to me. "No intelligence, no air support, nothing."

"Let's first see if it is possible," I said. I could tell from Natan's expression that he did not like the idea of telling Arik it might not be possible. "If we can't do it," I promised Natan, "I'll tell him."

Natan gave in. We worked for an hour, scouting the edges of the plantation, trying to formulate a plan. But we could not see beyond the thick green line of vegetation. Without a single aerial photograph or a single observation from inside the groves, we had nothing to work with. I decided to tell Arik about our reservations. But Arik surprised us when we went back to him. "Because of the cease-fire, we're postponing the mission," he said before I had the chance to tell him that Natan and I found inherent flaws in the plan. He relieved Natan and asked me to stay

"Listen, the cease-fire won't hold. I'm sure of it. So here's what we'll do. You go in with your boys. No armor—on foot. I'll be ready with artillery in case you need it. If we can get through, we'll be able to speed all the way to Ismailiya."

It made a little more sense than his original plan. By going in on foot, without armor, we could use all our skills as stealthy fighters instead of announcing our arrival with tanks and guns firing. I organized my troops and we began moving forward slowly and quietly, two columns leapfrogging from cover to cover, everyone on alert in the dark dusty road.

Only an occasional ruffling leaf from a soft breeze disturbed the quiet. But inside the groves, where in any tree around us a sniper might be watching, even this method seemed too risky. It made no sense to take a large force of fighters across the orchards without any intelligence.

The treetops blocked the starlight of the desert. For all I knew, there might be snipers up in one of the huge branches of the palms or an artillery spotter able to radio back our position to an artillery unit somewhere far beyond our reach. A hundred meters into the groves, with at least another four hundred to go and the cease-fire only a few hours away, I made a decision. Instead of risking the entire force, I'd go across alone to find a route for the troops.

"Amit," I called to my deputy. A reserve captain, Amit hailed from Kibbutz Ein Hashofet. I picked him as my deputy when Amiram gave me the command over the force after he was wounded at Fa'id. Pedantic and meticulous, Amit enjoyed the calculations of risk in an operation and the hard work involved to reduce the risk to a minimum.

"We're a big force," I said, "and we'll make noise no matter how hard we try to keep quiet. And cease-fire or no cease-fire, they'll open fire on us if they see us moving. Any movement is going to be a threat—and an excuse for opening fire. People will get hurt."

"So what do you want to do?" he asked.

"You and I will go in alone, cross all the orchards, get to the other side, and get the intelligence we need to move the whole force across safely."

Amit agreed my method carried the least risk. We summoned the officers and told them our plan. "Amit and I are going in alone," I said. "We'll maintain radio contact. If anything happens, you come get us out."

We crossed the five hundred meters in a crouch and crawling, moving as silently as possible. About halfway into the grove we passed a tank that had managed to penetrate the woods, only to be destroyed by an Egyptian anti-tank missile.

I do not know if our concern before entering the groves was justified, but as we crawled the last few yards out of the groves into a suddenly different terrain of soft sand dunes, I felt relieved to be out of the dark maze of the plantation.

We crawled up the first dune, peering into the darkness through night-scope binoculars. Only sand dunes appeared in the scopes. No signs of enemy positions disrupted the view. In daylight, I expected to see the Ismailiya-Cairo road on the horizon.

We retraced our steps, and then took the men through the groves along the route we found, digging in beyond the grove before dawn. We posted guards, to give everyone a chance for a nap.

An excited fighter crouching by my side woke me at daybreak.

"Two Egyptian peasants on donkeys are heading directly toward us. It looks like they'll walk right into us," he said.

For the peasants, it was a season for harvesting, not war. "Stay put," I ordered my soldiers. I climbed to the top of the dune, peering over it to watch the peasants approach.

When they were about twenty-five meters away, an Egyptian officer suddenly appeared from behind a dune about thirty meters beyond the peasants.

We did not know about them and they did not know about us, even though the whole night we lay there, forty meters apart, separated by a sandy white depression between the two dunes.

"Yalla, yalla," the Egyptian officer shouted. "Beat it. Get out of here!" It startled the peasants out of their early-morning daze.

Obviously unhappy, the two farmers slowly turned their donkeys around. I kept my eye on the Egyptian. To my dismay, out of the corner of his eye, he spotted some of my soldiers. He gave a shout and ducked down into his hiding place. Seconds later, accurate heavy fire from assault rifles and machine guns rapped at us.

"Return fire!" I ordered. The noise level grew quickly as my soldiers scrambled to return the fire.

A few tanks behind us began to move, firing an occasional shell. If they moved up to our position, we could outflank the Egyptians, whose fire grew more intense.

I ran across the sand to my radio man, wanting to report our position and predicament back to division and demand that tanks immediately back us up. For some reason he forgot the frequency.

"Who remembers Arik's frequency?" I shouted. Yoav, a fighter from Nahalal, shouted out the number. The radio man made the connection. "I need tanks!" I reported. "Immediately! The groves are clear!"

Suddenly, Arik's voice came over the radio. "Muki," he said in a fatherly tone. "It is time to withdraw."

"No, I want to attack. We can get them."

"No," he said. "Come back."

I put down the microphone and looked around. The casualties mounted. One soldier nursed a wounded leg, another lay bleeding heavily from a wound in his chest. Altogether, seven soldiers were knocked out of action. The Egyptians on the other side of the dune outgunned us. Reluctantly, I gave the order to pull back. One by one the crews left the dune until I was the last to crawl away from the Egyptian fire, back into the groves that had so frightened us the night before.

About a hundred meters back inside the grove, wounded pride made me change my mind. Instead of falling back all the way to the other side of the grove, I gave the order to dig in and prepare for a new round of combat. If the Egyptians did not keep the cease-fire here, I figured, they will be breaking it elsewhere. A cease-fire announcement does not necessarily end a war.

Arik authorized my decision. The Egyptians continued to fire into the groves, but we evacuated our wounded and dug into our foxholes. After a little while, a tense quiet prevailed, giving me a few moments of solitude to mourn Amit Ben-Horin, who, just a few hours before, had been at my side as we sneaked across the mango grove.

"He jumped up when the Egyptians started firing," a soldier who saw it told me. "He managed to get out 'There's a cease-fire!' when the bullet caught him."

His death only strengthened my determination to stick to the grove, to hold the ground—and move forward again if the Egyptians violated the cease-fire.

But suddenly, Menachem Digli, a former commander of Sayeret Matkal and now head of the collection branch in intelligence on the general staff, was on the radio network looking for me.

I gave him a report—casualties, and Amit's death. The radio fell silent for a few minutes. But then he was back with orders to fall back.

I explained to him that I was at the easternmost point on the Israeli front inside Egypt, after an engagement with the enemy. They would interpret the move as retreat. "It's a sensitive place, and there's no logical reason to give it up," I emphasized.

"No choice," Digli told me. "You're the only special force in the area for the job, and it's extremely important."

But if we left before replacements arrived, we'd lose the position to the Egyptians. I didn't want that to happen. I decided to go through the front's command—to Arik directly, a few hundred meters behind me.

I started back on foot, but found a jeep and started driving toward Arik's, but I ran into Uzi Yairi, the paratroops brigade commander, and his deputy, Amnon Shahak, at his side.

They had led the fight for the Chinese Farm, misnamed because of the Asian calligraphy left behind by Japanese agricultural advisers who worked there with the Egyptians before the Six-Day War. The battle for the Chinese Farm on the east bank of the Suez Canal became one of the toughest the army faced in the first days of the war in Sinai. Uzi lost fifty-eight soldiers, but now he wanted to know how Amit had died. I told him, and added my reasons for not leaving the line at the deepest point of Israel's penetration of Egypt. A former commander of Sayeret Matkal, Uzi understood my point of view.

"Don't agree," Uzi suggested.

"I have no intention of leaving," I said. "And that's it."

A few minutes later I was at Arik's field command, trying to convince him that he should let us stay.

"This assignment's more important," he finally said. "You're going to helicopter to the top of Jebel Ataka," he told me. I knew it as the site of an Egyptian radar station, about twenty-five miles south of Fa'id and the highest peak on the west bank of the Suez Canal. The air force had managed to take out the Egyptian radar station on its peak in the first hours of the war. "You'll take the position, and use it to help Bren," he said as we studied the map.

From the top of Jebel Ataka we would be able to look down on the besieged Third Army, east of the Canal, inside Sinai. Avraham "Bren" Adan was racing south with an armored division on the west side of the Canal, to close off the Third Army's rear door back into Egypt across the Canal.

Spotting enemy positions for Bren's long guns was a good job, I thought. But I wanted to take out the Egyptians who had killed Amit.

Arik finally convinced me. "If anything will make the war stop, this is it," Arik said. "It will be the siege of the Third Army."

A few hours later, sitting up front near the helicopter pilot and listening through the headsets to the air traffic, I heard that anti-aircraft guns ahead had just shot down a chopper on the same flight path we were taking on our way to Jebel Ataka. Nobody expected survivors.

The pilot glanced over at me, wondering if I would tell my troops in the hold and on a second chopper beside us. I decided the nerve-wracking ride over the battlefields was ugly enough, looking down on the huge graveyards of twisted, burnt equipment like huge tombstones in a chaotic cemetery. I warned them of the ack-ack ahead, but said nothing about the downed chopper.

Landing, we expected resistance. Instead, it felt like a deluxe trip to a magnificent view. The ragged peaks of Jebel Ataka looked down over a vast territory. Due east was the Egyptian Third Army, blanketing the flatland between the Suez Canal and the Mitla Pass, inside Sinai. To our northeast, Bren's division advanced toward Suez to complete the siege, at the southern mouth of the canal on the Suez Gulf. It all looked like pieces on a vast chessboard.

We immediately began relaying our information to headquarters. It became like a game, radioing in a report about Egyptian attempts to stymie Bren's advance and within minutes seeing Bren's armor change position in response to our calls.

With the enemy oblivious of our position and the air force keeping control of the skies in the area, it almost did feel like a picnic. But within a few hours of our arrival, one of my scouts reported Egyptian soldiers approaching from another peak of the mountain. I took my binoculars for a look. Even from the distance, their demeanor said they wanted to go home, not look for a fight.

Within minutes we deployed into an ambush for the fifteen approaching Egyptian soldiers. They walked right into a short burst that cut down a few in front. The rest dropped their weapons and surrendered.

We had a dozen hungry prisoners on our hands, and gave them food in exchange for information. But before we learned much more than that they had abandoned their position after their officers abandoned them, we saw more dejected troops coming our way.

By the end of the day we needed to share our water and hard-tack rations with forty Egyptian prisoners.

I reported back to division headquarters about the prisoners, and we continued our work. But over the next two days, someone at general headquarters decided that the reports of Egyptian troops on the mountain meant that we were in danger.

The radio began squawking commands at me to get ready to withdraw from the mountain. "Everything's fine," I tried to tell them. "They pose no danger to us," I said. "We can handle it."

"No," came back orders. "Get your force organized and be ready to move. We've already sent choppers."

I saw no reason to leave the mountaintop, with its perfect view of the Egyptian Third Army on the plains below. But I realized someone back at headquarters had got butterflies in his stomach when he heard of our contact with the enemy. Sure enough, barely an hour later, two helicopters landed. We took the few officers from amongst the prisoners and freed the rest before leaving on board the choppers.

The cease-fire in the south went into effect the day after we left Jebel Ataka, with the culmination of the IDF siege of the Egyptian Third Army. The Americans and Soviets negotiated it, with Henry Kissinger shuttling around the Middle East to arrange it. By laying siege to the Third Army, we forced the Egyptians to negotiate for the first time. It began with water deliveries, but eventually turned into a disengagement of forces – and ultimately helped produce the 1978 Camp David peace accords, Israel's first peace treaty with an Arab neighbor, five years later.

However, the fighting continued in the north along the lines we helped draw in the first week of the war. As the helicopter began its descent at the air base, I decided that until a full-fledged cease-fire with Syria went into effect, my unit and I belonged at the front.

Getting out of the chopper, three helicopter pilots approached me. We knew each other from years of working together. "Muki," asked one of them, "did you know that a helicopter crashed in front of you on your way to Jebel Ataka?"

"Yes," I said wearily.

"Gilad E. in your force?" he asked.

"Yes."

"The pilot was his brother, Ofer."

A shiver ran through my body. They were from Kibbutz Yifat in the Jezreel Valley, and everyone in the valley knew the brothers' family. Their father was principal at the Yifat High School, where many of the kibbutzniks of the valley went to school.

I waited a few minutes before telling Gilad, as if by delaying the news I could have made it never happen. I even walked slowly, trying to pick out Gilad from the dust-covered fighters. The three pilots followed silently behind me.

"Gilad," I said, finding him. Deciding to give it to him straight, I added only, "Ofer's fallen."

"Ofer!" he cried, his voice breaking. I continued telling him what happened, doubting he even heard me as the sorrow broke him. "He was ahead of us in a chopper flying through a canyon on our flight to Jebel Ataka," I told him, putting a hand on his shoulder, hoping to ease his pain. "Anti-aircraft fire caught him."

"There's a helicopter waiting for us," said Shefi, the senior pilot. "Come, we'll take you home," he said.

I watched the four climb on board the chopper, saddened by my soldier's personal loss, proud of the traditions of comrades-in-arms of the Israel Defense Forces and the way they came to their friend's brother to bring the tragic news and take him home.

SOUL-SEARCHING

———

The Egyptians and Syrians made a huge mistake attacking on Yom Kippur. Only ten days earlier, on the Jewish New Year, Rosh Hashanah, most Israelis would have been away from home—traveling, picnicking, hiking, or simply at the beach. If the Arabs had attacked on Rosh Hashanah, it would have taken many more hours than it did to get the reservists to battle and the roads would have been choked with tens of thousands of cars driven by panicked drivers trying to rush home—or to the front.

And obviously, the dastardly nature of the attack on our holiest day did not crumble our morale; it elevated it.

The Yom Kippur War taught me that we did not learn the right lessons from the Six-Day War. Passive after the Six-Day War, we waited for a phone call from the Arabs asking us to give back the land in exchange for peace. And gradually, for many, the possession of biblical homelands became more important than the security of the State of Israel.

If I understood one thing about Zionism, I understood that it meant our ability to control our own destiny. We should have phoned the Arab leaders, making suggestions of our own for a peace settlement. Instead, the government, the military leadership, and most of the people went into a state of euphoria, believing in our invincibility and the Arabs' incompetence, believing we could wait for peace.

So the Yom Kippur War forced many people to do some serious soul-searching about certain beliefs we had carried around since 1967, when the Arabs ran instead of fought. Eventually, Golda and Dayan resigned. I don't know if she ever understood why the people wanted her to go. I believe Dayan did understand, and he eventually returned to office as foreign minister under Menachem Begin, becoming one of the architects of peace with Egypt.

Dado became the first IDF chief of staff forced to resign in midterm. He died brokenhearted a few years later. Gorodish went into exile, digging for diamonds in Central Africa in the hopes of striking it rich enough to mount a campaign to clear his name.

Almost everyone in Israel paid a price for the hubris that led to the war. Nearly three thousand soldiers died on our side. Tens of thousands of Arab soldiers died.

Inside the army, we also had soul-searching to do, even though our military performance in 1973 outdid 1967 for success. Too many errors of judgment by Intelligence, poor maintenance of emergency stores, and too much confusion in the reinforcement of the front lines called for a serious accounting. Nonetheless, brilliant field command by a few outstanding senior officers, combined with the determination of the rank-and-file soldiers to fight to the last bullet in battles like the Valley of the Tears, combined into a great military victory.

For Sayeret Matkal too, I believed, the war proved to be both a success and a failure. I began my soul-searching in those first hours on the Golan, when I saw the Syrian tanks that reached Nafah, but it was my encounter with Arnan the next day, arguing about the Unit's presence in the war, that firmed my opinion.

I wanted to add a new vocation to the list of responsibilities Sayeret Matkal carried. For a special operations unit like ours to be truly effective, we needed to find a much different approach. We needed to define professional needs and develop and acquire equipment. We needed a military doctrine to develop dossiers for action that would pre-define the framework for our activities during wartime, so that everyone knew his job in advance.

As soon as I returned to base from Sinai and we finished our debriefings and written reports, I began pushing Giora to call a meeting of the commanders, to talk about what we learned in the war—and to press for my idea to add new responsibilities to our mandate.

But in those days between the cease-fire with Syria in November 1973 and Kissinger's mediation between Jerusalem and Damascus for a formal separation of forces, we conducted missions.

Typical of those months of nearly non-stop action was a night mission to destroy several Sherman tanks left behind in Syrian territory after the cease-fire. With their broken treads, we could not drive them out under cover of night, and towing them would be too risky as both a violation of the cease-fire and for the soldiers involved. But we obviously did not want the Syrians to get them as spoils of war.

I took a force to handle three such tanks, and Uzi Dayan took another force to deal with one further behind the line. After planting chemical-fused bombs on each of the tanks, we crept back across the lines to our side. While the rest of the force went home to base, I waited to make sure we had indeed accomplished the mission. Chemical fuses are tricky, especially in the cold of the Golan in winter.

I decided to take a nap while waiting for the blasts, figuring it would take an hour or two, and lay down on a cot in the corner of the bunker. "Wake me up as soon as the first one explodes," I asked an officer.

But dawn, not an explosion, woke me. I ran to the forward position and found the officer. "Why didn't you wake me up?" I demanded angrily, bursting in on the officer with a few of his colleagues.

"You said to wake you when the charges went off," the officer said innocently. "They didn't."

I pulled out my binoculars and stepped forward to the sand-bagged observation window. As I raised them to my eyes, one of the distant tanks burst into flames, and a moment later, an explosion echoed across the plain. It took another half hour for the second tank, and after that, the third tank and fourth tanks went up. All the while, through my binoculars, I watched the Syrian soldiers at their position opposite us depressed by the sight of the exploding tanks.

Finally, in the spring of 1974, Kissinger succeeded in brokering a deal between Israel and Syria for a disengagement of forces, freeing us to begin planning. One weekend, Giora invited seven key officers of Sayeret Matkal to his apartment for a meeting: Ehud Barak,

Yonni Netanyahu, Amiram Levine, Menachem Digli, Avashalom Horan, Uzi Dayan, and me.

Informally, we referred to the retreat as "Whither the Unit?" Anything and everything could be raised, like a brainstorming session to plan an operation, only in civilian clothes and in a relaxed atmosphere. For this session, we sipped our tea and black coffee slowly, and those who smoked took the time to empty the ashtrays. A few beers came out, but I stuck to my black tea with sugar.

They all knew that I wanted to use special operations forces to develop full dossiers on wartime targets. But going into the session, the consensus said implementation of my plan would disrupt the routine of Sayeret Matkal.

We began with a review of the war as we experienced it. Unlike during the Six-Day War, when Sayeret Matkal, like the paratroops *sayeret*, sat on runways waiting for assignments that never came, we had participated in the Yom Kippur War. However, as a result of the character of the war and its length, the Unit's product could have been better—if plans had existed for missions before the war broke out. I argued that the Unit needed to become like the air force, where every pilot knows well in advance his tasks and goals in wartime, because they prepare for it months, indeed years, ahead of time.

Without going into who said what, I can say that all sorts of ideas came up. Some said nothing should be changed. Others pointed to the APC shortage as the only problem. A couple admitted they would have preferred to be on special operations.

I went well prepared to that meeting, and gradually they came around to my point of view. But it became clear that with the end of the meeting, people would return to their routine: this one in school, that one in the armored corps, this one at the paratroopers, and that one in the Unit.

By the end of the meeting, I knew my next step. I told Giora I wanted leave without pay, but to continue serving as the senior reservist commander. From outside the army, I could go to anyone in the system. From within, I would be limited by the hierarchy of the bureaucracy. And meanwhile, I would incrementally implement my plans for adding a wartime capability to the best special forces unit in the IDF.

From the start Giora understood what I wanted. He agreed. Turning down some tempting offers to become a battalion commander, I took a civilian job with ChimAvir, a small crop-dusting aircraft company, with offices in Tel Aviv near the Defense Ministry compound and IDF general headquarters. ChimAvir's owner/operator understood I regarded it as a part-time job, but was glad to have me. The army called the rest of the time, and I commuted from Nahalal, using my rented apartment for overnight stays in Tel Aviv when work called.

Giora agreed to my most important condition: the Unit would call me for any emergency operation involving the rescue of hostages held by terrorists.

And the terrorists kept us busy. A few days after I began work with ChimAvir, a call from the Unit came to my office.

I ran the four flights down the stairs to the street and to my parked car, where my *chimidan* duffel bag was, as always, in the trunk, stocked with my needs: uniform, boots, and helmet; Kalashnikov, six 30–bullet magazines crisscrossed and taped for quick loading. In the web-belt I kept two canteens, six grenades, a flare-gun, and pockets packed with incidental neccessities—a jackknife, bandages, a shank of rope, and other tools. I raced through traffic to the base, leaving my car at the edge of the tarmac and racing to the helicopter just before it lifted off. I threw the *chimidan* onto the Sikorsky's deck and climbed aboard, joining fighters from the Unit on their way to answer the call.

During the flight north Giora briefed us with what he knew: a Palestinian terror group had crossed the border into Kiryat Shmona, a town on the Lebanese border, and had taken over an apartment in the northernmost neighborhood in the town. Holding a family hostage, they wanted Israel to release all the terrorists in our prisons. Our task: to take over the building, rescue the hostages, and capture or kill the terrorists.

We knew about hit-and-run terrorist infiltration across the border and hit-and-run attacks on cars on the road or isolated buildings along the border. Like any combat force, the terrorists had planned an avenue of escape from the scene. But as more information from Kiryat Shmona flowed to us through the radio while we flew north, it sounded like a completely new situation.

They had crossed the border, and held a building. Instead of blowing it up and retreating as usual, they held hostages, demanding the government negotiate with them. Until then, the only terrorists on suicide missions that we had encountered came from the Japanese

Red Army, PLO allies who arrived at the international airport in Lod disguised as passengers and pulled out machine guns, spraying the terminal with bullets. Twenty-four had died—mostly Puerto Rican Christian pilgrims to the Holy Land—before police and guards shot the terrorists dead. One terrorist survived—a Japanese student named Kozo Okamoto, who was eventually released from a life sentence in our jails during a prisoner exchange with Ahmed Jibril's terrorist group after the Lebanon war in the 1980s.

Now, as the chopper flew into Kiryat Shmona, it became obvious we had arrived too late. Smoke poured out of the building. The outdoor balcony hung from broken beams, destroyed by explosives, a gaping hole in the wall behind it.

Standard operating procedure in such cases is for the first troops on the scene to seal it off from curious onlookers—and to stay out of sight of the terrorists. According to officers on the scene, Golani soldiers and Border Police arrived on the scene and began creating a perimeter around the building. But then a Golani officer in an APC came into the terrorists' line of fire. Shot dead, his soldiers fired back. One of their bullets struck an explosive charge worn by a terrorist. The explosion set off a chain reaction of all the explosives the terrorists had carried into the building.

We ran up the stairs to the apartment. A horrific sight greeted us at the door. Sixteen civilians dead, including an entire family around a breakfast table. Two dead Golani soldiers, plus the terrorists.

Moshe Dayan arrived by helicopter a few minutes after us, and got a briefing on the spot from the commanders on the scene. His questions led to the question of whether the terrorists realized they had given up their escape route the moment they took hostages.

"Arabs do not commit suicide," Dayan summed up the conventional thinking after listening to his experts, who explained that the young Arabs probably expected to succeed in their mission.

"Wait a minute," I finally spoke up. "I don't understand," I said to the group. "Can you imagine a force of IDF soldiers crossing the border, going into an Arab village, taking hostages, and holding negotiations—without preparing any avenue of escape?"

"Well, us and them, that's two different things," someone said. "They have no regard for human lives."

"Maybe, maybe not," I answered. "But it's clear that even if they did not want to commit suicide, they fully expected to be surrounded by the army. They did not plan a retreat. They had nothing to lose. And that gave them unlimited options." I looked at Dayan, smiling at me with his piercing eye. He nodded at me to continue.

"With nothing to lose, they were free to kill the hostages, kill the negotiators, kill themselves, anything. I'm telling you, these people went on a suicide mission. And if this is the start of a pattern, we have a much more serious problem than you guys are talking about." I understood it clearly the moment I saw the remains of the terrorist who wore the booby-trapped explosives.

Dayan raised an eyebrow, and that evening called me at the rented flat I used in Tel Aviv during the work week, asking me to come visit at his home in Zahala, a suburb north of Tel Aviv. We met occasionally that way, informally. Sometimes I saw him when he visited Nahalal. He loved Nurit, his sister's daughter, and of late he had been using his influence to get her the best medical treatment for her ailment.

It was a warm spring evening. We sat on the patio in the back of his house, amidst the antiques that he collected, drinking dark, sweetened tea.

"Talk to me about what you said this morning," he asked.

"Listen, Moshe," I began. "It's clear to me that we should treat this as a first, and expect more just like it. We have to come up with some clear doctrine, or we're going to find ourselves chasing after terrorists on suicide missions. By definition they will be able to surprise us every time they act, since they'll be ready to take risks that never would occur to us—unless we think like them."

"I still do not believe that Arab fighters would agree to suicide missions," he said.

"They took a suicidal risk today," I insisted. "I know what your experts say. 'The Arabs aren't brave enough for it.' But we can't ignore what happened today, Moshe. They came ready to die. We don't have a doctrine for it," I added, "But we're going to need one."

The big army moves slowly, the small army faster, but terrorists on the offensive can be the quickest of all. It took a couple of weeks for an official order to come down from the defense minister's office, instructing Sayeret Matkal to develop a combat doctrine for hostage situations. Even before the official orders, we began working. But before much could be done, the terrorists struck again.

MA'ALOT

On Sunday morning, May 15, 1974, less than a month after the Kiryat Shmona incident, I was on my way to Tel Aviv from Nahalal as usual at six-thirty in the morning. At seven, near Yokne'am, south of Haifa, I heard the radio news:

"Terrorists holding hostages in a school in Ma'alot," the broadcast began, "are demanding the release of twenty convicted terrorists in Israeli prisons." I thumped on the brakes and pulled over to the side of the road. The announcer continued while I spun the wheel and made a U-turn against traffic, cars screeching to a halt around me. "The army surrounded the school," said the announcer, "and the government is going into an emergency session."

I floored the gas pedal, heading north to the town just south of the Lebanese border, realizing that the Unit had probably tried reaching me just after I left home. I sped north to Ma'alot, cutting the normal hour's drive to forty minutes.

Eight kilometers from the Lebanese border, Ma'alot is built on a tree-covered hill. The school was on the northern slopes, a large three-story building overlooking a grove of trees and empty fields. A few hundred yards away stood a new neighborhood of apartment houses, some under construction, others already inhabited. Driving up toward the school, I saw the first Sikorsky, carrying the Unit, hovering over the football field at the entrance to town, beginning its descent.

An intelligence colonel from Northern Command gave us a briefing. The terrorists penetrated from Lebanon two days ago, said the colonel. A patrol along the border discovered their tracks about ten kilometers northeast of Ma'alot, and gave chase. After a day of fruitless searching, the general assessment concluded the terrorists had returned to Lebanon, about five kilometers away from where the tracks had disappeared.

But they did not head back to Lebanon. Instead, they went through the hilly forests and fields along the border, heading west.

On the second day in Israel the terrorists began to leave a bloody trail. First, they ambushed a van carrying textile workers from the Arab village of Fasuta, killing two of the women on board and wounding the driver, who lost control of the van. It plunged into a wadi beneath the road, injuring the rest of the passengers. By the time a search party found the missing workers at the bottom of the gully, the terrorists were long gone. But instead of retreating, the terrorists wanted more. They reached Ma'alot sometime past midnight. They shot the only person they found on the sleepy town's streets, a city hall worker named Ya'akov Kadosh, then moved on to the nearest apartment building, finding the Cohen family.

Fortuna Cohen died clutching her three-year-old son, Edi, also killed by the terrorists. Jojo Cohen, Fortuna's husband, tried to save their other two children. The terrorists killed Jojo. But their deaf and mute year-old baby survived, apparently because, by not uttering a sound through the entire event, the terrorists missed him.

"After all that killing," said the intelligence colonel, "you might think they had enough. But no. They wanted more."

From the Cohens' apartment, they headed north in the direction of the school, where they found the hundred high school kids from Safed. After hiking through the Galilee, their field trip group stayed overnight in the Ma'alot high school, closed for a holiday.

By dawn, army units and police had surrounded the school. Thankfully, the army had already learned the first lesson of Kiryat Shmona: no random firefight as soon as the army arrived.

"We waited for you," said the intelligence officer. Now we all waited for Golda and Dayan to decide whether to give in to the terrorists or use The Unit. Not an easy decision under any circumstances, the Yom Kippur War had undermined the self-confidence and authority of both Golda and Dayan. Demonstrations after the war forced the government to appoint a commission of inquiry to determine responsibility for the failures in the opening phases of the war. The commission forced Dado's resignation, among others'. Less than a month before Ma'alot, they decided to name Motta Gur as chief of staff, replacing him with Raful as the Northern Command commander.

But the commission of inquiry did not blame the political level for the failures of the war, though it decried a conceptual blindness that imbued the entire defense framework.

So, Golda and Dayan both lost enormous amounts of political strength in the face of the demonstrators demanding someone pay for the 2,569 dead soldiers of the Yom Kippur War. The commission of inquiry's refusal to blame Golda and Dayan only increased public pressure on them to quit office. They did, but meanwhile remained in power as a transitional government until a new one could be formed. Eventually, Yitzhak Rabin, the chief of staff from 1967, would replace Golda for his first, two-and-a-half year, term as prime minister.

Meanwhile, Dayan still ruled in the field. He showed up in the morning to personally handle the situation. He wore his usual khaki trousers and a short-sleeved shirt, with a cap on his head against the hot sun. He set up headquarters at an apartment building not far from the school, and took control.

One element of the crisis also helped us prepare for its military solution. When the terrorists broke into the school, a number of adults traveling with the group as guides and chaperons jumped out of the second-floor windows, along with some of the children, leaving eighty-five inside with one teacher. The adults who escaped claimed they sought help. At least they provided some intelligence on the terrorists' weapons and explosives. The school's principal— one of those adults who escaped rather than lead the kids—told us the terrorists held the kids in two separate classrooms on the second floor of the three-story building.

Driving to Ma'alot, I thought of the time when as a child I encountered my first challenge from "an enemy" and how I froze, not knowing what to do. My teenage camp counselor did know what to do—disarm the assailants with an assault of his own. The schoolkids from Safed might do that to their captors, I hoped, if they moved quickly. They only needed one person to lead them. A teacher, the bus driver, some adult might be able to lead them. But, abandoned, the kids inside the building were like me and my friends at the water spigot outside Hadera.

After the briefing, I took a walk around the perimeter, staying out of the sight of a terrorist who kept lookout over the scene by patrolling an outdoor porch corridor on the second floor, and others on the second floor watching through a classroom window.

Coming around a locked shed at the construction site with a view of the school, I came across Dayan.

I approached silently from behind, watching him. Always brave in the field, he stood with one hand on his hip, the other holding the binocular lens to his single eye to survey the scene, a step away from entering the terrorists' line of sight from the balcony. He lowered the binoculars.

"Moshe, from here on, only on your belly," I said, afraid he might take that step.

He turned around and smiled. "How are you, Muki?" he asked, shaking my hand. "What do you think?"

"I still have to go completely around the building," I said, "but from what I've seen up to now, the conditions are relatively good for an assault."

"I think so too," he said. "I'm on my way to call Golda, to let her know."

I followed him back to the emergency field headquarters in the apartment building nearest the school. While Dayan conferred with aides, Giora worked out a basic plan, and we began filling in the details.

Without any formal doctrine about adequate break-in points, optimum firepower, the use of grenades, small caliber or large caliber weapons, we improvised. We set up a net of snipers around the school, looking for all three of the terrorists in our sights at the same time. But the terrorists also knew we waited for such a moment and took care to give us only one target at a time, whether the lookout on the porch or through the window into one of the classrooms where they held the kids.

Obviously, one assault force, running up the stairs to the second-floor classrooms, would not suffice. We already agreed the operation could begin if snipers hit two of the three terrorists, if not all three. I suggested that I take a team up a ladder to the window looking into the classroom where the third terrorist guarded the children. The first fighter up the ladder could get the terrorist, right after the snipers hit. Meanwhile, Amiram Levine's force, rushing up to the second floor for the break-in, would take out the third terrorist.

A negotiation crew with loudspeakers meanwhile kept the Arabs calm, telling them that the ambassadors they wanted as mediators were on their way and that the government meeting in Jerusalem continued deliberating over their demands to free the terrorists in our prisons.

Hundreds of soldiers laid siege to the school. Military jeeps and cars converged on the area, but we kept everything camouflaged from the terrorists, to make them feel safe, staying out of their line of sight, watching the building and waiting for our moment.

Everything seemed fine until a Kalashnikov shot from the school startled us all. A terrorist had spotted a Golani soldier, who at his own initiative had climbed the town's water tower for a better view. Thinking the soldier was a sniper, the terrorist fired. The soldier was killed on the spot and fell to the ground. For a long stretch of silence, the tension grew until the translator explained to the terrorist that he killed a soldier on home leave for the weekend. The poor soldier was probably the only one in the area not under orders to stay out of sight.

We presented our plan to Raful at eleven, and began moving into position, figuring the whole thing could be over by noon if the snipers got two terrorists in their sights. Meanwhile, the terrorists doubled their efforts to stay out of sight.

And Motta began to have second thoughts about a military solution. Dayan called Jerusalem.

In the apartment he used as a field headquarters, I remember hearing his voice and turning to watch his face as he spoke with the prime minister. "Golda," he said. "I'm in the field and have seen the forces. They are ready to break in." Moshe's face did not change as he listened to what she said to him.

But I saw the twitch of Dayan's brow over the eyepatch when Motta asked for the phone to speak with the prime minister. It never could have happened before Yom Kippur, when Dayan reigned supreme as the ultimate military authority in Israel. The war had taken its toll. Dayan handed the phone to the new chief of staff.

"This is Motta," the chief of staff began. "I'm also in the field, but I recommended continuing the negotiations."

A short silence followed. She must have asked him a question, I realized. "I think it is too big a risk," Motta said. "At least right now."

Furious, Dayan decided to fly to Jerusalem to explain the situation to the government. Time is against us, he would tell them. Night would begin falling at five, and in the dark, the situation becomes much more dangerous.

While Dayan choppered to Jerusalem, the terrorists released a hostage—one of the last three adults left among the kids, a teacher. She came out with a letter. But nobody paid any attention to the terrorists' message. I heard that the French ambassador showed up to mediate, if not negotiate, but nobody gave him access to the chief of staff. But the teacher's release gave us some more intelligence. The three terrorists "have rifles like yours," she said, pointing to my Kalashnikov. "And hand grenades. And they set up boxes with wires and explosives."

"What about the kids?" I asked, thinking of the water faucet in Hadera all those years ago.

She shivered, clutching a coffee cup with both hands. "Everyone is frightened, on the floor, panicked." It dashed my remaining hopes the hostages might take the initiative and overcome the terrorists.

The snipers stayed in position all the hours we waited for the okay from Jerusalem. Sometimes they had a view of the terrorist in the classroom, whom I planned to take with my team through the window. Others watched the terrorist on the balcony. But never again that day did all three terrorists enter the snipers' sights at the same time.

Five o'clock remained our final deadline. Minutes, then hours, ticked by, and the tension grew while the government deliberated. Giving in to the terrorists' demands would open a Pandora's box much more difficult to close than open. But Dayan could not promise a casualty-free operation.

Meanwhile, like overwound springs, my squad waited with a long ladder around the corner of the building, a blind spot to the terrorist's view. I put Micki first, Max second, and I went third. Amiram Levine's main assault force meanwhile crawled into place, ready to make the dash for the school door and up the stairs to the second floor.

Dayan finally returned to Ma'alot, and we waited for the ministers in Jerusalem to decide. The waiting became torture. Finally, just before five, we got the okay. Giora told the snipers to fire when ready. Now we waited for their shots to set the entire operation into motion.

No more than five seconds could pass from the time the snipers first fired to when we should be up the ladder and in the classroom window. By then, Amiram's team should be on the second floor, breaking into the classrooms. We waited for the snap of the snipers' shots while the seconds ticked by and the light began changing in the final minutes of daytime.

Suddenly, Giora's "Fire" came over the radio. Gunshots cracked. "Move!" I ordered, and we threw the ladder up against the wall, unaware that the snipers had only wounded the terrorist on the porch—and he managed to crawl back inside the classroom, to warn the others.

A massive cacophony of shooting and explosions and screaming burst out of the window along with shattered glass. We ignored the flying shards, racing up the ladder, while children leapt from the shattered window above, trying to escape the mayhem.

Out of the corner of my eye I saw an elderly man running from the woods nearby to help the shrapnel-wounded kids lying on the ground, their legs broken from the two-story jump. The seconds flew by as Micki scrambled up, followed by Max and me. Just as Micki reached the last rungs of the ladder, a grenade flew out the window.

"Grenade on the right!" I shouted. The three of us instinctively jumped off the ladder to the left, away from the grenade. We never managed to get off a single shot. Raising our heads after the grenade's explosion, I saw the elderly man fall, wounded by shrapnel in the back. He lived another five years, paralyzed from the waist down.

Back on our feet, we knew we had lost the time to get to the window before Amiram's crew arrived. "To the main entrance," I ordered, and the three of us ran around the corner to the doorway, up the stairs to the second floor.

The acrid stench of a smoke grenade hung in the air. I knew we faced disaster, but did not know its horrible extent—until I entered the first classroom, a scene from my worst nightmare.

The terrorists had crammed eighty-five kids into a room usually overcrowded with forty. The terrorists sprayed the kids with Kalashnikov bullets and exploded grenades in their midst. Dozens lay on the floor, piled on top of each other where they fell, wounded or dead. In the corner, a terrorist lay dead on top of a detonator. Luckily, he died before using it. The explosives could have brought down the building. The shooting over, chaos reigned. Dozens of wounded, frightened children screamed for help. Others shivered in shock. Out of the whole group, eighteen died on the spot (three more died later in the hospital) and fifty suffered wounds ranging from light to serious. Only a handful of the kids escaped without harm.

Medical crews ran in after us, to evacuate the wounded. Stunned by the gruesome scene, we helped load wounded onto stretchers. Dayan, Motta Gur, and Raful came into the chaos and confusion of the evacuation. Just as they entered the room, Shai, an officer from the Unit, shouted, "Terrorist!"

I turned. From amidst the broken bodies of dead children, a teenager in an IDF uniform stood up, fumbling with a Kalashnikov. He was wounded but must have hid among the kids when the shooting began, I realized.

He swung the barrel up, aimed in the direction of Dayan and Raful. I pulled the trigger on my own Kalashnikov, letting off a short burst that threw him backward, killing him instantly.

Moshe glanced at me and barely nodded, like all of us too horrified by the disaster to comment.

On the spot, we held a preliminary debriefing, listing all our mistakes. It began with the sniper hitting the terrorist on the porch in the chest instead of the head. His crew commander made a terrible mistake, whispering a last minute word to the shooter. "It's up to you," he told the sniper. "The responsibility for all those children is on you, so make sure you hit." Feeling the pressure, the sniper went for the sure shot to the chest rather than the riskier one to the head.

But the sniper's mistake only started a chain of events that included many other mistakes. Amiram's force, running up the stairs, went a flight past the second floor of the building, reaching the third floor. Retracing their steps, they made another mistake when someone threw a phosphorous grenade, filling the corridors with smoke and making visibility impossible, losing more precious seconds. Eventually, one of Amiram's fighters spotted a terrorist through the smoke and managed to kill him.

It was a national tragedy. I believed that in addition to all our mistakes, the government's hesitancy lay behind the failure. Their hesitation in fulfilling a policy of no negotiations with terrorists proved costly.

An inquiry into the events, headed by Amos Horev, a reserve general from the general staff that won the Six-Day War, turned out like the Agranat Commission that exonerated Dayan and Golda from responsibility for the Yom Kippur War.

But at least his report established a policy giving the three regional command generals—Northern, Southern, and Central—the authority to okay a military solution in the field without waiting for a government decision.

We felt that when Dayan gave his okay in the morning we could have done it properly. But that did not free us from responsibility to learn from the tragedy, the only balm for the pain we felt.

We analyzed each step of the operation and it all led back to the bloodied room on the second floor where we held the first impromptu debriefing and counted our mistakes. Into our new doctrine for hostage situations went a string of lessons for future incidents.

The day after Ma'alot, Raful ordered the Unit's commanders to his office in the Northern Command for a briefing. Raful listened, but already knew what he wanted to say. "Maybe you know how to fight and conduct special missions and night raids. But when push comes to shove, I should have used the Golani forces and let them do it right away. As long as I'm in charge here, you guys can stay out of the Northern Command."

A few weeks later, Golda and Dayan finally left office. Yitzhak Rabin became prime minister in the summer of 1974. Shimon Peres became defense minister.

And Sayeret Matkal received orders to redouble our efforts in preparing a full-scale doctrine for counterterrorism in hostage situations. To help, the army gave us authority to recruit forty more soldiers.

The recruits learned a whole new set of skills and tools. They learned to break into a room crowded with hostages, identify the terrorists, and selectively shoot to kill terrorists while avoiding hostages. The specialized teams learned how to take over houses, apartment buildings, ships, trains, planes, buses—any target that terrorists might capture. Every type of structure needed its own doctrine regarding entry, firepower, adequate numbers of teams. Ladders became an obsession for us. We developed easily transportable folding ladders, and invented special ladders for traversing from one building to the next. I called my best fighters on these ladders "the monkey crews," for they seemed to move up the ladders as quickly as the tree-climbing monkeys I used to see in Uganda.

Extraordinary skills are required for these operations, and every member of Sayeret Matkal needed to learn those skills. Though one officer took charge of the overall training, all the officers, both regulars and reserves, became involved in developing the doctrines and methods. We constantly practiced on models and real targets, from planes and trains to houses and apartments. Basic methodologies for snipers, communication networks, sabotage substances, and combat means needed to be developed. In quite a short time we put together a doctrine, which we kept improving all the time and the Unit continues to improve to this day.

Officially still a civilian on leave without pay, as always I remained on call for any emergency that came up, and a few weeks after Ma'alot came Bet Shean.

This time they caught me at home, before I left for work. Hilla Elazar, Dado's daughter and a secretary at the Unit, called, catching me in the kitchen, making coffee. "Muki, there's an incident in Bet Shean," she said.

After Ma'alot, I added a street atlas for all the towns and cities of Israel to the emergency supplies I kept in my car. I turned on the radio as I sped out of Nahalal. The news broadcast named the street where the terrorists had attacked. I quickly located the street in the atlas and sped to the town. Bet Shean is a few miles down the Jezreel Valley Road from Nahalal.

The police had already thrown up roadblocks to prevent people from getting near the danger zone. I realized that while I wore my uniform, my civilian vehicle would undoubtedly be stopped by a police roadblock around the danger zone, slowing me down on my way through the quiet little town overlooking the Jordan Rift Valley.

Ahead, I saw a police barrier, two portable fences partially blocking the two lanes of the road. Realizing that my car fit between the two blue fences, I drove slowly up to the barricade, as if readying to listen to the policemen. The cops approached to ask what I wanted. I gunned the engine, spun the wheel, and sped through the opening, the policemen jumping backward out of the way while I raced through the town toward the street I had found on the map.

Less than a minute later, I came to a halt in the front yard of one of the little four-story apartment buildings on the street, thinking I had reached a parallel road to the one where the terrorists held the house. I turned off the engine. Suddenly, a familiar sound snapped in the air near the car. A grenade's detonator. In another four seconds, an explosion would erupt.

Leaping from the car, I ran for cover to the side of the house. The grenade burst like a thunder clap, followed by a long burst of bullets at my car. The fire came from the third floor of the apartment house overlooking the yard where I had parked my car. As soon as the burst stopped, I raced back to my car, grabbed the duffel bag from the backseat, and high-tailed it to where Raful and some officers from his command made a field command in a yard behind an apartment building across the street from the building where the terrorists were holed up.

Raful smiled at me as I ran up to him and his officers, apparently forgetting his earlier reprimand of the Unit. "I came straight from home when I heard," I explained, joining the circle of officers from Northern Command.

"Listen," Raful said to me. "There's a ladder in place to get to the third floor. You get up there and see what's going on inside."

"No problem," I agreed, buckling my web-belt. I crossed the quiet street in a zigzagging run, but no shots rang out in the street after me. Beneath the building, out of the terrorists' view, I found the ladder and propped it to an open window on the second floor. Raful's intelligence officer told me that the ladder led to an apartment next door to the one the terrorists held.

I climbed quickly, and discovered an elderly woman in her living room, petrified with fear. I held up a finger to signal her to stay quiet. "Get me out of here," she wept.

"Just sit quietly and everything will be all right," I promised her. I went through her tiny flat to the doorway and stepped into the stairwell. I put my ear to the hijacked apartment's door, hearing a muffled conversation in Arabic.

The job looked very straightforward. Break down the door, identify the terrorists, and kill them. I went back to the elderly woman's apartment. "I'll send someone for you," I promised her, and headed back down the ladder.

"Okay, Raful," I said, back at his command post across the street. "We have to break in. That's all."

"Good," he said. "Put together a crew," he suggested, pointing to soldiers from his command arriving on the scene, "and I'll provide covering fire with the Border Police."

I spent a few minutes trying to find soldiers ready to join me. But nobody volunteered. It is not the kind of job that you can make someone you don't know do, just by giving an order.

But as I rejoined Raful to break the news, the familiar sound of Sikorsky rotors beating the air came from the south. A minute later, Giora Zorea, Sayeret Matkal's commander, appeared on the scene.

I took Giora back through the elderly woman's flat to show him the situation. She sat quietly, not saying a word as we came through the window and crossed her little living room. For a few minutes we stood in the corridor, listening to the muffled voices speaking Arabic inside. Using hand signals to communicate, we agreed that we could do the job with half a dozen fighters.

It only took a couple of minutes, and we went back down through the woman's apartment, finding a second Unit chopper had arrived, led by Nehemia Tamari. Giora's deputy at the time, he eventually rose to become a general, but died tragically in a helicopter accident in 1994.

Giora and I agreed that I'd wait for Nehemia, brief him, and we'd break in together at the head of a team of six to eight soldiers. It took a few minutes, and Nehemia and I were moving quickly to the building's front entrance along the edges of the wall, out of sight of the terrorists in the second floor apartment.

I gave the fighters Nehemia picked for the job a brief run-down: second-floor apartment, hostages, at least two terrorists. The idea was simple: move quickly—and quietly—up the stairs, take out the front door to the flat with a burst at the lock, break in, and take out the terrorists.

We exchanged quick glances, I gave the nod, and we went up the stairs to the front door of the apartment. In place around the doorway, a short burst at the door lock from one of the fighters blew the door open, and we raced in. Bullets cut down one terrorist in the living room before he managed to get off a shot. A second ran into the little side room off the living room.

"Grenade!" shouted Moshe from the break-in crew, announcing that he was tossing one into the little room after the fleeing terrorist. We all leapt for cover into the corridor, pulling the door closed behind us.

The four seconds to the explosion went quickly, especially when we realized that, in our haste, we had left Moshe behind, pushing at the door to let him out. One of his comrades flung it open, and Moshe lunged out as the grenade's blast shattered the apartment. Nehemia's face twisted in pain in front of my eyes as a sliver of hot metal sliced into his upper left arm while we burst back in, ready to fire.

A dead terrorist lay bullet-riddled in the living room, his partner blown apart by the grenade in the little room. We found the hostages in their bedroom, an elderly couple already killed much earlier that morning when the terrorists broke in.

Done with the job, we found Shimon Peres waiting with Raful and Giora. We gave them a brief report, and after Peres made a short speech congratulating us, we dispersed. The two helicopters lifted off, carrying the Unit back to base. I went back to my car.

Only then did I discover that a bullet pierced its roof when the terrorists fired at me on my arrival. It shattered the windshield on a trajectory that would have pierced my head if I had not gotten out in time. I smiled at my luck and, after stashing my duffel bag in the trunk, brushed the broken glass off the driver's seat and went on my way.

Later, on the radio going home, I heard that a mob stormed the building to take revenge on the bodies of the terrorists, throwing them out the window while people below waited to make a bonfire from the dead bodies.

In their hysteria, the mob also burned the bodies of the elderly couple killed by the terrorists. It shamed us that our people acted in such a barbaric manner. Terrorists or not, it was detestable behavior.

DOSSIERS FOR ACTION

I never liked the idea of medals. Usually, they are rewarded when something went wrong, and by isolating some people's courage, they ignore others'. I understand that armies need medals. But I never allowed one to be sought for my work and I never argued for or against a medal for anyone else.

My ambitions were different. I wanted to make real my theory that standing battle orders could be prepared for special operations during warfare. I did not care about the big army. Indeed, I often felt the ranks of bureaucracy to be no less a battlefield for me than the Golan or the Sinai. I wanted special operations to make the IDF more efficient protecting the state, the land, and the people of Israel.

As reserve commander of Sayeret Matkal, I sat down with every man under my command, planning to do something unprecedented in the Unit—clean the stables. I knew who had done well in the war and who had not. I knew who had missed reserves for a long time and who had aged prematurely. It shocked everyone, even the handful of supporters who knew my goal, but I cut a couple of dozen men from the Sayeret Matkal roster, making sure they ended up in another unit of their choice. In addition, under orders from the chief of staff, I moved another thirty fighters and officers from Sayeret Matkal to the armored corps, which was mauled during the Yom Kippur War and needed talented officers and combat-experienced soldiers.

But more than winnowing out fighters no longer fit for the Unit, I needed to create an infrastructure to support my plans to buck more than a decade of tradition set by Avraham Arnan.

I began with only two supporters: Giora and Yekutiel "Kuti" Adam, then deputy chief of staff and in line for the top job in the army. As deputy chief of staff, Kuti held the purse strings to any preliminary budgets I needed to create dossiers for action for the Unit in time of war. We needed specialized equipment and logistical support from the air force and, sometimes, the navy. We needed to be able to requisition whatever we wanted for an operation, without the need to go through the quartermaster's office.

For a long time I worked half-time at ChimAvir and half-time in the reserves, lobbying for my plan from outside the army. But that summer Yonni came back to the Unit, appointed commander after Giora left. Yonni had spent two years in the armored corps after the Yom Kippur War, serving as a battalion commander. He was knowledgeable about my operational concepts and asked me to come back to the Unit on a full-time basis.

I worked systematically inside the bureaucracy, going to officers with influence, whether generals or captains. When I ran into opposition, I moved on to someone more influential. A lot like battle, my strategy aimed at creating a *fait accompli*, and my tactics depended on finding the soft spots in the opposition. Some opponents had functions so critical to my success that I could not let go. I sat them down and let them pour out their arguments, and then I argued back until I won them over.

Benny Peled, commander of the air force, saw the need for the air force to have a special warfare unit and supported my cause.

But while I worked for a long-term goal, a more pressing need seemed to be upon us. The terrorist buildup in southern Lebanon was being met with heavy use of airpower. It was clear to me that the airpower could be effective but that it had some very serious disadvantages. Planes could miss their targets, hitting innocents and undermining our moral position, and more often than not, the terrorists managed to get out of the buildings before they were hit. I believed in the lesson of el-Hiam and Spring of Youth—the most effective way to challenge terrorists was to hit them face-to-face, surprising them.

And, once again, just as the PLO picked up where the Arab armies left off after the Six-Day War, they did the same after the Yom Kippur War. Fatahland, in south Lebanon, became even more violent. The army responded with two methods—big sweeps into sectors of south Lebanon, to push the terrorists north, and precision bombing by the air force to hit their command posts in Lebanon.

I lobbied for the IDF to use us the way they had when we went to el-Hiam with Egoz or into Beirut in Spring of Youth. I remembered my lessons well: surprise an enemy on his home turf. Pinpointing the military commanders and avoiding any harm to innocents would be far more effective than a hundred tons of explosives. It held true in between wars, and it held true during wars, as well.

I went into meetings with the bureaucracy with a prepared speech in my head and a readiness to answer any question they threw at me. "Gentlemen," I always began. "There is a big difference between hitting buildings and hitting people. The terrorists know the air force can hit them. They are on alert for the air force. But the air force hits buildings, not terrorists. Nothing is accomplished by that. They just move to another building."

But the army, especially Motta, was so taken with the air force's ability to inflict physical damage from the air without putting people at risk that it began canceling special operations for the Unit, just because the air force could handle the target.

I tried to explain to them that less risk exists in a special operation planned ahead of time, down to its most minute detail, than in any large-scale operation involving thousands of troops, heavy vehicles, and artillery support. A well-prepared operation gives the advantage, through initiative, to the attacker, not the defender. "That's why terrorism works—and that's why counterterrorism works," I explained to all who would listen.

Chief of operations Moshe Levy backed us in the Unit, but the chief of staff's policy focused on bringing technology and firepower to bear on the battlefield. I felt we were forgetting the traditions of the early Jewish defense movement. Our strength never lay in our sheer force but in our creative use of that force. From the Unit, we kept sending plans for special operations to hit terrorist command-and-control centers in Lebanon, but while we generated support for our plans from members of the general staff, the chief of staff,

Motta, remained opposed. And in the army, the chief of staff has the final word.

So I decided to go over his head and take the very rare course of action of initiating a meeting with Moshe Dayan. I usually waited for him to ask for my ideas. Moshe still lived in Zahala, outside Tel Aviv. After years of being a hero, he suddenly found himself regarded as a villain by many Israelis, who blamed him for the Yom Kippur War. I still regarded him as a friend and an extraordinarily original thinker.

I called and asked to see him. I took Amiram with me. "Fine," Dayan said after we finished the presentation. "I agree. But what do you want from me? I'm not defense minister anymore."

"Motta's opposed, we believe," I said. "How do we get past him?"

Dayan thought for a second. "I can speak with Shimon," he finally decided, referring to Defense Minister Peres, a longtime political ally. "I'll ask him to meet with you two."

Sure enough, a few days later I got a call from one of Peres's advisers. Since it was entirely outside of channels, I was told to make the arrangements to see Peres through his wife, who told me to come to their apartment in north Tel Aviv at ten o'clock the next night.

While Sonia plied us with tea and sandwiches, Amiram and I talked to Peres for two hours, concluding our presentation by handing over a paper outlining our ideas for using special forces, in addition to airpower, against the terrorists in Lebanon.

Peres listened carefully, occasionally asking a question. He never served as a rank-and-file soldier, but he spent most of his life working for the defense of the country.

When we finished, Peres thanked us for coming and showed us to the door, with a promise to take the plan to his people. We did not know whether that meant Rabin or Motta.

But a few weeks later, when we were presenting yet another proposal for a night operation by the Unit against a terrorist base in Lebanon, the chief of staff surprised us by authorizing our mission.

The lesson I learned was clear. I wasn't a career officer, so I was unafraid of the bureaucracy. I could stand up for what I believed, just as my parents had taught me. And in this case, if what I believed meant going over the chief of staff's head, so be it.

OPERATION THUNDERBALL

Neither day nor night exists in the Pit, a huge underground bomb shelter containing a warren of concrete tunnels and cinderblock offices under the Defense Ministry compound in Tel Aviv.

Bustling non-stop with young secretaries, technicians, and both desk officers and senior front-line officers, the Pit is the central junction of information flowing into the army and orders for action flowing out to units in the field. All year round, twenty-four hours a day, that windowless, fluorescent-lit complex is the thumping heart of the IDF.

I was in the pit on June 27, 1976, in a meeting with colleagues from operations, intelligence, and the air force. With Sayeret Matkal commander Yonni Netanyahu and his new deputy, Yiftach R., down in Sinai that week on an operation, I was also duty officer for the Unit in case of an emergency.

A major stuck his head into the narrow office where half a dozen of us sat around a long table working on plans for an operation under consideration. "We have a hijacking," he said. "An Air France plane out of Greece."

I reached for the phone. "Air France flight 139," the major continued. "It left Tel Aviv for Athens this morning. They landed fine. Took off fifteen minutes ago to Paris." I checked my watch. It was a few minutes before one o'clock in the afternoon. "The hijackers took the cockpit a few minutes ago. Signals intelligence picked up the communications with Athens control tower," he was saying when Rami answered the phone at the base.

"They just called from operations," Rami said.

"Good. Get the team to the airport on the double," I ordered. "I'll meet you there." Fifteen minutes out of Athens meant barely an hour from Israel. Sayeret Matkal teams were well practiced at the routine to get to the airport quickly for just such an emergency. And I could reach the airport in half an hour, if traffic permitted.

Nowadays, a modern four- and six-lane highway connects Tel Aviv to the airport. In those days, the route to the airport led through the residential towns east of Tel Aviv. My mind raced along with the car as I dodged through traffic, running an occasional light, thinking about which method to use to take down the plane if it landed at Ben-Gurion.

Ever since the Sabena rescue in the spring of 1972, the Unit had kept developing doctrines and methods for rescuing hijacked planes on the ground. We never use the same ploy twice. Just as we learn from each incident, so do terrorists.

A few weeks earlier, we had showed the general staff a new way to handle a hijacked plane on the ground, totally different from the method used for the Sabena rescue four years earlier.

As I pulled into the airport, I decided on our latest method as the first option. We could be ready in time for the hijacked plane's landing, if it headed for Israel. I flashed my ID to the guard at the main gates to the tarmac and drove onto the landing field, where I could see the Unit's crews already organizing their gear. But as I got out of the car near the small hall we used in such instances, word came that the plane was heading to Libya.

Nobody was surprised. Libyan leader Moammar Qaddafi's oil-financed support for international terrorism, especially Palestinian terror against Israeli targets, was well known. We began preparing for the plane's arrival, suspecting it could yet return to Israel.

Sure enough, within an hour of the first report of Libya as their destination, the terrorists radioed ahead to Benghazi airport demanding fuel be readied to top off the passenger plane's tanks—and that representatives of Wadi Haddad's Popular Front meet them. Wadi Haddad, head of one of the most radical of the Palestinian groups, regarded Yasser Arafat's Fatah as too moderate. Haddad worked hand-in-hand with Western European terror groups like the German Bader-Meinhof gang and the Italian Red Brigades. The news that the terrorists wanted more fuel could mean they still wanted to try landing in Israel.

A few minutes later, Ran Bag showed up. A lieutenant colonel, he headed the counterterrorism branch in the chief infantry and paratroops command, under Dan Shomron. A full participant in the Unit's development of new methods and doctrines for handling terror incidents, he spent the rest of the day and much of the evening with us, while we refined details on plans we already knew by heart, waiting for the plane to take off from Benghazi.

Yitzhak Rabin, then in his first term as prime minister, was running the weekly cabinet meeting when his military liaison officer informed him of the hijacking. Rabin immediately formed a working committee of relevant ministers and issued a statement reiterating government policy that Israel never negotiates with terrorists. Jerusalem regarded the French government as responsible for the safety of the passengers aboard the Air France plane, said the statement.

Meanwhile, three IDF officers back at general staff headquarters began considering options if the plane remained in Benghazi under Libyan protection. Major Amiram Levine, the "dancing blond dervish" from Spring of Youth, who graduated from Sayeret Matkal to become an intelligence-branch officer specializing in operations planning; Major Gadi Shefi, commander of the Shayetet, the naval commandos; and Major Ido Embar, air force branch chief for combined operations raised ideas ranging from a helicopter rescue to hijacking a Libyan plane or Libyan strategic facility and holding it in exchange for the hostages. If any harm came to any of the Israeli passengers, they planned a punitive action to make the Libyans think twice about cooperating with any terrorist group again.

A few minutes after ten o'clock that night, word arrived that the plane took off from Benghazi, about three hours away. I called the troops into the briefing room at the airport and conducted a final review of the plan.

Chief of operations and deputy chief of staff Yekutiel "Kuti" Adam was there with his assistant, Col. Avigdor "Yanosh" Ben-Gal, the former armored corps commander who had asked us to rescue Yossi Ben-Hanan at Tel Shams during the Yom Kippur War.

But by one-thirty in the morning, the plane had still not arrived and Defense Minister Shimon Peres appeared with his own entourage. Kuti asked me to go over the plan's essentials for the defense minister. So once again, I recited the plan, tapping at the airport map hanging on the wall behind me and counting off "positions one, two, three, and four" for each of the squads.

"Here's the runway; the control tower will direct the plane to here," I pointed out, tapping at a runway marked on the map. Then I ran through the reasoning behind the chosen method.

"As always," I concluded, "if we take the initiative, we can control the events." With that, I ended the briefing.

"Does anyone here want to comment?" Peres asked from his position at the rear of the small hall. Nobody spoke up. Peres looked around. "Anyone here take part in the Sabena operation?" he tried.

Danny, sitting on the floor to my right, raised his hand.

"Do you want to make any comment on the plan?" the defense minister asked the soldier.

"No," Danny said, shaking his head.

"Well then," Peres said. "I wish you all luck." But instead of leaving, he asked Kuti, me, Ran Bag, and Yanosh Ben-Gal into a side room.

"Why this way and not the Sabena method?" the defense minister asked as soon as the door closed behind us. Kuti nodded at me to provide the answer. For the third time in an hour I ran through the explanation about not wanting to repeat the same tactic twice.

When I finished, Kuti spoke up. "They demonstrated it last week to the general staff," he said. "It works."

"Okay," Peres finally decided. "Approved."

We settled in to wait for the plane's appearance. But as the night wore on, so did reports that the plane did not head east toward Israel. It went south, over the Sahara, into Africa, and far from our purview. They might still be coming our way, we figured, on a surprise route over southern Egypt and then up the Red Sea. But by dawn the plane had disappeared into central Africa, and we finally called off the alert at the airport, and headed back to base.

THE IDF OPTION

Around noon on Monday, a foreign radio report provided surprising news. The Air France plane had landed in Uganda, at Entebbe airport, where President, Field Marshall, and erstwhile Israeli paratrooper Idi Amin Dada (who never did jump and didn't deserve the wings) offered his services as a mediator for the release of the plane, its passengers, and the terrorists in our jails.

In the years since he threw us out of Uganda so ignominiously, his appearances on the international stage had grown increasingly bizarre. He took dozens of women from the villages of his country to serve in a harem and fed his political opponents to crocodiles living on the banks of Lake Victoria. Ambassadors out of favor were made to kneel before him if their government wanted good relations with Uganda, a country rich in natural resources. Yet despite his bizarre behavior the Organization of African Unity chose Amin as its chairman for 1976.

Extremely sketchy reports came in from Uganda, mostly from the BBC, relying on stringers in Kampala, the capital. Amin's first declarations said he wanted to mediate the dispute. It was impossible to determine if he let the plane land because the pilot said he desperately needed fuel or because Amin was aligned with the terrorists. In any case, he had already proved his treachery to us in the past.

In the afternoon, the BBC reported the terrorists had allowed the hostages off the plane. Later the BBC said the terrorists had hustled the passengers into the old terminal building at Entebbe airport. And that Amin had surrounded the building with what he called his best troops—the paratroops I had begun training four years earlier.

By mid-Monday, the terrorists released their demands: $5 million in cash and a hostages-for-prisoners exchange on the tarmac at Entebbe. They wanted terrorists freed from jails in Kenya, France, Switzerland, Germany, and of course Israel. They set a deadline of Thursday at one in the afternoon, and their demand for the release of their jailed comrades from the Bader-Meinhof gang confirmed that the operation was a clear-cut case of international cooperation by terrorist groups. Amin immediately proposed that the government in Jerusalem surrender to the terrorists by releasing their comrades in exchange for the hostages. Rabin's government kept referring the matter publicly to the French government as being responsible for the safety of passengers aboard an airplane from the French national carrier's fleet.

I knew the troops and the airport. Not only had I flown in and out of Uganda through that airfield, I visited it on routine supply missions during my three months in Jinja, meeting incoming military air transports from Israel bringing supplies to our delegation. I wasn't surprised when Ehud Barak's office called, asking me to attend a meeting about the hijacking. Now assistant to the chief of Intelligence, responsible for research and special operations, he worked out of a Defense Ministry office a few floors above the Pit.

Coming into his office, I saw the IDF's leading counterterrorism experts—Sayeret Matkal veteran Amnon Biran, now an intelligence-branch major; Amiram Levine, Ido Embar, and Gadi Shefi, who began planning an attack on Libya when the plane landed in Benghazi; Lietenant Colonel Ran Bag and Haim "Ivan" Oron, both from the staff of Dan Shomron's chief infantry and paratroops Command in the IDF. We were all friends and colleagues from past operations.

They filled the chairs around the T-shaped table, with Ehud leaning back in the seat at the top of the T. He smiled at me standing in the doorway. "Muki, you know Entebbe. What do you think of Ugandan soldiers?" he asked.

"They must be good," I said. "After all, I trained them." It raised a laugh around the table.

But then Ehud's expression changed. "How good?"

"They're afraid of the night. In the best of circumstances they don't have much in the way of motivation. In this case? I really don't see what motivation they'd have to fight us." I rattled it off as I saw it.

Ehud grinned as if I had just proved the point he was making before my arrival.

I went on. "So, I don't think Ugandan soldiers will be our problem." Then I thought of something. "You know, Solel Boneh built the terminal," referring to the Israeli construction firm.

"We already sent for the plans," said Ehud. And with that, the planning for the Entebbe rescue mission began.

No order came down from the government, or even the general staff, for the planning to begin. Although from the start air force commander Benny Peled told a meeting of the general staff that the air force could be ready in twenty-four hours to fly to Entebbe for a rescue, without any solid intelligence from Entebbe, issuing an order for a rescue operation was impossible.

Indeed, with the hijacked plane so far away, the top ranks of the entire IDF—except for those of us in Ehud's office—continued functioning as previously scheduled. Chief of staff Motta Gur kept to his schedule. So did Kuti, as chief of Operations the deputy chief of staff, as did Dan Shomron, the chief infantry and paratroops commander.

But meanwhile we worked. The telephones rang constantly, and information flowed into the office. An engineer from Solel Boneh provided the original plans, sworn to secrecy and astonished to find himself part of a planning team for what appeared to be an impossible mission.

We called in pilots who had flown the Israel-Uganda shuttle in the years we maintained a mission, and brought in former IDF flight trainers who had trained Uganda's little air force. We made extensive use of international directories of the world's civilian airports, used by all commercial pilots. The directory gave us an up-to-date picture of Entebbe airport, where the Ugandans had added a new terminal about two kilometers away from the old one, as well as a new runway to handle eleven MiGs—not Mirages—the Libyans had given them.

The enthusiasm for the operation infected everyone. From the start, we felt we had almost everything we needed to make it work:

pilots who knew the route, knowledge of the airport, and of course, our special skills in hostage situations.

The seven of us became the ad hoc operations group, making plans for a military solution to the hijacking. We had all worked together in the past on missions—those we executed and those scotched at the last minute, those that never went beyond theory to those we practiced and honed but never set into real motion.

More than colleagues or associates, we felt like members of a team in which we all knew our positions, with a natural dynamic of give-and-take. Sometimes it felt like a Ping-Pong game, with someone throwing out an idea and someone else hitting it back with a spin. Sometimes it felt like a basketball team, passing ideas like a ball down-court. With each pass the idea developed a new twist that enhanced the plan.

I called in Amnon M., one of my reservist officers, to act as my intelligence officer for the planning, and Bicho, another reservist officer, to be operations officer. They would stick with me throughout the coming week as my assistants, putting together the dossier for action.

It went on all night, over endless coffees and teas, with Ehud subtly directing the brainstorming. But over and over we came across major problems, holes in the intelligence. The biggest was that we still did not know what Idi Amin wanted. Even states like Libya and Iran, which sponsor terrorism, pay public lip service to peaceful air traffic. But Amin remained totally unpredictable.

The intelligence officers noted that Amin was due to chair an upcoming meeting of the Organization of African Unity, scheduled to open in Sudan at the weekend. The hijacking guaranteed just what he wanted—an international stage. Meanwhile, his statements to the press promised his guarantee of the hostages' safety—but pleaded with Israel to agree to accept the terrorists' demands.

All of us in that room during that long first night of thinking about Entebbe felt a tremendous responsibility. If Jerusalem gave in to an exchange, our humiliation would be a victory for terrorists everywhere.

By dawn we had moved to the Pit with four plans sketched out. Advantages and disadvantages accompanied each one. All depended on surprise.

At the top of our list we put a parachute drop into Lake Victoria, a combined operation with fighters from the Shayetet. Landing in the water and riding into shore on Zodiacs para-dropped into the lake, we could reach the shore, where the airport sat at the edge of a swamp on the lake's banks. We would move into the airport on foot, overcome the terrorists, and then give ourselves up to the Ugandans. The plan assumed Amin wanted a rescue to relieve him of responsibility.

The second plan depended heavily on Israel's diplomatic ties with Kenya, one of the few Third World countries that maintained relations with us in those years. A lake-faring ship could carry us across Lake Victoria to Entebbe. Like the first plan, our going in by ship assumed Amin wanted a rescue as much as we did.

So did the third plan. The terrorists wanted a prisoner exchange at Entebbe. We could give them one. If we painted an air force Boeing with civilian colors, put together some uniforms for the pilots, and disguised soldiers from Sayeret Matkal as prisoners, we could come out of the plane fighting. But again, the success of this plan depended on Amin guaranteeing us safe passage out of Uganda.

Indeed, all three blueprints for action also required the major involvement of the Mossad, whether arranging affairs in Kenya, dealing with the other countries holding terrorists the hijackers wanted freed, or getting us Air France uniforms.

So, while we put the Mossad on to those ideas, we dubbed our fourth design "the IDF option."

A straightforward show of force, it called for flying into the African country with enough soldiers to hold off hostile Ugandan troops while we eliminated the terrorists, collected the passengers, and flew out.

But the larger the fleet flying to Uganda, the more likely its discovery. The flight down the Red Sea and then west into central Africa took us within radar—and fighter—range of three Arab countries sworn to our destruction.

Ido Embar's confidence that the air force could do the job inspired us all. The planes needed to fly more than eight hours—with a large portion of the flight within radar range of enemy countries: Saudi Arabia, Sudan, and, of course, Egypt—the largest and most powerful of our Arab enemies at the time.

Furthermore, he convinced me a plane could land unnoticed in an airport. "Believe me," he said. "I live on an air force base. I know what I'm talking about. If a plane manages to avoid radar detection up to its landing, it could land and come to a quiet halt at the end of a runway without anyone noticing."

His idea became a cornerstone of an air operation. Just in case the Entebbe air traffic controllers did pick us up on radar and ask for identification, we could name a regularly scheduled flight in the area. But ideally, we wanted to land in radio silence, without any contact with the control tower. And we needed to work on the assumption that the Ugandans might turn off their runway landing lights, whether to save electricity or foil just such an unexpected landing. We needed camouflage.

Ehud assigned each member of the team a job appropriate to his skills and function in the army. As Sayeret Matkal's representative, I became responsible for all aspects of the plan involving the break-in force that would eliminate the terrorists and free the hostages.

"Battalion commanders in the Ugandan Army ride around in Mercedeses with chauffeurs and a couple of Land Rovers of soldiers behind them," I suggested. "With that disguise, we could drive through into any military installation in the country without stopping. By the time they figure out who we really are, we'll be on the job."

Indeed, my suggestion for the Mercedes became the second cornerstone of all the plans. The Mossad, at work on what we needed if we decided to sneak into Entebbe, whether disguised as terrorists aboard a faked civilian plane or on board a ship carrying us across Lake Victoria from Kenya, added it to their plans.

But we took things a step further with them, pressing them for up-to-date photographs of the airport. We had the plans for the old terminal, where the hijackers held the hostages. But even the Jeffison airport directory only gave us a schematic map of the airport, with little about the buildings, very little about the Ugandan military presence at the airport, and nothing about the squadron of MiGs the Libyans had given Amin. And since Amin threw us out of Uganda in 1972, no Israeli had visited the country.

Defense Minister Peres called in Burka Bar-Lev, the former mission chief in Uganda. Amin had always liked Burka and now,

Peres hoped, Burka's conversations with Amin could reveal the Ugandan dictator's intentions. Peres listened in on the conversations, taking notes, looking for a clue to Amin's position. Burka reminded the crazy dictator that Amin's mother, on her deathbed, told her son "never to betray the Jews." Burka even promised Amin a Nobel Peace Prize if he released the hostages. Amin sounded tempted, and continued claiming innocence in the affair. But he told Burka that Israel should accept all the terrorists' demands.

We still did not know if Amin was in cahoots with the terrorists or whether the terrorists had hijacked his airport along with the passengers on board the Air France flight. But some new intelligence arrived that told us a little more about the terrorists.

A woman with dual Israeli-British citizenship, on her way to London, managed to get off the plane in Libya. A doctor on board the plane convinced the plane's captors that the woman needed hospitalization due to a complicated pregnancy. They agreed to let her off the plane. Reaching London, she contacted the Israeli embassy and gave her account of the hijacking, describing in detail everything she remembered.

According to the woman, two Germans and two Palestinian teenagers had pulled out their guns about ten minutes out of Athens. She reported that the German man led the hijacking. The German woman was being particularly vicious to the Jewish passengers, whether Israeli, European, or American. The woman's information helped us profile the four terrorists, but with the hostages now in Uganda, her report about what happened inside the plane and on the ground at Benghazi was old news.

In the Pit, under the Defense Ministry, day and night merged as we worked around the clock. Early Wednesday morning, Defense Minister Peres called Ehud to his office. Peres was pressing hard for a military solution to the hijacking, but Prime Minister Rabin, a soldier since his youth, knew that wanting an operation was not the same as being capable of producing one.

But Ehud could only report what the old Uganda hands remembered, what the Jeffison directory said about the airport, and what the radio reported about Ugandan Army troops surrounding the airport. And despite Burka Bar-Lev's conversations with Amin, we still could not be sure if the Ugandan troops at the airport were protecting the hostages from the terrorists, preventing their escape, or on guard against a rescue attempt.

I kept in touch with Yonni down in Sinai, to keep him up-to-date on our work. If things heated up, he'd come back, we decided. I told Bicho, the reservist operations officer, to make arrangements for the air force to keep a light plane or chopper available around the clock if necessary to bring Yonni back from Sinai.

Meanwhile, the work went on. The Shayetet naval commandos planned a practice jump with para-dropped Zodiacs into the Mediterranean. For the first time since the planning began, I left the Pit to collect my gear for the jump. But as I pulled up in the parking lot outside my office at Sayeret Matkal's base, a secretary ran out to the car with a message sending me back to the planning group.

I called back to the Pit, wondering what news had come in since I left. "The para-drop can't work," I was told about the plan to drop Zodiacs into Lake Victoria. "At least not yet." Ironically, only a few months later, I would see a drill in which para-dropped boats worked perfectly.

With the parachute drop off our list, we worked on three plans: stealing across Lake Victoria by boat from Kenya; pretending to be a civilian plane carrying the freed international terrorists in a negotiated exchange; or, as Benny Peled suggested from the start, airlifting a thousand troops to Entebbe.

"But it's too many," I kept saying about a major airlift. "If we want to keep the element of surprise on our side, we need to arrive in a much more compact formation. The more elements involved in the mission, the more likely something will go wrong." In any case, with the terrorists' deadline set for Thursday, July 1, it looked like we were running out of time.

None of the governments involved wanted to appear to cave in first, but as the appointed hour approached, it seemed more likely than ever that the Europeans were cutting a deal. Wednesday afternoon, radio reports, first from Uganda and then Paris, said the terrorists had agreed to free some hostages "as a gesture of goodwill." But as the details came in, we learned that there was no goodwill in the gesture for us. Indeed, our worst fears were coming true.

The terrorists, led by the German whom we now knew to be Wilfried Boese, a member of the Bader-Meinhof gang, distinguished between the Jews and non-Jews among the hostages. He freed the non-Jews. The Jews remained in Uganda. To their credit, the Air France flight crew stayed with the remaining hostages.

It reminded us all of the Nazi *selektzia*, the process whereby they selected who would die and who would live in the concentration camps. The discrimination between Jews and non-Jews proved to us that we were alone.

But the freed hostages in Paris could provide important intelligence. We immediately decided to send someone to Paris to interview them. The natural candidate for the trip was Lt. Col. Amiram Levine, at the time director of operations planning in Military Intelligence.

Amiram, the blond dervish of Spring of Youth in Beirut, rose through the Unit: from soldier through crew commander, company commander, deputy commander of the Unit, to next in line to replace Yonni as commander. Eventually, he would go on to become a general, commander of the Northern Command. Someone who can be dropped anywhere and immediately know how to get around, Amiram knew what to ask to get the answers we needed.

Amnon Biran provided Amiram with an intelligence kit for the trip. Amnon organized the Solel Boneh blueprints, and in a neat, clear handwriting he listed the essential elements of information that interested us, attaching a set of drawings based on what we knew about Entebbe airport. While Biran coded and photocopied the material, Amiram rushed home for civilian clothes and then came back for a final briefing before flying to Paris.

One unexpected problem faced him. Rabin sent his adviser on terrorism to Paris to handle Israel's side of the political negotiations in case of a hostage-for-prisoner exchange. Former general Rehavam "Gandhi" Zeevi knew nothing of a military plan in the works. If he saw Amiram at Orly Airport, he would immediately understand that a military option was being planned. It could affect his judgment during the negotiations. So, we reminded Amiram, "No matter what, don't let Gandhi see you."

That night, forty-two freed French hostages celebrated with their families and friends at home. With help from the French government and the Israeli embassy in Paris, Amiram managed to meet with five of the hostages. Without revealing that Israel was planning a rescue, Amiram questioned them, digging for the kinds of details we needed. One of the five freed hostages was a veteran officer of the French Army, who had spent his three days in Entebbe making mental notes of all the military options, wanting revenge on the terrorists who so humiliated him and his fellow passengers. Reading between the lines of Amiram's questioning, the retired French officer understood Israel planned a rescue. Displaying a prodigious memory, the Frenchman poured out a gold mine of details for Amiram to relay back to us over a scrambled phone line.

The *selektzia* began when Ugandan soldiers silently came into the terminal and broke a hole through the main hall into a smaller room. The terrorists then ordered the Israelis and Jews into the much smaller room.

The terrorists maintained round-the-clock guards on the hostages, said the Frenchman, who described what appeared to be explosive charges laid out throughout the room.

But the most critical piece of information concerned the relationship between the terrorists and the Ugandans. First of all, Amiram reported, while four terrorists had hijacked the plane, at least another six had showed up in Entebbe when the hostages landed. That meant we faced as many as ten terrorists. It also meant that Amin was involved.

"The Ugandans definitely are working with the hijackers," Amiram quoted the Frenchman as saying. "They are there to prevent the hostages from escaping." But, Amiram added hopefully, "from what the Frenchman's saying, the last thing that the terrorists expect is for us to show up."

Ships across Lake Victoria or fake identities as Palestinian terrorists aboard a plane painted to look like a civilian jet—all the other planning suddenly become irrelevant. With the product from Amiram's gold mine, everything became clear: the only plan that counted involved landing at the airport, freeing the hostages, and flying out.

I went to Col. Shai Tamari, then assistant to Kuti Adam. "I suggest dropping everything else and working only on the IDF option," I said, briefing him quickly on what we had learned from the retired French officer.

He reached across his desk for the button on the direct intercom to Kuti's desk. "Here's what we have," Shai told Kuti, outlining the scope of information the Frenchman had provided and how it narrowed our options down to the airborne rescue.

Despite all the pressure on him from Motta Gur to come up with a plan to bring to the government, Kuti remained calm. "I want a written brief on all four options," he said over the intercom. "*All four plans,*" he emphasized, "including the failed naval one. I want a concise report on the advantages and disadvantages of each one."

Shai and I looked at each other impatiently. But Shai shrugged, and pulled out a clean sheet of paper. With the rest of the team now crowded in around him in case he had a question, he neatly and concisely listed all four options, with their pluses and minuses in meticulously drawn columns. Finished, he nodded to himself, looked up, and announced he was off to see Kuti.

It only took a few minutes before he was back with authorization. We finally could get down to details.

The radio played constantly in the office. Every hour we all paused to listen to the latest news. The government appeared impotent. Demonstrations by anguished relatives of the hostages turned violent outside the prime minister's office. With 104 Israelis and Jews held hostage, the entire country shared the anxiety of the families. Nobody in the media even raised the possibility of a military solution. Indeed, they discounted it because of the huge distances involved. But while those of us deep in the Pit could feel the frustration of the people outside, we had an important advantage over everyone else. At least we could work on turning a theoretical possibility to free the hostages into a real plan of action.

Nonetheless, the gap remained large between planning an operation and reaching a reasonable level of feasibility in its execution. Until Rabin saw a feasible plan, he would not recommend a military solution to the government. Feasibility meant a minimum of casualties and a successful escape from Uganda.

When the clock struck one o'clock in the afternoon that Thursday, reaching the deadline set by the terrorists, Jerusalem surprised the world by announcing a reversal of the years' long policy of never negotiating with terrorists.

Made with a heavy heart, the government's statement noted that such an exchange takes time to arrange, and called on the terrorists to extend their deadline.

A few hours later, while we redoubled our efforts, the terrorists announced a new deadline—one in the afternoon on July 4, seventy-two hours away. It gave us the extra bit of time we needed.

All Thursday we worked on the compromise between the need for an unobtrusive airlift and the need for the firepower necessary to take the airport from the Ugandan Army.

Ido Embar calculated and recalculated fuel and cargo weights for the Hercules transport planes recently acquired from the Americans. I concentrated on the most important cargo the first of those planes would be delivering to Entebbe—the Unit—planning the landing, the ride to the terminal, the break-in, the elimination of the terrorists, freeing of the hostages, and holding the building against Ugandan opposition until the arrival of troops from the second plane in our air convoy. I had to find ways to minimize the size of that "package" while maximizing the amount of firepower we could bring.

Amiram's French gold mine continued to yield important intelligence. For example, we learned that at midnight, the terrorists ordered the hostages to lie down on the straw mattresses the Ugandans provided. By one in the morning, most indeed slept. The hour gave us a cornerstone for our timetable.

With the hostages at the old terminal, Entebbe's international airport remained open and operating at the new terminal, about a mile away from where the hostages languished. A regularly scheduled British cargo flight was due to fly into Entebbe a little after midnight on Saturday night. We decided to sneak in behind the British plane, before the Ugandans turned off the runway lights.

By Thursday afternoon we narrowed the mission down to four Herculeses, with each plane loaded far past its recommended capacity. We needed the break-in crews on the first plane to take out the terrorists, neutralize any interfering Ugandan troops, and hold the old terminal until the second Hercules landed seven minutes later with reinforcements, including two armored vehicles.

Booty from the Yom Kippur War, the Soviet-made APCs, known as BTRs, were lighter than our usual APCs but carried plenty of firepower to protect a perimeter around the old terminal building.

Once the second plane landed, the third and fourth would immediately follow. The third plane would carry more reinforcements, including two more BTRs, while the fourth plane was devoted to medical facilities. We prepared for 25 percent casualties among the hostages and the soldiers. The break-in and rescue were to take no more than seven minutes, but the planes would need an hour on the ground to refuel from the airport's fuel depots—unless the Kenyans agreed to let us refuel at Nairobi airport after the operation. But to preserve field security, no mention of the operation could be made to the Kenyans until we landed at Entebbe.

Dan Shomron, chief infantry and paratroops officer, arrived in the Pit at four in the afternoon on Thursday, for the first time joining the ad hoc planning group Ehud put together. He knew nothing of the four plans we began with, let alone the details of our plan for only four planes. He began with an explanation that he figured ten planes would be necessary for the job, and I lost my patience.

"Dan, I think there is a misunderstanding here," I began. He raised an eyebrow, but I plunged on. "You're making it sound as if we are going to start planning. We're almost done with the planning. We don't need hundreds of soldiers. Let us brief you on the essentials of the plan, give you an idea of what we have. Then you can make up your mind."

In the Pit's war-room, the walls were covered with the documentation of our planning: old aerial photos taken in the days when Israeli planes flew into Entebbe, up-to-date civilian flight paths for East Africa, architectural schematics of the old terminal building provided by Solel Boneh, outlines of the intelligence provided by the French officer through Amiram.

I gave the floor to Amnon Biran, the chief intelligence officer for the operation. He detailed the intelligence in our hands for Dan, running down everything we knew, from the Solel Boneh architectural plans to Amiram Levine product from Paris.

Then it was Ido Embar's turn, as air force branch chief for combined operations. He didn't need to point out that the IDF had never undertaken an operation so far from home. He emphasized that the best planes for the job were the U.S.-made Herculeses we nicknamed Rhinos. They were also relatively new planes in the air force fleet at the time. So, only four Hercules crews fully trained for a night landing in an unfamiliar airport were available in all of Israel, he explained.

Nonetheless, his expression of the air force's confidence in its ability to deliver us to Entebbe—and get us and the hostages back—inspired us all. For the infantrymen in the planning group, the conceptual hurdle of the vast distance to Uganda was one of the biggest problems to overcome. Ido's confidence made us certain. "We can land the first plane without the Ugandans noticing—or thinking something's amiss," Ido summed up, just as he had promised those of us planning the break-in. More than anything, our operation depended on the Ugandans—and the terrorists—not knowing we had arrived, at least until we eliminated the terrorists.

"If we can reach the terminal in secret," I said, picking up from where Ido left off, "we can succeed." It had been my motto from the start.

Dan's expression said he was waiting for me to explain how we would get to the old terminal without being detected. "The break-in force from the Unit will land in the first plane. It's a kilometer and a half from the new terminal building to the old one. We're going to drive."

He raised his eyebrow. I went on. "I know the Ugandan soldiers," I told him. "I trained them. We don't need hundreds of soldiers. Instead we use a Mercedes. Every battalion commander in Uganda rides around in one. A soldier spots a Mercedes, he snaps to a salute. They'll see us in the Mercedes with a couple of Land Rovers carrying soldiers, and they'll assume a general's about to drive by. They aren't going to shoot to stop us." I smiled at him. "You know, it's possible I'll run into one of the soldiers I trained," I pointed out.

"It's lucky you trained them for only four months and not four years," someone in the room cracked back.

We all laughed, but I wanted to make a serious point. "While we're driving to the target, we'll probably see Ugandan troops, and they'll probably see us. We can ignore them. Indeed, for the plan to work, we must ignore them, to avoid alerting the terrorists to our

247

arrival. That's what makes a hostage situation so unique," I explained, speaking as one of the four Sayeret Matkal officers at the time who were capable of commanding a hostage-rescue force. "Our first concern must be eliminating the terrorists—or else they'll start harming the hostages. We're not going all that way to fight Ugandans. We're going down there to eliminate the terrorist threat to the hostages.

"So," I went on, "even if a Ugandan soldier sees through our disguise and starts shooting, we should speed on to the terminal, to the break-in. Only then should the backup force deal with the Ugandans, while the break-in crews do their job.

"So, to sum up," I said. "Five minutes for us to drive across the airfield to the old terminal. Two minutes for the break-in. Seven minutes after we land, the second and third planes come in carrying reinforcements. In an hour, we're all on our way home."

Dan has a lot of field experience. To his credit, he immediately understood the operational principles of the plan.

Just then, a messenger came in with the message that Kuti wanted to hear the plan so he could take it to Motta and Peres.

"Ivan," Dan said to the colonel from his staff who had been on the job with us from the start. "Grab the maps. Let's go."

Ido, Amnon, Ivan, Dan, and I headed for Kuti's office, a few floors above the underground war-room. Kuti was waiting for us in the corridor outside his office.

"Can you present the plan in a minute?" he asked Dan, who ten minutes before knew nothing of it.

"Sure," Dan said confidently.

"Good. Motta's waiting for us with the defense minister."

Everything picked up speed at that point as we marched down the corridor to the minister's office. For a moment, the last four nights and five days flashed before my eyes—all the work, all the effort, all the hopes. I could see it coming together. Our plan already slated one in the morning on Saturday night as the moment the first Hercules touched down at Entebbe. It was getting hot. Time to call Yonni.

As we reached Peres's office I told Bicho to get the light plane the air force had promised us into the air to pick up Yonni. While the rest of the officers trooped into Peres's office to make the presentation, I called down to Sinai. "Grab your kit and get over to the airfield," I told him as soon as we finally patched through.

"It's hot?" he asked.

"It's hot."

As I hung up, a beaming Dan Shomron came out of Peres's office and announced that the full plenum of the government would, of course, vote on final approval, but meanwhile we proceed full-steam ahead. He called an 8 P.M. meeting that night at the Paratroopers' House in Ramat Gan, a small civic center built in the memory of the IDF's fallen paratroopers. I immediately called back down to Yonni, telling him to come straight to the Paratroopers' House at eight.

Ido and Amnon came out of the office behind Dan. I asked them what I missed inside Peres's office. "Dan was a hundred percent," Ido said. "He presented the plan as if he had planned it himself. Peres asked everyone what we thought. So Dan added something. 'If we can reach the terminal in secret, we can succeed.' Exactly what you told him."

Thursday night, officers from the signals corps and the medical corps as well as commanding officers from Golani and the paratroops brigades joined us as Dan went over the order of battle from top to bottom, filling in the details of the plan.

The first Hercules rolls down the runway. A dozen paratroopers, under Matan Vilnai, run out the rear doors, laying electric lanterns along the side of the runway in case the Ugandans turn off the landing lights.

Disguised as a convoy of Ugandan troops in a Mercedes and two Land Rovers, a break-in force from the Unit, under the command of a regimental commander, drive off the plane to the old terminal building. Headlights on, they travel at normal speed to the old terminal building. That takes five minutes. Another two minutes should suffice for taking out the terrorists and securing the building.

Exactly seven minutes after the first plane lands, the second Hercules lands, carrying reinforcements: a second group of Sayeret Matkal fighters aboard two BTRs, commanded by Shaul Mofaz. His force patrols a perimeter around the old terminal.

The third plane lands a minute later, carrying two more BTRs manned by Sayeret Matkal fighters, plus more of Matan's paratroopers, plus a contingent of Golani troops under Uri Saguy. The paratroops take the new terminal building, the refueling station at the airport, and guard the new runway. One BTR, commanded by Omer Bar-Lev, takes the MiG airfield beside the old terminal, while the fourth joins Mofaz to patrol around the old terminal.

The Golani forces meanwhile cover the area between the old terminal and the new, and stand by to help the freed hostages on board the first Hercules. Medical crews on the fourth plane, carrying field hospitals, begin treating any casualties, who are then ferried by Land Rover to the plane, guarded by the Golani troops.

A second flying hospital in a converted Boeing 727 meanwhile lands in Nairobi, where the Kenyan government has been informed of the operation and asked for permission to land all four Hercules aircraft leaving Uganda.

During the entire operation, somewhere in the skies over Entebbe, a converted Boeing command-and-control plane carries Kuti, Benny Peled, and a host of radio technicians keeping communications open with the Pit in Tel Aviv.

Dan selected Sayeret Matkal's headquarters as the base of operation for all the forces involved. With our own runway to practice on and the strictest field security of any base in the army, we were also not too far from the airport from which the Herculeses would take off.

From the moment Dan ended his briefing, anyone on the base was to stay there until after the mission. All but the most necessary phone lines in the base were cut to prevent leaks, while the remaining few were monitored.

As Dan wrapped up his summary, Yonni burst through the doors. His smile made me realize I had missed him the week he was away. Our experiences together had created a friendship that transcended the differences between a farmer from the Jezreel Valley and someone educated in America.

We had shared so much—from the capture of the Syrian officers through Spring of Youth and the Yom Kippur War. I got up from the long table to shake hands with him, and we remained standing, eager to get going. Dan wrapped up his briefing, and we were on our way.

I rode with Yonni in his car back to the base, not wanting to lose a minute of time. Yonni knew nothing about the entire week. He had been in another place, another country, another operation. He was always very reserved, but when he became enthusiastic about an idea, he had a little chortle of excitement. As I outlined the plan, his little bursts of laughter punctuated my speech as I described how each element fit into the next.

Back at the base, Amnon M. handed over the dossier he had prepared during the week. A folder full of all the paperwork, it contained everything from Amiram Levine's reports on the French gold mine to the architectural plans of the old terminal building. Yonni quickly took up the baton and was conducting the Unit's operations for the plan, naming me his deputy for the operation, as well as commander of the four break-in teams. As deputy, my job was to fill in for him whenever he was absent. As commander of the break-in teams, the responsibility for success fell on my shoulders. Remembering the mistakes we had made at Ma'alot, I told him I wanted to be in the first break-in crew.

"C'mon, Muki, you know it's against doctrine." That was true. I was too senior an officer to be risked as first into the fire. But I didn't want a repeat of Ma'alot, where afterward I realized I should have gone up the ladder first. I wanted to make sure the job was done properly. "I insist upon it," I said bluntly to Yonni.

He knew me well enough not to argue. "You're impossible," he sighed, accepting my condition.

In overall command of the break-in teams, I broke them down first into three teams. Giora Zussman's team was assigned the VIP lounge, which the Frenchman had said the terrorists used as a rest area. We assigned the second floor, where Ugandan troops bivouacked, to Yiftah, Yonni's new deputy. I would take care of the main hall, where the terrorists held the hostages. I broke down the break-in team for the main hall into two separate teams, one for each of the entrances to the hall from the tarmac.

With only fifteen soldiers in four break-in crews, and another nineteen outside holding off a Ugandan opposition, Yonni's command-and-control post would remain outside, responsible for all the Unit's forces on the ground. A doctor, David Hessin, plus Tamir Prado, our communications officer, and Alek Ron, a reservist company commander, would stay outside during the break-in, to help fend off any Ugandan opposition.

The entire operation hinged on delivering the four break-in crews quietly to the front door of the terminal. While Yonni spent the night writing the order of battle, I put soldiers to work building a model of the terminal building according to Solel Boneh's architectural plans. Using two-by-fours for a frame, we hung burlap and canvas sheets to simulate the exterior and interior walls and doorways of the terminal building. As soon as it stood alongside our runway, just like in Entebbe, we began practicing.

All night, troops from the Golani and the paratroops brigade converged on our base, to begin practicing their function in the operation. Blue-uniformed air force techies responsible for handling the refueling from Idi Amin's fuel dumps stood out among all the green combat fatigues. But doing their best to keep up, the techies threw themselves into the drills and rehearsals alongside the combat fighters. At dawn the air force landed a Hercules on our runway, and we added its element to our drills.

Mid-morning, a white seven-seater Mercedes that obviously had seen better days as a taxi pulled into base. Danny Dagan, the Unit's munitions and automotive expert, inspected it with a grumble.

"It needs a lot of work," he said about the car that came off a used-car lot in Tel Aviv.

"Whatever it needs," I told him. "But just make sure it works for the ride from the plane to the terminal. Put in a second ignition, just in case. And," I added, "paint it black."

According to the Frenchman, the terrorists had put a permanent guard at one point in the hall, right beside the entrance where I would lead my break-in crews. But he had said to expect at least four to six terrorist guards with the hostages, and another two to four in the VIP room at the end of the building.

The memory of Ma'alot was uppermost in our minds. Again and again I drilled the essential concept into the troops. "When the Ugandan soldiers see the Mercedes, they are going to assume it is an officer's," I drummed into the troops. "They won't try to stop a senior officer," I emphasized. "As far as they are concerned, we will look just like a Ugandan brigadier and his escort. They are not going to shoot at us—at least not until we start shooting. And even if they aren't sure about our identity, the dilemma will make them hesitate long enough for us to reach the terminal.

"But, if for any reason they do start shooting," I told the break-in crews, "let the backup crews handle it. We concentrate on the break-in, eliminating the terrorists and then defending the hostages until the time comes to get them on the plane."

Two elements that became important in our planning evolved during those hours of drilling. We decided that one member of the two break-in crews slated for the main hall would be carrying a megaphone to shout, in Hebrew and English, "Everyone lie down! This is the IDF. Lie down!" when we entered the hall. And to prevent accidents, since we'd be wearing leopard-spot fatigues like Ugandan paratroopers, we decided that once the firefight began, we'd all pull on white caps, to identify friendly forces.

Chief of staff Motta Gur moved into a tent headquarters beside the tarmac at our base on Friday to watch the drilling with Dan Shomron. They studied us shortening the landing-to-break-in time-table minute by minute until we did it in less than seven minutes from start to finish.

For those seven minutes we would be alone on the ground. As long as we kept the initiative, we could finish off the terrorists and hold off the Ugandans, until the second plane landed with reinforcements, including the light armor.

Motta grilled Yonni and me over and over with questions. At one point, he decided that we had packed too many soldiers onto the Land Rovers and told us to remove two from each vehicle.

"They'll never forgive us if they miss this," I told Yonni, taking him aside after Motta issued his order.

"What do we do?" Yonni asked.

"At least offer a compromise," I told Yonni. "Tell him we'll give up two riders, not four. Tell him we need every extra man in case another regiment of Ugandans shows up."

Sure enough, Yonni convinced Motta that the Land Rovers could handle the load without attracting attention. But breaking the news to the two fighters Motta made us leave behind was not easy.

Much also depended on the skills of the pilot in the first plane. We wanted him to land a plane with neither its own lights nor landing lights on the runway. The lead pilot for the first plane, Yehoshua Shani, backed up by an old Uganda hand, Ram Levi, told Motta confidently he could do it.

"Prove it," Motta demanded. "Fly me down to Ofira and land me there in the dark." At the southernmost tip of the Sinai Peninsula, the Ofira airport, like Entebbe's, had a landing approach over water.

While Motta flew south, we continued practicing through the night. The Mercedes and two Land Rovers ready, we began fitting all the pieces together, from rolling off the Hercules to the ride across the tarmac to the terminal, coming to a halt in front of the building a few yards from the front doors. Yonni and I worked with stopwatches, keeping track of the time, making the soldiers run it over and over until everything clicked into place. The eight-hour flight to Entebbe would give us plenty of time for sleep.

When Motta returned, Yonni and I went to see him in his command tent.

"I made them land twice, just to make sure," Motta told us. "It went perfectly," he said. "How are your boys doing?"

"It's working like a clock," Yonni said.

Other commanding officers for the mission—Dan, Matan Vilnai, Uri Saguy, Ephraim Sneh, the medical officer in charge of the field hospitals—trooped into Motta's tent. They all reported that their forces were ready.

In another few hours dawn would rise in the east, marking the last twenty-four hours before the terrorist deadline ran out. It was now or never. We all waited for Motta's decision. His usually dour expression broke into a grin. "The cabinet is meeting at nine this morning," he said. "I'm going to tell them we can do it."

But we went back to work, just to make sure we had it right. By eleven, the first troops began heading by bus to the airport, fifteen minutes away. The four Herculeses waited there for us, and would fly to Ofira, to top off the fuel tanks and wait for the final okay from the government.

We loaded the Land Rovers and the Mercedes onto two large trucks and drove them under canvas to the airport. The last thing we needed was someone noticing fake Ugandan license plates on a Mercedes limo driving through the quiet suburbs of Tel Aviv on a Saturday morning.

While the ground forces from the Unit, the paratroops, and Golani headed for the airport on their buses, I conducted a last meeting with the break-in crew commanders. Yonni stayed for a little while but, needed at the airport, he left early. I worked another half hour with the crew commanders, going over last-minute questions, until finally we were out of time. We went out to the bus to take us to the airport.

"Stop!" shouted one of my soldiers just as the bus reached the main gate.

"What happened?" I jumped up from my seat behind the driver.

He looked at me sheepishly and then down at his feet. "I forgot my boots." I told the driver to turn around. But before the driver could finish his U-turn, the soldier shouted, "Here they are!" pulling the boots from his duffel bag.

Yonni waited for us in the rear Hercules doorway, the other three Herculeses lined up beside the first, propellers already beginning to spin. Yonni watched the men march aboard, finding places to stow their gear and get comfortable on the cargo floor between the Mercedes, the two Land Rovers, and Dan Shomron's command-and-control jeep, which took up most of the space in the hold.

Just as the rear ramp of the plane began to rise, a jeep raced across the tarmac to our plane. A fighter from the Unit jumped out, running to the rear door waving an envelope.

The flight engineer took it and wound his way through the hold to Dan Shomron, up front in the cockpit with the pilots. A moment later, Dan called for Yonni and me to join him.

The envelope came from the Mossad, containing photographs shot from a light plane over Entebbe airport that week. The pictures were snapshots, raw data with no legends or explanations about the buildings in view. But they confirmed everything we knew.

Nonetheless, as our plane took off toward Sharm al-Sheikh, I wondered if the eleven MiGs we counted in the pictures would be in the air to meet us as we flew into Ugandan airspace.

BACK TO AFRICA

The flight to Sharm al-Sheikh was horrible, with air pockets all the way making the plane buck in the sky like an angry rhinoceros. Around me, troopers vomited into air sickness bags, turning the closed hold into a reeking den of unhappiness. If it went on like this all the way to Uganda, I worried to myself, we wouldn't be fit for the job.

The temperature at the tip of Sinai that morning was close to forty Celsius (104 Fahrenheit). But we were grateful for the fresh air—at least we could breathe.

One soldier in particular, designated for my break-in team, was obviously too sick for the trip. I called over Amos Goren, a soldier from one of the BTR crews, reassigning him to my break-in squad, quickly bringing him up-to-par with a description of his job.

We sat in the hot dry shade of a hangar, waited for the planes to be topped off with fuel and for the government, meeting in an extraordinary Sabbath session, to decide whether to give us the green light. But to keep to our schedule, we couldn't wait in Sinai for the okay. Just after one o'clock, Dan ordered us back on board the planes, which were retopped with fuel.

The turbulence flying down to Ofira still a rude memory, we boarded the planes apprehensively. But like during my boat ride to Beirut for Spring of Youth, the turbulence miraculously disappeared

256

as soon as we took off from Sharm and began heading south over the blue waters of the Red Sea.

Twenty minutes into the air, as we were flying low to avoid Egyptian radar detection, word came to Dan via Kuti in the command-and-control plane. The government gave its okay.

The boys curled up in corners of the plane, leaning against the car and the jeep, sacked out on the floor of the rumbling airplane. It's true of soldiers everywhere—given the chance, they can always find a way to fall asleep, no matter how noisy the surroundings.

Yonni and I bunked in the Mercedes. As usual, he carried a book in a pouch. But for the first hour we mainly talked about what each of us had missed during the week we were apart. He told me about the operation in Sinai, and I told him about the days and nights in the Pit, planning the rescue.

I told him how the first thing Ehud asked when he called me to the ad hoc task force was what I thought of Ugandan soldiers; how Shai Tamari handled all the coordination with the other forces, while Ido Embar handled the planning for the air force's role. I told him how we sent Amiram to Paris, and how the Mossad decided that it would not be safe for him to fly back on any airline other than El Al, so he got stuck in Paris, eating his heart out that he was missing the action.

But after a while, exhaustion from a sleepless week of non-stop preparation took over. I settled into a deep sleep. Over Kenya, a massive African thunder-and-lightning storm outside the plane woke me completely. Appropriate, I thought, smiling to myself, considering the IDF computers named the mission Operation Thunderball.

The storm reminded me of all that I missed in Africa. The sky flashed with streaks of lightning outside the small portals of the Hercules. The thunder clapped louder than the Hercules engines' rumble. The plane rocked unevenly through the sky. But for a little while I enjoyed the view, remembering the red skies of Jinja, until the storm receded as quickly as it had begun and it was time to get ready.

I checked my gear and moved around the plane, patting boys on the back, giving them a wink or a smile. I noticed one of the paratroops officers having difficulty buckling his web-belt. Coming closer, I saw his hands trembling as he tried to rush through the buckles.

I smiled at him. "Relax," I said, checking my watch. "We're still twenty minutes away," I added with a grin. His pale face seemed to regain its color in front of my eyes, and he smiled back.

We all carried lightweight gear: mostly Kalashnikov AK-47s and some Galils, Israel Military Industries assault rifles still in experimental form at the time. Those carrying special equipment, whether silenced pistols or megaphones, double-checked their equipment one last time.

Yonni moved among the soldiers, shaking hands and patting backs, until we found ourselves facing each other beside the Mercedes. We shook hands, grinning at each other, and then climbed into the car as the plane began its landing approach.

Nine of us, three per bench, were crammed into the Mercedes. I sat directly behind Amitzur, whom I knew from Nahalal. Yonni sat in the same row, beside the right-hand passenger door. The rest of the break-in crews were aboard the first Land Rover behind us, while the third vehicle carried the force to protect us from the Ugandans once the shooting began. Their first job would be to take out the control tower, with its commanding view of the tarmac in front of the old terminal. Motta emphasized the point to Yonni several times during the preparations, reminding us that he was once wounded by a rooftop sniper in Gaza.

I let out a deep breath as the plane's wheels touched the runway. "So far, so good," I heard a soldier behind me mumble, perhaps a last prayer. Almost as soon as the plane touched ground, the rear ramp began to lower, and soon it was moving slowly enough to let the paratroopers on board run out to post lanterns for runway lights for the planes behind us.

Finally, the Hercules came to a stop. Flight crew yanked away the blocks and lashes holding the Mercedes and Land Rovers in place. Yonni tapped Amitzur on the shoulder. The car engine roared and then began to purr. The rear ramp clanked to the ground.

"Go," Yonni ordered.

The car lunged forward and memories poured into me as we came out of the Hercules into the fresh night air of Africa right after a rain. I felt calm, almost serene, looking out into the darkness as Amitzur drove slowly but steadily, like any convoy of VIPs in the Ugandan Army—not too fast to attract attention, not too slow as to cause suspicion. The silence of the night was absolute. Far ahead, the old terminal was but a glow in the dark.

I turned to look over my shoulder. Right behind us, the Land Rovers did indeed look like Ugandan troop carriers—though the soldiers' faces were white, not black. Nonetheless, everything felt right.

I broke the radio silence between the three vehicles with the code word to my break-in crews to prepare their weapons. The ratcheting sounds of seven assault rifles clicking their first round into the chambers filled the car. I used the code word to order the break-in crews to set their weapons to single-shot mode for selective shooting.

The distant halo of the old terminal's lights sharpened into detail as we rolled closer. I could see the canopied entrances to the building, just as we expected, and began the countdown in my mind to the moment when the car would stop in front of the building—and we'd rush out into action.

Out of the corner of my eye I noticed two Ugandan soldiers. One of them was walking away from his comrade, disappearing into the dark. But I concentrated on the building ahead. We could ignore the Ugandan guards—that's why we were in the Mercedes.

The lone Ugandan sentry noticed our arrival and, in the standard operating procedure of a Ugandan soldier, raised his rifle and called out, "Advance."

It was nothing to get excited about. Just routine. I used to see it all the time in Uganda. We could drive right by him. That's why we were in the Mercedes. "Eighty, seventy, sixty," I was saying to myself under my breath, concentrating on the first canopied entrance, where I would push through the doors and enter the hall where the terrorists held the hostages. When I reached zero, the action would begin.

"Amitzur," Yonni suddenly said, breaking the silence in the car, and my concentration. "Cut to the right and we'll finish him off." The car swerved to the right.

"Leave it, Yonni," I said quietly but emphatically. "It's just his drill."

There was a moment of silence. Then Yonni repeated his order. Like me, he and Giora were carrying silenced 22–caliber Berettas, useful for very close quarters shooting. Giora Zussman cocked his Beretta and aimed it out his window at the Ugandan. The car continued veering toward the Ugandan, away from the terminal.

"Giora, let's take care of him," Yonni said, cocking his own gun.

"No," I tried again. The entire effort of the last week was to deliver us to the front doors of the terminal in peace and quiet. The memory of Ma'alot raced through my mind. We were making a mistake, even before we reached the terminal. "Forget it, Yonni," I tried again. But I was too late.

Yonni and Giora both fired from the moving car from ten meters away, using the silenced .22s. They were the only guns at the time that could carry silencers. I knew them well from my El Al air marshal work. It was a shot I wouldn't have tried to make. But it was too late. The silencers turned the crack of the small handguns into bare whispers. The Ugandan fell.

I sighed with relief. We could still get there and get our job done before he caused us any trouble. I tried to resume my focus on the terminal building. Amitzur continued driving toward the old terminal, now barely fifty meters away. The Land Rovers kept to the path behind us.

Suddenly, from behind us came a terrifying sound—the long burst of a Kalashnikov cutting down the Ugandan.

I jerked my head around, just in time to see the Ugandan, back on his feet and aiming his rifle at us, cut down by a burst of Kalashnikov fire from the Land Rover.

The order was clear and simple: no shooting until the operation starts, but then heavy fire to keep the Ugandans away. Someone in the Land Rover behind us had seen the Ugandan soldier get up and take aim at us. Instinctively, he had wanted to protect us. But now all of us were in danger as shooting erupted all around us.

Fifty meters from the target, I was seeing the entire element of surprise evaporate in front of my eyes. The rattling gunfire certainly alerted the terrorists. At any moment the terminal building might turn into a fireball of explosions as the terrorists followed through with their threats to blow up the hostages.

From the very start of the planning, I had recited the lessons of Ma'alot. "We failed there because of our own mistakes," I warned. And now it was happening again.

"Drive!" Yonni shouted at Amitzur, who braked instinctively with the first burst of Kalashnikov fire from the Land Rover behind us. "Fast!" Amitzur sped ahead another ten meters. Fire came at us from the darkness around the tarmac.

Crammed together in the car, we became sitting ducks for the Ugandans. Yonni realized it, too. We shouted at the same time: "Stop!" Amitzur braked hard. The car slid to a stop, the Land Rovers behind us screeching to a halt.

I flung open the door and began running toward the building, still at least fifty meters away, instead of the five meters we planned for. I flanked left to avoid the pool of light on the tarmac directly in front of the terminal, hearing the thumping of the fighters' boots behind me. Long bursts of fire shattered the night air. But I continued running, still focused on the canopied entrance to the terminal building, my target, aware that I was pulling the fighters behind me in the same direction.

Some Ugandan fire blasted toward us from my right, screaming lead past my head. Still running, I flicked the Kalashnikov to automatic and aimed a long burst at the source. I needed to create cover for all of us—myself and everyone in the column behind me. It was just like this in el-Hiam, I thought for a second as I raced ahead at the front of the column, creating as much fire as possible. The African flew backward, and I ran on, followed by all the fighters.

Finally I reached the building, directly below the control tower, barely a dozen meters away from the entrances to the building. The rattle and crack of rifle and submachine-gun fire shook the air, kicking up bits of asphalt at our feet. And behind me, thirty-three Sayeret Matkal soldiers bunched up, instead of heading to the assigned entrances. It was a complete contradiction of the battle plan, indeed of any combat formation.

But then I realized that no explosions had yet rocked the building. We still could prevent another Ma'alot. I was first in line, and the only way to proceed was forward. I took a deep breath and resumed the race to my assigned entrance, knowing that my example would spur the fighters behind me to follow suit.

Half a dozen strides into my run, a terrorist came out of the building from the second canopied entrance. I knew I had used up most of the magazine creating the cover fire in order to reach the control tower. But I also knew that once inside, I only needed a few bullets to do the job. Now, surprised by the terrorist, I aimed and fired. Only a couple of bullets spat out of the barrel. And I missed. He ducked back into the terminal building.

Racing forward, I pulled out the empty ammo magazine and flipped it over, reloading on the run, all the while keeping my eyes on my target—the canopied entrance to the building a few meters away. Still, no explosion racked the building. The plan could still succeed.

Instead, a second disaster struck: no glass doorway opened at the end of the canopied path into the hall.

I found myself facing a blank wall. We had planned according to Solel Boneh's original architectural plans, and they clearly showed an entrance. Somehow, we had lost one of the most crucial pieces of information the Frenchman gave Amiram.

Withering machine-gun fire poured down at us from the control tower. Yonni's backup fighters were supposed to take out the machine-gun nest up there. But obviously, the fighters were still confused by the bad start. The fifty-meter run from the cars, instead of the few meters we had practiced, threw everything off. At any second, I feared, the terrorists would ignite the explosives they had planted in the hallway. I had no choice but to get inside, to prevent that from happening.

With my preassigned entrance blocked, I began running to the second entrance, where I had seen the terrorist duck inside. Amir, a fighter from my second break-in team, suddenly ran past me, followed by his team leader, Amnon. Later, Amir said that in the confusion he lost his crew and thought they had already made it inside. Meanwhile, he became the first of us to get into the building.

He immediately spotted a terrorist and cut him down with a burst. Just then, Amnon ran in and saw the German man and woman terrorists kneeling side by side aiming guns at Amir's back. Amnon fired at the two Germans, sending them flying, just as I came in through the door, with Amos Goren on my heels.

I immediately added my own shots to the two German terrorists, to make sure they were out of the action.

For a second, silence fell over the room. Then suddenly shooting erupted again from outside, and screaming began inside the hall. I stood in the doorway, Amnon to my left and Amos and Amir on my extreme right, totally focused on the fully lit hall, searching for more terrorists.

People were lying all over the floor on mattresses. Some were frozen with fear, others screamed and shouted. People covered their heads with blankets as if to protect themselves from the bullets.

To my left, about fifteen meters away, a man came out from behind a column, bringing a rifle up to firing position. Amos and I fired simultaneously, knocking the terrorist off his feet. Again we scanned the hall. A dark-haired young man jumped up from amidst the hostages. Bullets from all four Kalashnikovs cut him down.

The shooting continued outside. Suddenly, Amir remembered the megaphone he carried. "Lie down, we're the IDF. Don't get up!" He shouted the instructions in Hebrew and English. We stood that way in the room for a long moment, ready to fire again.

Hesitantly, one of the hostages raised his hand. "You got them all," he said. "All of them. But that one," he added sadly, pointing at the body of the young man we had just shot, "he was one of us. A hostage."

The radio clasped to my web-belt gave me no time to respond. "Muki, Muki," it squawked.

"Muki here."

"Giora here. Mission accomplished." He had taken the VIP room, which the terrorists had made into their dormitory. "Two terrorists down. No casualties on our side."

"Yonni," I called over the radio. No answer came back. I tried again. "Yonni?" I tried again, "Muki here. Mission accomplished." A long, foreboding silence followed, finally broken by a squawk.

But instead of Yonni's voice, I heard Tamir Prado, the signals man from Yonni's command-and-control team. "Muki," he cried out. "Yonni's down."

I gave orders to the medics to treat any wounded among the hostages and went outside. Yonni was lying flat on his back on the tarmac. The bullet had come from the control tower, which had now fallen silent. The slug ripped into his chest and exited from his hip. David Hessin, the doctor, kneeling by his side, had torn open Yonni's shirt and was trying to treat him.

Karameh flashed through my mind—Arazi's body on the stretcher in the chopper, the doctors working on him to no avail. I looked around. Shaul Mofaz and his BTRs, from the second and third planes, were already patrolling the perimeter. Omer Bar-Lev's BTR from the third Hercules was headed toward the MiG airfield.

I clenched the radio clipped to my belt. "Dan," I called Shomron, who was on the other side of the airport at the new terminal, overseeing the Hercules landing. "Muki here," I continued. "Yonni's wounded. I am taking command." Dan Shomron confirmed my report with a terse "Okay."

Shaul Mofaz reported in. "Muki, everything's fine with me," he said. Then Yiftach Reicher, who led the break-in to the second floor, reported that he and his crew had also finished their job.

I kept Dan Shomron informed as my medics and the doctors took care of the few wounded hostages and collected the terrorists' weapons. Dan showed up, his face grave and worrying as he watched Hessin work on Yonni.

The shooting was over. But the noise continued. The spinning propellers of the Hercules approaching us to collect the hostages and the clanging of the BTRs' metal treads on the asphalt protecting us from any potential Ugandan assault filled the air.

Dan left us to handle shepherding the passengers to the Hercules while he headed back to the fuel depots, where the air force technicians readied to refuel the planes. But by the time he reached the fuel depot, word came through the command-and-control communications center circling overhead that the Kenyan government, informed of the operation, had given permission for us to land in Nairobi for refueling.

We knew that we had killed six terrorists—four in the main hall, and two taken out by Giora's force in the corridor outside the VIP room. Yiftach Reicher's team took out some Ugandan soldiers on the second floor. But we found no other terrorists at the old terminal. The other four terrorists, we later heard, spent that night in Kampala, the Ugandan capital, a few miles away from Entebbe airport.

Three hostages died in the rescue: Pesko Cohen, hit by one of our bullets when we hit the terrorist near the column; Ida Bobovitz, killed by terrorist fire; and the young dark-haired man who we mistook for a terrorist when he jumped up—Jean-Jacques Maimon, a young French Jew on his way home to visit family before coming back to Israel to join the army. (One other civilian from the hostages died—Dora Bloch, a Tel Aviv matron who had been taken to a Ugandan hospital the day before, when she choked on some food. Amin's thugs murdered her after the rescue.)

We loaded a Land Rover with the wounded to take to the flying hospital plane. "Yonni first," I ordered. While the Land Rover disappeared into the darkness across the tarmac to the field hospital, I went back inside to find Amos Goren pleading with the hostages to leave their possessions behind, to free them for the race to the airplane.

But the same passengers who only a few moments before had listened to everything we told them now ignored Amos's request to leave behind their belongings. Realizing that Amos's efforts were in vain, I let the passengers collect their valuables before the crews organized them for the hike to the airplane across the wide tarmac at the front of the terminal.

The fighters formed a protective wall around the civilians to ferry them out across the tarmac to where the Hercules stood waiting about 150 meters away. The Golani troops waited by its open rear door to help the freed civilians aboard.

I took the lead position of the box, Amir beside me as we stepped out of the terminal building. A heavy burst of fire came at us from the control tower.

Nervous, Amir accidentally let loose a bullet. It whizzed past my ear. "Hey, Amir, don't overdo it," I joshed him as we ducked back inside the building.

"Shaul," I called to Mofaz in the BTR. "Take out the control tower, please."

A moment later, a powerful burst of heavy machine-gun fire and several rocket-propelled grenades slammed into the control tower, silencing its occupants.

Again I stepped out onto the tarmac, into view of the control tower. And for a second time a blast of machine-gun fire raced across the asphalt at me from the control tower.

"Shaul," I called over the radio again. "How about giving them something that will really convince them."

RPGs and machine-gun fire from the BTR again riddled the tower. Shaul's shooting went on for a full minute.

That should silence it for good, I thought. But I waited for a long minute to be sure. "That's it," I told the boys, and we began moving the passengers out to the tarmac and the plane, about 150 meters away.

I watched from the distance as they trooped to the Hercules, remembering the last Israeli departure from Entebbe airport barely four years before. Nobody helped us then as we climbed, heavy-hearted, onto the plane to Nairobi. Then we felt like refugees, helpless and defeated. Now, at first glance, the freed hostages boarding the Hercules also looked like refugees, struggling to carry a few precious possessions across the tarmac. But they were not helpless. Or alone. They were free citizens of Israel, and we had fulfilled our roles as their protectors.

The back door to the Hercules slowly rose and the plane began its lumbering run down the runway to take-off. I turned back to the business at hand. The forces scouted the building one last time looking for stragglers, and then we boarded the Land Rovers and the Mercedes to carry us to the planes waiting near the new terminal.

We threw out demolition slabs behind us as we started the trip across the tarmac, to create a smoke screen behind us for any Ugandans who might decide to be heroes as we left the old ter-minal. But suddenly someone announced that Udi Bloch, one of the fighters accompanying a BTR, was missing.

Everything froze as fighters went to find him, taking care to avoid the demolition slabs. Within a minute he showed up, and we finally began rolling, packed into the Mercedes, the Land Rovers, and the BTRs.

But as we drove away, shooting resumed from the machine gun in the control tower.

"God, he's stubborn," I said out loud. But, finished with our job, we had no good reason to stop to shoot back. Someone in the car laughed at my joke as we raced away from the tracers flashing past us. Our fight in Entebbe was over.

The final force to leave Entebbe, on the fourth plane, we took off exactly fifty-nine minutes after we had landed in the first plane, flying off into a night lit up by the flaring destruction of the Ugandan Air Force.

A row of eleven MiGs parked about a hundred meters away from the old terminal, were sitting ducks for Omer Bar-Lev's BTR. He and his fighters blasted them with machine guns and RPGs before driving onto their Hercules. Only afterward did we find out that he had acted without a direct order. Something disrupted his Motorola communication with me or Dan, so Omer decided to act on his own.

No joy broke out in the fourth plane as we lifted off from Entebbe. We all knew that Yonni was seriously wounded.

Ehud met us in Nairobi. He had flown to Kenya on Friday to help organize permission to land for the flying hospital in the Boeing and refueling for the planes on the way back from Uganda. The fighters stayed on board, but we opened the rear ramp for fresh air. I went down the ramp to greet Ehud.

He was probably aching to hear from me what had happened back in Entebbe. But only one thing interested me just then. "How's Yonni?" I asked as we shook hands and then hugged.

"Wounded," Ehud said, "but he's going to be okay."

"Ehud," I pressed. "I know it was serious. I saw him. Tell me the truth."

"The doctors are working on him right now."

"Please do me a favor, go see what's going on," I asked Ehud. "Find out about Yonni."

He grimaced a nod and left me waiting for him on the tarmac beside the plane.

While I waited for him, I called Giora, who had led the break-in of the VIP room, to tell me how his team took down the two terrorists they found.

"We broke in," Giora told me, "and found two people in civilian clothes. We couldn't tell if they were terrorists or hostages. 'Who are you?' I asked them. But they said nothing. I thought maybe they couldn't understand me. But before I could try asking again, one of them pulled out a grenade. I gave a shout and we took cover, but added our bullets to the explosion. The terrorists died from the blast and our bullets."

I smiled at him. But my joy was short-lived. Ehud had come back—and his face said it all. Yonni was dead.

I was left with the task of telling the fighters inside the plane.

I climbed the rear ramp of the Hercules back into the plane, where the Mercedes and Land Rovers were lashed to the floor, the fighters gathered close to hear the news.

"Yonni's dead," I began, pausing to let the news sink in. "We did our duty. We succeeded. Successfully. This is the painful price we sometimes have to pay in this kind of war. But we continue." I paused for a second, then added, "Now we go home."

Throughout the airplane, most of the fighters slept for the ride home. I couldn't sleep. I sat up front in the cockpit. The natural loneliness of the commander had never sat so heavily on my shoulders. Usually after such an operation, Yonni and I sat together, talking about what had just happened and what we planned next.

Now, alone, I tried to understand what Yonni had been thinking when he decided to take out the Ugandan. He had obviously believed that the Ugandan soldier was threatening us. He didn't know what I knew—that presenting arms and calling out "Advance" was routine drill for a Ugandan soldier.

We could have driven right past any sentry. And even if the sentry became suspicious after we passed him, in those few seconds of his confusion, we would have reached the terminal building and begun our real work. Indeed, the entire plan was based on the idea that we were ready to endanger ourselves by driving past "enemy" soldiers on our way to the canopied entrances to the terminal in order to go ahead with our mission.

Obviously, I realized, Yonni had believed that with his and Giora's silenced guns, they could quietly eliminate the threat from the lone Ugandan soldier. But he could not have foreseen that the Ugandan would be only wounded and, getting back on his feet, would then be cut down by one of our own soldiers using an unsilenced weapon.

I found comfort in the fact that despite everything—the wounded Ugandan, the bunched-up run to the building from fifty meters away, the blocked entrance to where I had expected to break in—the Unit knew how to react fast enough to nonetheless surprise the terrorists before they could harm the hostages.

Deep in my thoughts, I was startled when the pilot turned to the Voice of Israel's radio frequency and we heard a pre-dawn news report in which Israeli government "sources" confirmed international media reports saying Israeli troops had destroyed the Ugandan Air Force. Still facing another three hours of flight within reach of enemy aircraft from Egypt and Saudi Arabia, our mission was not yet over. Someone in Jerusalem couldn't wait to make the announcement and was endangering our lives by doing so.

We flew directly to the Tel Nof base, far from the public eye. Rabin and Peres waited for us at the plane's door, shaking our hands as we came off. Then they gave short speeches thanking us for our accomplishment. Rabin spoke to us like an army commander. Peres spoke of our contribution to the fight against international terror.

Amiram Levine came up to me right after the speeches, and while we waited for the choppers to take us back to base, he told me they had appointed him that morning to replace Yonni.

A few hours later, back at the base, Amiram ran the debriefing, which we held in the mess hall. Usually, only those who took part in an operation attend. But this time Amiram broke precedent. He invited all the members of Sayeret Matkal on the base.

First the officers, then the crew commanders, and finally each individual fighter reported on what he did and what he saw, especially in those few seconds between the time the Ugandan soldiers spotted us and the plan went wrong because of the silenced .22s and the long blast of Kalashnikov fire that followed. The soldier from the Land Rover who fired his Klatch explained that when he saw the Ugandan get back up on his feet and aim at us, he feared for our safety. The driver of the Land Rover said he also was worried and decided to try to run over the Ugandan.

We did not celebrate a victory that night. For the Unit, even one casualty is proof that our performance did not match our plan. To maintain its abilities, a unit like Sayeret Matkal must always learn from its mistakes, facing honestly and truthfully what went wrong.

Into the night we talked about what had happened, each of us, from our own point of view, trying to understand what went wrong on the night of our most famous initiative. This was mine.

Epilogue

One successful counterblow against terror does not put an end to the war. In March 1978, after terrorists hijacked an Israeli bus north of Tel Aviv and twenty-seven vacationers died, the IDF swept into Lebanon in what became known as the Litani Operation, pushing the terrorists north out of their bases in southern Lebanon.

But by 1981 they were back, and then-Prime Minister Menachem Begin declared Yasser Arafat to be Adolf Hitler's successor. With Arik Sharon his defense minister and Raful the chief of staff, no holds were barred to try defeating the Palestine Liberation Organization, whose aspirations for a state conflicted with the right-wing government's belief in the Greater Land of Israel.

For the third time in nearly twenty years in the army, I was assigned to get PLO chairman Arafat. This time, I scattered dozens of special-forces snipers into besieged Beirut, looking for him and other key PLO personnel. But by the time we found him in our scopes, the United States had brokered a deal giving Arafat safe passage out of the city. Nonetheless, my riflemen came back with the Polaroids proving they had indeed had him in their gun sights.

Operation Peace for Galilee was supposed to last a few weeks. By its third year, it was my son Shaul's turn to go to the army. Now, for the first time, I could understand my parents' silence about their fears for my safety. I was faced with an even worse dilemma. In my last job in the IDF, I would be involved in the planning of operations my son might be asked to execute. I did not want to spend long hours waiting behind a desk for him to come back from a mission instead of being there by his side to protect his flanks. And at forty, I had to admit to myself that no matter how hard I tried, the twenty-year-olds would always be in better physical shape for the job.

Proud, I watched Shaul enter the Unit just as I was leaving, and wished his mother had lived to see him full-grown. Nurit passed away shortly after Entebbe, finally freed from the tragic illness that debilitated her in the last years of her life. We laid her to rest in Nahalal's cemetery overlooking the Jezreel Valley, under a broad fir tree that shades her spot from the hot sun. She was twenty-nine years old. Shaul grew up in Nahalal, where my younger brother Eyal, who had married Nurit's sister, took over the family farm after Nurit's passing.

So, a decade after my most famous mission—though not at the pinnacle of my work in the army, a subject and period that await declassification for another book—I retired from the army at the age of forty. Since then, I've seen many of my friends and colleagues—Ehud Barak, Matan Vilnai, Amiram Levine, and others—rise to the highest levels in the army.

But I never wanted an army career. And as a civilian I chose a profession as rooted in the traditions of my family as service in the defense of Israel—settlement. But instead of government-subsidized settlements in the occupied territories, my friends from the army and the Jezreel Valley organized our new village in the hills overlooking Nahalal.

For the first time in Israel, private citizens undertook to build a new settlement without help from the government or from a political movement. Neither kibbutz nor moshav, nor merely a bedroom suburb to nearby Haifa, we planned it from the start as an independent community.

Asked to serve as chief executive officer for the group, I became involved while studying at Haifa University. I finally went back to school during a sabbatical the army gave me in 1980, studying the geography, botany, and zoology of the Land of Israel, just as I had for years. We began construction in 1981. A year later I remarried, to Nomi, and in 1983, we moved into our new home, and had two daughters, Tamar and Shani.

I began this book in the same September 1993 week as the historic handshake on the White House lawn between my former commanding general, Yitzhak Rabin, and my former enemy leader, Yasser Arafat. I wanted to leave the next generation an account of the wars and battles I saw from the tip of the IDF's spear, to help those future generations understand the value of peace.

As I have always said, I am a son of the Jezreel Valley, born in Nahalal, a village deliberately shaped as a circle. Indeed, an important circle of my life was closed that same week in September 1993 as the first steps on the long road to real peace in the Land of Israel took place—my father, Nahman, died.

A working farmer until the last weeks of his life, he was gladdened to live to see the beginning of a peace process with the Palestinians, an enemy he never hated. He was buried beside my mother, Sarah, who died in 1986, in the Nahalal cemetery at the other end of the same row as Nurit. Hundreds of old-timers and members of our extended family came to the shady grove overlooking the valley to pay their respects to him as the embodiment of the pioneering ideal of a man who devoted himself to Israel's safety and settlement.

In late 1973, a few weeks after the cease-fire at the end of the Yom Kippur War, while Henry Kissinger still negotiated the disengagement of forces and the IDF held positions on the west bank of the Suez Canal, my brother Udi and I both managed to get home for a few hours.

We told our father, Nahman, about the battles we had fought. He was interested, of course. But when we told him about the agriculture that we saw in Egypt, he became most excited. The Egyptian farming techniques fascinated him, for while we knew the best of Israeli agritechnology, the Egyptians used methods as old as the Bible. We decided to take him down to Egypt, to see firsthand.

We drove over the bridges Arik's engineering crews had put up to make the bridgehead into Egypt. We took him to Fa'id and to Deversoir, all the way to where Amitai Nahmani was killed, and then through the mango plantations to the dunes where Amit Ben-Horin died trying to invoke the cease-fire.

Only when we reached the irrigation canals of that huge plantation did his excitement finally break through his normally stoic expression. Finding some Egyptian peasants working in the groves, he questioned them for hours in his farmer's Arabic about when they plant and harvest, how they control the water, and which crops served them best. The farms, not the fighting, interested him.

Like him, I understood there was no realistic choice but mutual recognition between the two people—the Israelis and the Palestinians—who regard the Land of Israel as home. Not that I wanted to run to embrace Arafat. But no people can rule another people without their consent, and no realistic alternative exists to compromise in the Land of Israel between us and the Palestinians. For me, the historic mutual recognition was proof of the success of the Zionist revolution my grandparents helped begin at the beginning of the century, a revolution that believed in eventual Arab acceptance of our presence in the region.

The historic handshake in September 1993 also became the start of a process that enabled me to close two circles in my own life story.

In January 1994 I received a phone call from an Israeli journalist asking if I would be ready to go with him to Uganda to do a documentary, including a trip to the old terminal at Entebbe airport. No Israeli had visited Uganda since the Entebbe rescue.

"Sure," I said. But that was about all he had as far as his story idea was concerned. He had been sending faxes to the Ugandan government ever since the mutual recognition between Israel and the PLO when, suddenly, many of the Third World and developing countries that had long boycotted Israel announced their renewal of diplomatic relations. But Uganda was so far silent on the issue. Even the Foreign Ministry in Jerusalem couldn't help.

Over the years I had kept up my contacts for anything connected to the African country that had played such an important part in my life. I knew that the Ugandan president's brother was in Israel, having an operation at one of the country's best hospitals. The medical treatment had been arranged by an Israeli, with a company based in Nairobi, that did business in Uganda. I gave the journalist the name of the Israeli businessman in Nairobi. "Here's the intelligence," I told the reporter. "Now, let's see how good a reporter you are."

And sure enough, a week later, I was back in a jeep on the tarmac at Entebbe, but it was daytime, and instead of a web-belt and a weapon, I carried a tourist's flight bag and a camera. And instead of an officer leading the break-in teams to the old terminal, I was officially a "producer" for an Israeli television news crew.

Nothing had changed in seventeen years. Uganda had seen civil wars and coups, invasions, and finally peace, but nobody had used the old terminal since the night we flew out. The control tower at Entebbe was still riddled with the scars of Shaul Mofaz's fifty-caliber machine guns mounted on the BTR. I climbed a musty stairwell to the room at the top of the tower, astonished by the commanding view it had of the scene and amazed at how lucky we were that more of us didn't die that night.

The Ugandan president invited us to meet him at his home in the far north of the country. Not certain how he felt about the rescue, we did not mention my role in the raid. But he told us he regarded Idi Amin as an enemy of Uganda, and praised Israel for its action in 1976. Indeed, on camera, he announced the resumption of diplomatic relations with Israel. Promising Israeli tourists a warm welcome in his country, he took seriously a suggestion that the old terminal be turned into a museum for tourists interested in the rescue and its blow against international terror.

The second circle closed for me by the peace process began with an invitation from Prime Minister Rabin and King Hussein to attend the 1994 signing of the treaty between Israel and Jordan. That ceremony was an emotional moment for me, of course, but far more meaningful to me was the trip Rabin and Hussein's offices arranged in March 1995, enabling twenty-eight veterans of the paratroops brigade's *sayeret*, my original unit, to revisit the battlefield at Karameh.

This time, instead of helicoptering in before dawn, we rode an air-conditioned tourist bus across the tiny bridge over the Jordan River. Just like at Entebbe, at Karameh too, time stood still.

In the dry desert nothing had changed. The boulder where Arazi fell still marked the spot. No winter since 1968 had been wet enough to change the dry riverbed's bend. The weather was the same as that morning twenty-seven years earlier: end of winter, still cold in the morning, but by midday an oven of heat, relieved by sudden breezes that last only a few minutes and then pass, carrying a rough dust in the air up and down the valley.

My seemingly endless walk of 1968 turned into a five-minute stride across the plateau. Climbing the crumbly sandstone wall to the ridge overlooking the gravel-and-sand riverbed, I stumbled, more amazed than ever at how I survived then.

Yisrael Arazi's brother, Asher, led the twenty-eight veterans of the unit in a prayer of commemoration for all who died—Yisrael, Haim Prager, Yitzhak Shoham, and Zevik Alterman.

Engel was so excited that he forgot I had told him to keep firing when he was hit in the leg. And for a long hour we listened to Sergeant Alexander tell the story of Nissim, the tagalong from the air force who pulled rank and got the platoon into trouble. We finally held the debriefing after Karameh that must follow every operation, but especially the failures—to learn what went wrong and how to fix it.

Two Jordanian Army officers accompanied us as our hosts, and together with them we held a second moment of silence in the desert at the foot of their monument to the soldiers who fought and fell at Karameh trying to help the Palestinians. From Karameh we went to Amman and dined out, the next morning visiting the War Museum, to see relics from the battle of Karameh. An air force pilot's uniform, helmet, and personal weapon hung in a glass case. I knew the family of the pilot shot down that day, killed by the villagers who captured him, so I brought home pictures for his sister.

But the most important moment for me on my first trip to Jordan as a civilian came on top of Mount Nevo, the presumed resting place of the biblical Moses. From that point, he was allowed only to see the Promised Land, not to enter it.

I could see across the Jordan Rift Valley all the way to Jerusalem, perched on the top of the tawny Judean Mountains in the south, and to the green Samarian mountain ridge heading north. Far below, in the heart of the Jordan Rift, the Jericho oasis west of the Jordan glimmered emerald-green.

It is indeed the heart of the Land of Israel—but it is not the State of Israel. For more than a generation—from 1967, when it was captured in the Six-Day War, to the mid-1990s—Israel held that territory. Many hoped that one day the territory would be annexed to the State of Israel. Some undertook an effort to settle the lands named in the Bible.

But every government since 1967, right-wing, left-wing, hawkish or dovish, has been unable to do so, because it would mean undermining the idea of Israel as a democratic state with a Jewish majority.

Thus, for all the rhetoric of those opposed to the peace process with the Palestinians, I am confident that the sobering reality of responsibility for the lives of Israel's citizens will make any elected government in Israel in the future continue with the process. There is no alternative if we—and our Arab neighbors—wish to be a part of the new world of instant communication and free markets arriving in the twenty-first century.

In that new world, it is impossible for one people to rule another without their consent. So, just as we made peace with Egypt by returning the Sinai and just as the peace with Syria being made at the time of the writing of this book is based on trading the Golan Heights in exchange for peace, so will the territory I could see from the top of Mount Nevo go to the Palestinians.

Thus, as a realist, I understand that the West Bank is on its way to becoming a Palestinian state. I can only hope it will be a democracy and that it will be a sturdy neighbor for the State of Israel, whose borders will once and for all be set, recognized, and respected by our neighbors.

The end of the hundred-year war is in sight. To my grandparents and parents, it appeared it would go on forever. But already, despite all the difficulties, the reconciliation has begun.

I have traveled to Egypt and Jordan as a civilian, and soon, I believe, I will be able to travel to Syria and Lebanon as a tourist, carrying a camera instead of a gun, with my children, rather than my soldiers. For that I am grateful, knowing that it means all my efforts—and my entire generation's—in the service of my country have truly borne fruit. My only regret is for all my friends who did not live to see the peace for which we fought.